THE

PRESSURE COOKER

COOKBOOK

THE
PRESSURE
COOKER
COOKBOOK

Revised

Toula Patsalis

HOME

THE BERKLEY PUBLISHING GROUP
Published by the Penguin Group
Penguin Group (USA) Inc.
375 Hudson Street, New York, New York 10014, USA
Penguin Group (Canada), 90 Eglinton Avenue East, Suite 700, Toronto, Ontario M4P 2Y3, Canada (a division of Pearson Penguin Canada Inc.)
Penguin Books Ltd., 80 Strand, London WC2R 0RL, England
Penguin Group Ireland, 25 St. Stephen's Green, Dublin 2, Ireland (a division of Penguin Books Ltd.)
Penguin Group (Australia), 250 Camberwell Road, Camberwell, Victoria 3124, Australia (a division of Pearson Australia Group Pty. Ltd.)
Penguin Books India Pvt. Ltd., 11 Community Centre, Panchsheel Park, New Delhi—110 017, India
Penguin Group (NZ), cnr. Airborne and Rosedale Roads, Albany, Auckland 1310, New Zealand (a division of Pearson New Zealand Ltd.)
Penguin Books (South Africa) (Pty.) Ltd., 24 Sturdee Avenue, Rosebank, Johannesburg 2196, South Africa

Penguin Books Ltd., Registered Offices: 80 Strand, London WC2R 0RL, England

Copyright © 2006 by Toula Patsalis
Text design by Tiffany Estreicher
Cover design by Rita Frangie
Cover photo © by Cormier Photography

The recipes contained in this book are to be followed exactly as written. The publisher is not responsible for your specific health or allergy needs that may require medical supervision. The publisher is not responsible for any adverse reactions to the recipes contained in this book.

PRINTING HISTORY
Original HPBooks edition / November 1994
Revised HPBooks edition / January 2006

HPBooks is a registered trademark of Penguin Group (USA) Inc.

Library of Congress Cataloging-in-Publication Data

Patsalis, Toula
    The pressure cooker cookbook / Toula Patsalis.—Rev. ed.
        p. cm.
    Includes index.
    ISBN 1-55788-482-X
    1. Pressure cookery. I. Title.

TX840.P7P34 2006
641.5'87—dc22

                                                    2005052658

PRINTED IN THE UNITED STATES OF AMERICA

10 9 8 7 6 5 4 3 2

ACKNOWLEDGMENTS

First and foremost, my heartfelt thanks to my husband, Chris, for his confidence and encouragement to complete this book.

Gratefully and lovingly this book is dedicated to those who have taught me to enjoy the many delicious wonders of food preparation.

To my mother, who introduced me to the healthy flavors of our Greek heritage.

To my father, who instilled the fine delicate flavors of quality.

To my editor, Jeanette Egan, who was there every step of the way.

To the many food mentors and instructors who helped orchestrate my knowledge of methods and techniques: Julia Child, Jacques Pepin, Nick Malgieri, Lynne Kasper, Marlene Sorosky, Cleo Gruber, Jane Schermerhorn, and Guilda Krause, to name only a few.

CONTENTS

INTRODUCTION

Pressure cooking has certainly added a new dimension to my culinary life. I have discovered that the pressure cooker is a marvelous kitchen tool that can be conveniently used for speedy meal preparation, producing nutritious, mouthwatering dishes with enhanced flavors and vibrant eye appeal. In addition to saving time, a pressure cooker also saves energy. Yes, pressure cooking is perfect for today's active lifestyles. Within these pages I offer you tested and retested recipes that will soon become your favorites.

As you leaf through the chapters, you will be inspired by the shortcuts that can be accomplished in planning menus for entertaining and cooking for everyday meals. Timesaving appetizers filled with flavors of many countries will surely be a hit with family and guests. The soups and stews are filled with fresh and healthy ingredients, perfectly balanced with fresh herbs and spices. It will soon become apparent that leaner, less expensive cuts of meats can be cooked until tender and succulent in minutes. Fish and shellfish dishes will be cooked to perfection when you follow the easy instructions. And the dessert chapter, filled with creamy cheesecakes, lemon curd, chocolate pudding, bread puddings, and sauces, is not to be missed. There are jams and chutneys to be enjoyed at home or given as gifts.

Pressure cooking is uniquely different. The methods, techniques, and timing are altered from conventional cooking. In some recipes, cooking time is reduced by 70 percent. Once the steps for converting standard conventional recipes to pressure cooking are followed and learned, you will find a new culinary world of convenience and ease that will encourage you to become more adventurous.

Yes, I am a pressure-cooking convert. Unlike those pressure cookers of the 1940s, the new technology is safer. I am intrigued by the science and technology behind these wonderful units and astonished at the marvelous results. The testing and development of the recipes was a lengthy procedure and one idea led to another. I felt an urge to push the pressure cooker to its limits, only to find that its boundaries were endless.

While testing and developing these recipes, I became a pressure-cooking addict! Although I have not come to the point of giving up my quality skillets, saucepans, or microwave oven, I truly feel the pressure cooker is a fine tool that should be in every kitchen next to the finest kitchen tools and equipment. The pressure cooker can make it possible for all of us to cook and enjoy good, healthy meals. This hassle-free method of food preparation will be your right hand, whether preparing casual snacks, fabulous meals, or beautiful foods for entertaining.

I hope you will come to enjoy the ease and convenience of pressure cooking. The recipes are designed to be followed step-by-step, leading to wonderful results. Overcome your fear and use your pressure cooker frequently. Soon it will prove itself in value and you will find yourself reaching for it every day.

I can't remember having more fun and feeling more enthusiasm about a cooking method during my many years involved in food preparation. Now I invite you to share the pleasure and flavors of the adventure of pressure cooking.

BASICS OF PRESSURE COOKING

UNDERSTANDING THE PRESSURE COOKER

The first-generation pressure cookers popular in the thirties and forties were complicated, had many parts to deal with, and lacked safety features. We've all heard the horror stories our grandmothers and mothers told about using the older models such as lids blowing off or soup all over the kitchen. Technology has advanced by leaps and bounds since then. The new generation of pressure cookers introduced to the public since 1985 offers easy-to-use equipment without the hassle of feeling like you must be an engineer instead of a cook. The new-generation pressure cookers and their lids offer safety features, including a system where extra steam escapes, preventing any accidents. The new-generation pressure cooker is perfectly safe, and the new materials used in construction seal the steam under the lid, penetrating the food fibers, and resulting in extremely quick and delicious meals.

The newly designed lids allow very little steam to escape. This means less liquid is required to pressure-cook, helping retain nutrients during the cooking process.

Combining and layering courses is easy and can be accomplished in a pressure cooker with excellent results. Simply refer to the timing charts. Plan to cook compatible foods. Interrupting the pressure-cooking process can easily be done. Meats take longer than vegetables. Pressure-cook the meat first, interrupting the cooking process to add the vegetables for the last few minutes.

It has long been recognized that the pressure cooker is a great energy saver. During World War II, when energy was necessarily conserved, it was the pressure cooker that prepared most home-cooked meals. As much as 60 to 70 percent of the time is saved, and the shorter cooking time cuts the consumption of energy by two-thirds. Today, with rising gas and electricity costs, it is a sensible alternative to save dollars in the household budget.

SELECTING THE RIGHT PRESSURE COOKER

Even though the principles of pressure cooking remain the same, there are great variations in the craftsmanship and materials of the various models. Deluxe, standard, large, and small pressure cookers are available in the marketplace. The 6-quart pressure cooker is the industry standard, and all the recipes in this book can be prepared in it. Pressure cookers vary in construction, type of metal, and accessories. Everything should be considered and examined before the initial purchase is made.

Pressure cookers are constructed of either aluminum, enamel-coated carbon steel, or stainless-steel metals. Even though aluminum is known for

fine heat conduction, the stainless steel or enamel-coated carbon steel should seriously be considered, because there is no interaction between these metals and the foods. Aluminum will darken when in contact with acidic foods such as tomatoes or citrus products, and a metallic taste will penetrate the food. Look for a pressure cooker of heavy-gauge metal, with an easy-to-clean surface and interior. Preferably, the handles should be constructed of heatproof material and include a helping handle on the opposite side for easy lifting.

All it takes is a little preplanning. Remember, quality will indeed endure long after the price is forgotten.

ELECTRIC PRESSURE COOKERS

The electric pressure cookers are convenient and easy to operate. They are available in a variety of materials, usually with a heatproof exterior and nonstick interiors. They come in a variety of sizes beginning with 4-quart up to 8-quart sizes. Look for a manufacturer that offers a removable insert for easy cleaning. If not, there may be concerns while washing the pressure cooker, because the electrical gauge should not be submerged in water at any time. It is a convenience that is soon appreciated. Most electric pressure cookers can be used conventionally for stocks, rice, or warming foods. They offer the three standard means of pressure measurement beginning with low, medium, and high, and a gauge or button that enables the user to determine where the pressure is at all times. There is also a steam release on each unit for easy adjustment of pressure and also for release of pressure at the end of the cooking time. Look for a lid with a removable rubber seal, because after approximately 150 uses it will have to be replaced. Of course, reading the instruction manuals should always be the first step to cooking with the electric pressure cookers.

FEATURES OF THE PRESSURE COOKER

Pressure valves: Always review the manufacturer's manual first. Examine the construction of the unit. Is the pressure valve secure and built into the lid, or is it a freestanding plug that balances on top of the lid? The well-constructed pressure cooker has pressure valves that are attached to the lid with gauge lines to indicate the various pressures. Look for a well-designed, easy-to-read gauge that can be disassembled for thorough cleaning. The wobbly, balancing plugs may cause difficulty in determining when the exact pressure level has been reached. Amount of pressure and timing are key factors to pressure cooking success.

The new pressure cookers have technically improved valves that will not explode. They are designed so the excess steam will escape before a disaster can occur! Forget about the horror stories of the 1940s.

Rubber seal ring: The rubber ring around the lid plays a very important part in the functioning of the pressure cooker. Double-check the rubber ring for firmness, cracks, or peeling. It should be smooth and fit snugly. It can easily be removed for cleaning and should be washed thoroughly and rubbed with mineral oil after every use. The oil will preserve the ring, and properly cared for, the ring should last for approximately 150 meals. It is a good idea to have a spare rubber ring on hand. They are available from the merchant where the pressure cooker was purchased, or write to the manufacturer. Address and parts information will be found in the manual.

When should the rubber ring seal be changed? The steam pressure will not develop and you will see the steam flow from around the edge of the lid. When this happens, double-check the ring for cleanliness. Remove any food particles that may have adhered to the seal. Check positioning of the lid. Is it sealed correctly? If all of these have been checked thoroughly and everything seems to be in order, your next step would be to replace the rubber ring seal.

Pressure release: Many units offer a pressure/steam escape button near the valve. There will be times when the pressure should be adjusted during cooking, and this is when you will most appreciate the convenience of the steam-escape button, which may be used instead of transferring the pressure cooker to the sink so cold running water can be run over the cooker to release the steam or reduce pressure for delicate foods. The button release is an extremely useful feature.

Steam basket: Found packed with most units, the steam basket is great for fresh vegetables, fruit, or fish. It is designed with elevated feet to keep the unit away from the liquid and has little holes for steam penetration and circulation.

Heat diffuser: A heat diffuser is a wire or metal plate that prevents direct contact between the heat and the bottom of the pressure cooker. Most manufacturers include a heat diffuser with the pressure cooker. If, however, it is not a part of the package, they can be found in most cookshops very inexpensively. Heat diffusers should be used when preparing all rice, pasta, or bean recipes. It prevents sticking and scorching.

Cake pans or pudding molds: Many times a recipe will call for a cake pan, pudding mold, or tart pan. These should be made of any heatproof material, such as metal or tempered glass.

Timer: A timer won't come with the pressure cooker, but it should. It is important that all recipes be accurately timed, so purchase a good-quality timer.

PRESSURE-COOKING TERMS

Lock the lid into place: First and foremost, read the manufacturer's manual carefully. Most units have symbols on the lid handle and the vessel handle. Once these symbols are lined up, the lid slips into the proper position and is secured in place. Practice positioning the lid and locking it into place several times until confidence is developed before starting to cook.

Secure the lid: Align the lid with the lower part of the vessel and lock it into position.

Develop pressure: Bring the pressure up to the level indicated in the recipe.

Release the steam: Releasing steam can be done in three ways.

Rapid release is great for vegetables or fish dishes. Carefully carry the pressure cooker to the sink, release the lock as the manufacturer directs, and run cold running water over the top of the lid.

The steam-release latch or button works well for soups and stews. This handy addition to the newer units allows the steam to escape without transferring the vessel to the sink. Simply unlock the latch and release the steam until all pressurized steam has escaped. The lid will easily open.

Slow release is simply sliding the cooker off the burner and allowing it to stand until the cooker cools, releasing the pressure. This slow process usually takes 15 minutes or so, affecting the texture of the food. It is not a recommended method; the extra time causes foods to overcook.

Precaution: If the pressure cooker is left unattended after the cooking time is completed, the lid can form a seal and it will be impossible to release the lid. Simply put the pressure cooker back on the heat and bring the pressure up to low. Then release the steam and the lid can be removed. Redeveloping the pressure breaks the seal.

Remove the lid: The lids on the new pressure cookers will not come off until all pressure is released. It is important to read the manufacturer's manual for instructions on properly removing the lid. Practice a few times, adding a cup of water to the pressure cooker, developing pressure, releasing the pressure, and removing the lid.

Adjust heat to maintain pressure: Once the desired pressure has been reached, it is important to reduce the heat to medium or lower to maintain the pressure at the correct level. Because the heating units of cooktops vary, it will be necessary to keep adjusting the heat until the correct amount is achieved.

Insert heat diffuser between pan and heat: The heat diffuser (page 6) prevents scorching and burning, especially while preparing starchy rices or pastas. The heat diffuser should be put over the heat after pressure has been reached.

Interrupting the process: This method is used most often when ingredients requiring long periods of cooking are combined with ingredients that require shorter cooking periods. Pressure is released quickly, usually under cold running water, and the lid is removed. At this point the second batch of ingredients is added for the last few minutes of cooking, ensuring perfect results and texture. The lid is secured into position and the cooking time completed. The pressure is once again released and the lid removed.

Amount of liquid: The manufacturer's manual will recommend a minimum amount of liquid for the pressure cooker. Never use less than recommended. The liquid is the key to developing the steam that creates the pressure under the tightly fitting lid. The magic of pressure cooking develops when the water is heated to above boiling (212 degrees F, 100 degrees C) temperatures. The pressure continues to climb under the tightly sealed lid and is measured by pounds of pressure thereafter and will be indicated on the valve gauge of the pressure cooker or a weight that is added to the exhaust valve of the pressure cooker. The deluxe pressure cookers' gauges have lines that appear as the steam rises. Standard models create steam and jiggle the gauge at a slow, even pace.

Amount of pressure: Low pressure is developed when steam under the sealed lid is around 220 degrees F (105 degrees C). Low steam pressure is used for custards, puddings, and delicate fruit and vegetables. As the steam develops under the sealed lid, the pressure continues to increase, unless the heat is reduced to adjust the steam.

Medium pressure is developed when steam reaches 235 degrees F (115 degrees C) and is recommended for poultry, fish, and some firmer fruits and vegetables.

High pressure is developed at about 250 degrees F (120 degrees C), which again is indicated by lines on the deluxe units and a rapid juggling of the gauge on the standard models. High pressure is recommended for tough cuts of meat, wild game, dried fruits, firm vegetables, beans, rice, and pasta.

High-altitude cooking: Above 3,500 feet, always increase cooking time by 10 percent.

Pressure	Pounds	Temperature
High	15	250°F (120°C)
Medium	10	235°F (115°C)
Low	5	220°F (105°C)

EIGHT STEPS FOR PERFECT PRESSURE COOKING

1. Always read the manufacturer's manual thoroughly so you will understand each part. Have on hand spare rubber rings. Always double-check the flexibility of the valve.

2. Read recipe through. Does the recipe fit the unit? Meat, poultry, or fish pieces must be of same thickness. Trim fat from meat and cut all vegetables the same size. Assemble all ingredients for the recipe before starting to cook.

3. Use more, never less, liquid as required by the manufacturer. Tomato sauce, stocks, and juices are all considered liquid. Oil is not included.

4. Use a heat diffuser on the heat source when cooking rice, pastas, or beans.

5. Secure lid according to manufacturer's directions and develop pressure. Once pressure is reached, timing begins. Adjust heat to maintain pressure.

LET'S PRESSURE COOK

1. Make sure the manual has been read and is understood.

2. Examine ring and seal on unit.

3. Read selected recipe thoroughly.

4. Organize ingredients and prepare as required.

5. Use proper measuring utensils. Check liquid measurements at eye level. Loosely pack dry ingredients and level off straight across top with a spatula.

6. All recipes in this cookbook were tested in a 6-quart pressure cooker.

7. Regardless of whether there are one or four people in the family, it is recommended that you prepare the entire recipe. Leftovers can easily be frozen in portioned packages and enjoyed at a later time.

6. Invest in an accurate timer. It is as crucial as developing the pressure.

7. Follow manual instructions to bring pressure down. For quick steam release, run the unit under cold running water or release and press the pressure release button. When preparing soups and stocks, the pressure is best released slowly. Once pressure is released, shake the unit several times before removing the lid. The shaking adjusts the inner temperature.

If the lid is left on long after the pressure is gone, a seal will form. To release the lid, develop low pressure over low heat once again. Release steam rapidly and remove lid.

8. Thoroughly cleanse the unit in hot, sudsy water. Make sure the valve area is thoroughly clean. Remove the rubber ring and wash with sudsy water. Rinse, dry, and rub mineral oil all over rubber surface. This extra step adds endurance to the ring. The rings last for approximately 150 uses. Store unit with lid inverted, not locked into position.

CONVERTING YOUR FAVORITE RECIPE

1. Separate ingredients according to length of pressure cooking time (see charts in each chapter).

2. Make sure all ingredients are cut into uniform pieces.

3. If cooking a soup or stew, sear meat or poultry to seal in juices.

4. Add the minimum liquid required for your unit. This includes stocks, tomato puree or sauces, water, or juices.

5. Begin cooking meat or poultry first until almost completely cooked (see timing chart for meat, page 64).

6. Interrupt cooking process by releasing steam according to manufacturer's directions and adding vegetables or fruit in accordance with pressure-cooking timetable. Redevelop steam and continue to cook.

7. Flavors will be more pronounced in pressure-cooked meals; therefore, reduce amounts of herbs and spices by one-fourth. For example, if your recipe calls for 1 teaspoon dried oregano, use ¾ teaspoon dried oregano.

8. When cooking is complete, release pressure according to manufacturer's directions. Remove lid and stir well.

9. Taste and correct seasonings.

10. If the recipe seems to have too much liquid, cook over high heat, uncovered, to reduce excess liquid, stirring occasionally.

(APPETIZERS)

Great beginnings for any festive get-together, appetizers and hors d'oeuvres are always a welcome sight for hungry guests. Set the mood with a welcoming display. Many of the recipes in this chapter can be made ahead and frozen.

Plan a balance of cocktail hors d'oeuvres for a stand-up party. Try to have at least eight servings of cocktail hors d'oeuvres per person. The variety should include fresh vegetables and fruit pieces for dieters. Be prepared to refill platters throughout the party.

If you are planning appetizers for a dinner party, keep it light. One hot and one cold appetizer is plenty before you invite your guests to sit down for dinner.

Include bowls of munchies such as a mixture of nuts or seasoned popcorn and position the bowls around the entertainment area.

BLACK BEAN DIP WITH JACK CHEESE

The hot flavors in this recipe can be varied with the type of chiles used. Jalapeño chiles are moderate in flavor, yet give some heat to these ingredients. If a milder flavor is preferred, use canned green chiles.

MAKES 12 SERVINGS

1 cup dried black beans, soaked overnight

3 slices bacon, finely diced

1 tablespoon olive oil

1 small onion, finely diced

3 garlic cloves, crushed

1 cup canned diced tomatoes

1 cup water

2 small canned jalapeño chiles, finely chopped

1½ teaspoons salt

1 teaspoon chili powder

½ teaspoon dried oregano

¼ cup finely chopped fresh cilantro

1 cup (4 ounces) shredded Monterey Jack cheese

Corn chips

Drain beans; set aside. In a pressure cooker over medium heat, cook bacon with the olive oil until the bacon is almost cooked. Add onion and sauté, scraping bottom of cooker with a wooden spoon to loosen any browned bits. Stir in beans, garlic, tomatoes, water, chiles, salt, chili powder, and oregano. Secure lid. Over high heat, bring pressure up to high. Reduce heat to medium to maintain pressure and cook for 12 minutes.

Release pressure according to manufacturer's directions. Remove lid. Stir in cilantro. Transfer mixture to a food processor or blender. Process until smooth. Place in a bowl or fondue pot. Top with cheese. Serve warm or cold with corn chips.

❑ ❑ ❑

CARIBBEAN HUMMUS WITH FRESH TOMATO RELISH

Perfect for picnics, pool parties, and barbecues, the refreshing island flavors of this unusual hummus fill each bite. It is colorful and delicious. Serve chilled as an appetizer or side dish.

MAKES 6 SERVINGS

6 ounces red or white kidney beans, soaked overnight

4 cups water

1¼ teaspoons salt

1 tablespoon tahini paste

3 tablespoons crushed pineapple, drained

2 garlic cloves, crushed

⅛ teaspoon ground cumin

⅛ teaspoon ground ginger

⅛ teaspoon freshly ground white pepper

¼ cup finely chopped fresh cilantro

1 medium tomato, seeded and diced

3 green onions, diced

¼ cup canned or frozen whole-kernel corn

2 tablespoons canola oil

Corn chips

rain beans and place in a pressure cooker with the water and a dash of salt. Secure lid. Over high heat, bring pressure up to high. Reduce heat to medium to maintain pressure and cook 10 minutes.

Release pressure under cold running water. Remove lid and drain. Place the beans, 1 teaspoon of the salt, tahini, pineapple, garlic, spices, and cilantro in a food processor or blender. Blend until chunky. Transfer to a bowl, cover, and chill.

Combine tomato, green onions, corn, canola oil, and remaining ¼ teaspoon salt in a bowl. Toss until blended. Serve hummus in a bowl surrounded with tomato relish. Or serve in individual dishes garnished with tomato relish. Serve with corn chips.

◻ ◻ ◻

CHORIZO WITH RED AND GREEN PEPPER

Chorizo is a pork sausage used in Mexican and Spanish dishes. It is traditionally flavored with garlic, chili powder, and a combination of spices. This recipe could also be used as an enchilada filling.

MAKES 12 SERVINGS

3 tablespoons olive oil
4 garlic cloves, crushed
1 large onion, sliced
1 large red bell pepper, sliced
1 large green bell pepper, sliced

1 pound chorizo (Mexican sausage), cut into 2-inch pieces
Pinch crushed red pepper flakes
1 teaspoon salt
½ teaspoon chili powder
1 cup beef broth
Corn chips

eat oil in a pressure cooker. Add garlic, onion, and bell peppers and sauté 1 minute. Add sausage, pepper flakes, salt, chili powder, and beef broth. Stir to distribute ingredients. Secure lid. Over high heat, bring pressure up to medium. Reduce heat to medium-low to maintain pressure and cook for 5 minutes.

Release pressure under cold running water. Remove lid. Using a slotted spoon, transfer sausage and vegetables onto a serving platter. Spoon ¼ cup of the juice over sausage and vegetables. Serve with corn chips.

MEXICAN MEATBALLS IN SAUCE

The tangy tomato-cheese sauce is a grand finish to the flavors of the meatballs. If a milder meatball is preferred, eliminate the jalapeño chile. Low-fat cheese may be substituted in the recipe.

This combination also makes a wonderful, juicy meatball sandwich.

MAKES 6 SERVINGS

Meatballs

1 pound ground turkey or pork

1 large egg white

1 medium onion, diced

3 garlic cloves, crushed

3 tablespoons finely chopped fresh cilantro

¼ teaspoon ground cumin

¼ teaspoon ground chili powder

1 jalapeño chile, seeded and finely chopped

¼ teaspoon salt

⅛ teaspoon freshly ground white pepper

1 cup crushed canned tomatoes

1 teaspoon dry oregano

½ teaspoon salt

½ red or green bell pepper, chopped

1 cup (4 ounces) finely grated Monterey Jack cheese

Shape the meatballs: Blend together turkey, egg white, onion, garlic, cilantro, cumin, chili powder, chile, salt, and pepper. Form into 1½-inch meatballs; set aside.

Combine tomatoes, oregano, salt, and bell pepper in a pressure cooker. Layer the meatballs in the sauce. Secure lid according to manufacturer's directions. Over high heat, bring pressure up to high. Reduce heat to medium to maintain pressure and cook 5 minutes.

Release pressure according to manufacturer's directions. Remove lid. Gently stir in the cheese. Serve warm in a chafing dish.

▣ ▣ ▣

POLENTA DISCS WITH RED PEPPER TOPPING

These polenta discs are very versatile. Top with either the Hot Sauce (page 15) or the Red Pepper Topping.

MAKES 6 SERVINGS

2 slices bacon, finely diced

4 tablespoons olive oil

1 small onion, finely diced

2 garlic cloves, crushed

2¾ cups chicken broth

1 cup cornmeal

Dash crushed red pepper flakes

1 teaspoon salt

1 teaspoon sugar

1 tablespoon butter

3 tablespoons freshly grated Parmesan cheese

Red Pepper Topping

2 slices bacon, finely diced

1 tablespoon olive oil

1 medium red bell pepper, sliced

½ teaspoon dried basil

Dash salt

Dash freshly ground white pepper

Cook bacon with 1 tablespoon of the olive oil in a pressure cooker over medium heat 3 minutes. Stir in onion and garlic and cook 1 minute, scraping bottom of cooker with a wooden spoon to loosen any browned bits. Add remaining ingredients, except butter and cheese. Secure lid. Over high heat, bring pressure up to high. Reduce heat to medium to maintain pressure, and slide heat diffuser between pressure cooker and heat. Cook for 15 minutes.

Release pressure according to manufacturer's directions. Remove lid. Stir in butter and cheese. Cover and allow to sit until warm. Polenta will be very thick. Lay out a 30-inch piece of plastic wrap. Spoon polenta lengthwise down center of plastic wrap. Fold wrap over polenta and form a log 2 inches thick. Secure ends and refrigerate for 4 hours. Remove plastic wrap. Slice polenta into ½-inch slices. Heat the remaining 3 tablespoons olive oil in a large skillet over medium heat. Brown each side of polenta slices. Set aside.

To make the topping: Sauté bacon with oil in a skillet over medium heat until bacon is browned. Add bell pepper and cook over medium heat. Sprinkle basil, salt, and pepper over top. Stir well.

To serve, place polenta on a platter or individual serving dishes. Crisscross bell pepper slices over top and drizzle with pan juices.

HOT SAUCE

To serve with polenta, drizzle sauce over polenta discs. This versatile hot sauce is also great served with corn chips or enchiladas.

MAKES ABOUT 1 CUP

1 cup canned diced tomatoes

2 garlic cloves, crushed

2 tablespoons olive oil

⅓ teaspoon ground cumin

¼ teaspoon dried oregano

1 teaspoon salt

Large pinch crushed red pepper flakes

1 teaspoon sugar

¼ cup finely chopped fresh cilantro

3 tablespoons seasoned bread crumbs

Place all ingredients, except bread crumbs, in a pressure cooker. Secure lid. Over high heat, bring pressure up to high. Reduce heat to medium to maintain pressure and cook 3 minutes.

Release pressure according to manufacturer's directions. Remove lid. Stir in bread crumbs. Transfer to a heatproof bowl. Refrigerate at least 4 hours before serving.

VEGETABLES WITH HONEY MUSTARD DIP

Mustard sauce makes a delightful salad dressing. It may be doubled in quantity and stored for up to a week in a jar with a tight-fitting lid.

MAKES 12 SERVINGS

1 cup water

1 small cauliflower head, cut into bite-size pieces

1 small broccoli head, cut into florets

20 miniature carrots

⅓ pound green beans, ends removed and cut in half

Honey Mustard Dip

1 large egg, boiled 3 minutes (see below)

1 tablespoon mayonnaise

½ teaspoon honey mustard

1 tablespoon butter, melted

1 tablespoon apple cider vinegar

⅛ teaspoon salt

Dash freshly ground black pepper

¼ cup olive oil

Pour water into the pressure cooker. Layer cauliflower, broccoli, carrots, and then green beans in order listed into the steam basket. Secure lid. Over high heat, develop pressure to medium. Reduce heat to maintain pressure and cook 2 minutes.

Release pressure under cold running water. Remove lid. Transfer veggies into a colander and run cold running water over them. Transfer to a plastic bag or bowl and chill.

Prepare the dip: Combine egg, mayonnaise, mustard, butter, vinegar, salt, and pepper in a bowl. Whisk until blended. Slowly drizzle olive oil into mixture, whisking vigorously. Keep refrigerated in an airtight container until ready to use.

Pour dressing into a ramekin and place in center of a large platter. Arrange veggies all around in a colorful manner. Serve as an appetizer or side dish.

EGG SAFETY

Uncooked or undercooked eggs should not be eaten by young children, the elderly, or anyone with a serious illness or compromised immune system, because they may contain salmonella bacteria that can cause serious illness. Cooking eggs to 160 degrees F will destroy any salmonella that may be present.

BLACK BEAN APPETIZER WITH SOUR CREAM, CHOPPED TOMATO, AND AVOCADO SLICES

Cilantro resembles flat-leaf parsley. If you're not sure which is which, pinch off a leaf and smell to make sure in fragrance it isn't parsley. Cilantro is more pungent smelling than parsley.

MAKES 6 TO 8 SERVINGS

½ cup dried black beans, soaked overnight

3 slices bacon, cut into ½-inch pieces

1 small onion, minced

2 garlic cloves, crushed

1½ cups beef broth

1¼ teaspoons salt

1½ teaspoons chili powder

½ teaspoon crushed red pepper flakes

¼ teaspoon ground cumin

⅓ cup chopped fresh cilantro

1 tablespoon sherry

1 large tomato

1 ripe avocado

1 (8-ounce) carton sour cream

Drain beans; set aside. Sauté bacon in a pressure cooker, stirring, until crisp. Add onion and garlic; cook 2 minutes, stirring often. Add broth, salt, chili powder, pepper flakes, cumin, cilantro, sherry, and beans, mixing well. Secure lid. Over high heat, bring pressure up to high. Reduce heat to maintain pressure and cook 10 minutes.

Release the pressure according to manufacturer's directions. Remove the lid. Drain the beans through a sieve.

Beans may be served hot or chilled. Cooked beans can be refrigerated for up to 2 days or frozen for up to 1 month.

Seed and coarsely chop tomato. Cut avocado in half, remove pit, peel, and cut into slices. To serve, mound about 3 tablespoons beans on a small dish. Top with a dollop of sour cream, spoon several chunks of the tomato over sour cream, and garnish with an avocado slice. Repeat with remaining ingredients.

LAYERED TORTILLA DIP

Enough to feed a crowd, the pressure cooker helps put this together quickly.

MAKES 16 SERVINGS

Meat Sauce with Beans

1 cup dried kidney beans, soaked overnight

¼ cup olive oil

1 large onion, chopped

2 garlic cloves, crushed

1 pound ground beef or ground turkey

1 (8-ounce) can tomato sauce

1 cup beef broth

1 tablespoon light brown sugar

1 teaspoon salt

2 teaspoons chili powder

1 teaspoon *each* crushed red pepper flakes and
    ground cumin

Guacamole

2 ripe avocados, peeled and pits removed

2 tablespoons fresh lemon juice

2 garlic cloves, crushed

3 green onions, cut into pieces

3 tablespoons salsa

2 tablespoons olive oil

⅓ cup sour cream

½ teaspoon salt

1 (14- or 15-ounce) package tortilla chips

½ head iceberg lettuce, shredded

2 cups (8 ounces) shredded Monterey Jack cheese

3 tomatoes, seeds removed and chopped

6 green onions, chopped

1 green bell pepper, chopped

1 cup pitted ripe olives, cut in halves

Prepare Meat Sauce with Beans: Drain beans and set aside. Heat oil in a pressure cooker. Add onion and garlic and sauté until softened. Add beef to onion mixture and cook, stirring to break up meat, until no longer pink. Add beans, tomato sauce, broth, brown sugar, salt, chili powder, pepper flakes, and cumin; mix well. Secure lid. Over high heat, bring pressure up to high. Reduce heat to maintain pressure and cook 10 minutes. Release pressure according to manufacturer's directions. Remove lid. Set aside.

While mixture cooks, prepare Guacamole: Combine all ingredients in a food processor. Process until smooth. Cover surface with plastic wrap to prevent darkening.

To serve, place chips in center of a 14- to 16-inch round platter or pizza pan, leaving a 2-inch-wide space around edge. Arrange lettuce around edge of platter. Sprinkle half of the cheese over chips. Spoon meat sauce over cheese. Scatter tomatoes, green onions, bell pepper, and olives over meat layer. Sprinkle with remaining cheese. Place spoonfuls of Guacamole over cheese.

COOK'S NOTE: Prepared meat sauce may be frozen up to 3 months. Thaw overnight in the refrigerator before reheating. The sauce is also great for Coney Island hot dogs.

HUMMUS

The flavor of the freshly cooked dried garbanzo bean, or chickpea, is sweeter and nuttier than the canned ones.

MAKES 6 SERVINGS

1 cup dried garbanzo beans, soaked 4 to 6 hours

2 cups water

3 sprigs fresh parsley

1 teaspoon dried spearmint, rubbed between palms

1 teaspoon salt

1/4 teaspoon freshly ground black pepper

2 garlic cloves, crushed

1/3 cup olive oil

1/4 cup fresh lemon juice

2 teaspoons tahini (sesame seed paste)

1/2 cup plain yogurt

Pita bread wedges or toast points to serve

Drain garbanzo beans. In a pressure cooker, combine garbanzo beans, water, parsley, spearmint, salt, and pepper. Secure lid. Over high heat, bring pressure up to high. Reduce heat to maintain pressure and cook 15 minutes.

Release pressure according to manufacturer's directions. Remove lid. Drain garbanzo beans through a colander. Remove parsley sprigs. Combine garbanzo beans, garlic, oil, lemon juice, tahini, and yogurt in a food processor or blender. Blend until smooth.

Serve hummus with pita bread.

MEXICHICKEN TACOS

Always a winner, these tacos are a real treat for football Sundays!

MAKES 24 TACOS

3 slices bacon, cut into 1/2-inch pieces

2 tablespoons olive oil

1 medium onion, sliced

3 garlic cloves, crushed

1/3 cup finely chopped fresh cilantro

1/3 cup jalapeño salsa

1/4 cup ketchup

1/2 cup chicken broth

1 teaspoon salt

1 teaspoon chili powder

2 chicken breasts, skin removed, boned, and cut into 2-inch strips

1/3 cup sour cream

1 tablespoon potato starch or all-purpose flour

1 (24-count) package miniature taco shells

1 cup (4 ounces) shredded Monterey Jack cheese

2 cups shredded lettuce

1 green bell pepper, coarsely chopped

1 large tomato, seeds removed and coarsely chopped

2 avocados, thinly sliced

Sauté bacon with oil in a pressure cooker over medium heat 1 minute. Add onion, garlic, and cilantro; sauté 3 minutes. Stir in salsa, ketchup, broth, salt, chili powder, and chicken strips. Secure lid. Over high heat, bring pressure up to medium. Reduce heat to maintain pressure and cook 5 minutes.

Release pressure according to manufacturer's directions. Remove lid. Stir chicken and sauce. Combine sour cream and potato starch. Stir into chicken and sauce and cook, stirring, over medium heat 1 minute, or until mixture thickens.

Place taco shells on a large tray. Spoon chicken and sauce into shells. Add a little cheese, lettuce, bell pepper, and tomato to each filled shell, topping with sliced avocado.

COOK'S NOTES: Potato starch is a thickener that also adds flavor to recipes.

The chicken filling may be frozen up to 3 months. Thaw in refrigerator overnight before reheating.

SALMON MOUSSE

It makes a lovely presentation to mold the mousse in a fish-shaped mold. Invert onto a platter. Unmold by wrapping hot towels around bottom of mold. Cut a cucumber into very thin slices and use the slices to cover the fish in rows resembling the scales. Use pimiento-stuffed olives for eyes.

MAKES 16 SERVINGS

1 envelope unflavored gelatin

⅓ cup fresh lemon juice

¼ cup butter or olive oil

3 shallots, minced

1 cup bottled clam juice

1 bay leaf

1 teaspoon salt

¼ teaspoon freshly ground white pepper

1 teaspoon dried dill weed

1 pound 1-inch-thick salmon steaks

1 tablespoon sherry

½ cup sour cream

½ cup mayonnaise

Lemon slices to garnish

Hearty dark bread or crackers

Soften gelatin in lemon juice in a small bowl and set aside. In a pressure cooker, melt butter. Add shallots and sauté over medium heat until softened. Stir in clam juice, bay leaf, salt, pepper, and dill, mixing well. Place salmon steaks in clam juice. Secure lid. Over high heat, develop medium-high pressure. Reduce heat to maintain pressure and cook 3 minutes.

Release pressure according to manufacturer's directions. Remove lid. Place salmon steaks on a platter, reserving cooking liquid. Remove bay leaf. Remove skin and bones from salmon and discard.

Combine salmon, cooking liquid, dissolved gelatin, sherry, sour cream, and mayonnaise in a food processor or blender. Blend until smooth. Pour into a 6-cup mold or serving bowl. Refrigerate, covered with plastic wrap, overnight or at least 6 hours. Unmold on a serving plate if desired. Garnish with lemon slices and serve with bread, cut into triangles.

COOK'S NOTE: Salmon Mousse can be made up to 2 days ahead.

STUFFED GRAPE LEAVES

Make these ahead and serve as part of an appetizer tray.
MAKES 16 SERVINGS

1/3 cup olive oil

4 green onions, minced

3 garlic cloves, crushed

1/3 cup minced fresh parsley

1/3 cup minced fresh mint, or 2 teaspoons dried
     mint

1 cup long-grain white rice

2 cups chicken broth

1 1/2 teaspoons salt

1/4 teaspoon freshly ground black pepper

1/2 teaspoon grated lemon zest

1 (16-ounce) jar grape leaves

2 cups water

1/2 cup fresh lemon juice

Heat oil in a pressure cooker. Add green onions, garlic, parsley, and mint and sauté in hot oil 2 minutes. Stir in rice and cook, stirring, 1 minute. Stir in broth, 1 teaspoon of the salt, pepper, and lemon zest, mixing thoroughly. Secure lid. Over high heat, bring pressure up to high. Reduce heat to maintain pressure and cook 8 minutes.

Release pressure according to manufacturer's directions. Remove lid. Transfer rice mixture to a bowl. Rinse pressure cooker.

Drain grape leaves and rinse well in warm water. Place grape leaves, rib sides up, in a row on work surface. Trim thick rib from bottom of each leaf. Spoon 2 teaspoons of rice filling on each leaf. Fold sides of leaf to center of filling, then roll from bottom to top. Place in steam basket, seam side down. (Extra grape leaves may be tightly wrapped in plastic wrap and frozen.) Pour the water and remaining 1/2 teaspoon salt into pressure cooker. Insert steam basket with grape leaves. Pour lemon juice over stuffed grape leaves. Cover leaves with heavy plastic wrap, pressing around edges. Secure lid. Over high heat, bring pressure up to high. Reduce heat to maintain pressure and cook 10 minutes.

Release pressure according to manufacturer's directions. Remove lid. Remove steam basket and let stand, covered, 5 minutes. Serve stuffed grape leaves hot or cold.

COOK'S NOTE: Refrigerate stuffed grape leaves in an airtight container up to 2 days. Also, they may be frozen up to 3 months; thaw in refrigerator before serving.

SOUPS

The basis for a hearty, rich soup is a good stock. The pressure cooker quickly and easily extracts all the flavors and nutrients from bones and vegetables.

Several stock recipes are offered in this chapter. They are all moderately seasoned and offer a well-balanced base for soups or stews. However, if a canned stock is preferred, select one with a low-sodium content.

Favorite soup recipes are easily adapted to pressure cooking. Begin with a good stock, keeping in mind that because very little evaporation occurs during cooking, the liquid should be decreased by a cup. Begin with ingredients that require longer periods to cook and interrupt the process (see "Eight Steps for Perfect Pressure Cooking" on page 8) to add ingredients that require less time. Refer to time charts for guidance.

VEGETABLE STOCK

This low-fat, flavorful stock may be substituted for any poultry, meat, or fish stock. Vegetables may be used with peels.

MAKES 2 QUARTS

3 tablespoons olive or canola oil

3 large leeks, coarsely chopped

2 garlic cloves, crushed

½ cup minced fresh parsley

2 tablespoons all-purpose flour

4 carrots, cut into 1-inch pieces

6 celery stalks with leaves, cut into 1-inch pieces

10 cups water

¼ cup fresh lemon juice

2 large zucchini, cut into 3-inch chunks

1 (10-ounce) package fresh spinach, rinsed

1 large sweet potato with peel, cut into 1-inch cubes

2 bay leaves

½ teaspoon dried tarragon

1 teaspoon dried thyme

¾ teaspoon ground fennel

2 teaspoons salt

½ teaspoon freshly ground white pepper

Heat oil in a pressure cooker over medium-high heat. Add leeks, garlic, and parsley and sauté 3 minutes. With a wooden spoon, stir in flour and cook 3 minutes. Add carrots, celery, water, and lemon juice. Stir well, scraping bottom of the cooker with a wooden spoon to loosen any browned bits. Add remaining ingredients and stir well. Secure lid. Increase heat to high, and bring pressure up to high. Reduce heat to maintain pressure and cook 20 minutes.

Release pressure according to manufacturer's directions. Remove lid. Strain stock into a 5-quart saucepan and return to high heat. Boil 10 minutes.

COOK'S NOTE: You may use stock immediately in your favorite soup recipe, store in the refrigerator up to 2 days, or freeze in airtight containers up to 2 months. Thaw in refrigerator.

◻ ◻ ◻

CHICKEN OR TURKEY STOCK

Stock may be reduced for sauces by boiling over medium-high heat 10 minutes. The flavors will intensify.

MAKES 2½ QUARTS

3 pounds chicken or turkey pieces (wings, necks, and bones)

2 large leeks, sliced

2 garlic cloves

1 carrot, cut into large chunks

2 celery stalks, cut into 2-inch pieces

2 teaspoons salt

½ teaspoon freshly ground white pepper

1 bay leaf

2 tablespoons bouquet garni in a cheesecloth bag (page 205)

3 parsley sprigs

3 quarts water

In a 6-quart pressure cooker, combine chicken, leeks, garlic, carrot, celery, salt, pepper, bay leaf, bouquet garni, parsley, and water. Secure lid. Over high heat, bring pressure up to high. Reduce heat to maintain pressure and cook 1 hour.

Release pressure according to manufacturer's directions. Shake cooker to release pressure pockets. Remove lid. Stir stock. Remove cheesecloth bag, bay leaf, and chicken pieces. Strain stock through a fine colander, sieve, or cheesecloth into large pot or container, lightly pressing with back of a large spoon to extract juices from vegetables.

Refrigerate a few hours, allowing fat to rise to top of stock for easy removal.

COOK'S NOTE: You may use stock immediately in your favorite soup recipe, store in refrigerator up to 3 days, or freeze in airtight containers up to 2 months. Thaw in refrigerator.

BASIC BEEF STOCK

Make your own stock and forget the canned ones. This is so much better.

MAKES 2 QUARTS

¼ cup olive oil

2 carrots, cut, into ¼-inch cubes

2 celery stalks, cut into ¼-inch slices

2 medium onions, chopped

3 pounds meaty beef bones, split by butcher

1 cup dry white wine

3 garlic cloves, mashed

1 teaspoon dried thyme

½ teaspoon dried tarragon

2 bay leaves

3 large parsley sprigs

1 teaspoon freshly ground black peppercorns

2 teaspoons salt or to taste

1 teaspoon light brown sugar

10 cups water

Preheat oven to 425 degrees F. Combine oil, carrots, celery, and onions in a baking pan, stirring to coat vegetables with oil. Add beef bones. Bake, stirring frequently, 35 minutes, or until vegetables and bones are a deep, golden brown.

Transfer vegetables and bones into a pressure cooker.

Place baking pan over medium heat and add wine. Scrape to dislodge caramelized cooking juices clinging to bottom of pan. Add wine mixture, garlic, herbs, peppercorns, salt, brown sugar, and water to pressure cooker. Secure lid. Over high heat, bring pressure up to high. Reduce heat to maintain pressure and cook 1 hour.

Release pressure according to manufacturer's directions. Shake well to release pressure pockets. Remove lid and stir vegetable-bone mixture.

Using a slotted spoon, remove bones and set aside. Strain stock through a fine sieve into a 4-quart pan. Using back of a large spoon, press vegetable pulp through sieve into stock. Remove meat from bones and add to stock or reserve for other use. Boil stock 8 minutes.

VARIATION Veal bones may be substituted for beef to make veal stock.

COOK'S NOTE: You may use stock immediately in your favorite soup recipe, store in refrigerator up to 3 days, or freeze in airtight containers up to 3 months. Thaw in refrigerator.

□ □ □

AUTUMN CABBAGE AND SAUSAGE SOUP

Cabbage can be found in the produce department in vibrant colors of green, red, or white. Chinese cabbage or Savoy cabbage is considered more flavorful than standard white. It's always fun to experiment with different types.
MAKES 6 SERVINGS

2 tablespoons olive or canola oil

1 large white onion, coarsely diced

¼ cup coarsely chopped fresh parsley

3 cups chicken broth

1 large bay leaf

1 tablespoon dried dill weed

1½ pounds cabbage, coarsely sliced

¼ cup tomato sauce

1 teaspoon light brown sugar

1 teaspoon salt

⅛ teaspoon freshly ground white pepper

½ pound cooked turkey sausage, cut into 1-inch pieces

¼ cup sour cream

Parsley sprigs to garnish

Seasoned Croutons (page 43)

Heat oil in a pressure cooker and add the onion and chopped parsley. Sauté until onion is softened. Add remaining ingredients, except sausage, sour cream, parsley sprigs, and croutons. Secure lid. Over high heat, bring pressure up to medium. Reduce heat to medium to maintain pressure and cook 3 minutes.

Release pressure according to manufacturer's directions. Remove lid. Discard bay leaf. Stir in turkey sausage. Ladle ⅓ cup broth into sour cream and whisk until smooth. Add to the soup. Cook over high heat for 2 minutes; do not boil. Serve in individual soup bowls and garnish with a sprig of parsley and croutons.

□ □ □

BELGIAN ENDIVE SOUP

Two leafy greens have been combined in this soup. Endive is traditionally used, but here I have used escarole to balance endive's bitterness with a little sweetness.
MAKES 6 SERVINGS

½ pound Belgian endive (about 2 heads), rinsed

½ pound escarole (about 2 heads), rinsed

3 tablespoons butter

3 large leeks (white parts only), rinsed and thinly sliced

4 cups chicken broth

¼ teaspoon ground nutmeg

1½ teaspoons salt

⅛ teaspoon freshly ground white pepper

2 tablespoons fresh lemon juice

3 tablespoons all-purpose flour or potato starch

Croutons

Cut away the base of the greens. Separate the leaves and rinse two times in warm water. Drain and set aside. Melt butter in a pressure cooker. Add leeks and sauté until tender. Add remaining ingredients, except lemon juice, flour, and croutons. Secure lid. Over high heat, bring pressure up to high. Reduce heat to medium to maintain pressure and cook for 8 minutes.

Release pressure according to manufacturer's directions. Remove lid. Stir well. Combine lemon juice and flour in a small bowl. Stir in ⅓ cup of the hot broth and whisk until smooth. Stir into soup and cook over medium-high heat, stirring, 3 minutes. Serve hot with croutons.

⊡ ⊡ ⊡

BUTTERNUT SQUASH BISQUE WITH SHRIMP

Sweet butternut squash is a large pear-shaped vegetable, as long as 12 inches and weighing 2 to 3 pounds each. The smooth, rich colorful flesh is sweet and the rich orange color has delicious eye appeal.

MAKES 6 SERVINGS

3 tablespoons olive or canola oil

1 leek (white part only), rinsed and thinly sliced

2 medium butternut squash, peeled, seeded, and cut into 3-inch pieces

2 cups water

1 teaspoon salt

⅛ teaspoon freshly ground white pepper

1½ teaspoons dried dill weed

½ pound shrimp with shells

¼ cup half-and-half

½ cup finely chopped fresh parsley

Heat oil in a pressure cooker. Add leek and sauté 2 minutes. Add squash, water, salt, pepper, and dill. Secure lid. Over high heat, bring pressure up to high. Reduce heat to medium to maintain pressure and cook 10 minutes.

Release pressure according to manufacturer's directions. Remove lid. Transfer squash to a colander and run cold running water over the squash 1 minute. Add shrimp to pressure cooker and cook over medium heat 2 minutes. With a slotted spoon, transfer shrimp to a platter; remove shells and devein. Cut shrimp in half. Add squash pulp to soup broth.

In a blender or food processor, or using a hand blender, blend soup until smooth. Add shrimp and half-and-half. Stir well. Heat over medium heat until hot. Stir in ¼ cup of the parsley. Ladle into soup bowls and sprinkle with remaining parsley. Serve hot.

CANADIAN CHEESE SOUP

Cheddar has become a favorite cheese. It originates from a village in England called Cheddar. It is available from mild to sharp in flavor, and is also available in orange-yellow or white colors.

MAKES 6 SERVINGS

3 slices bacon, finely chopped

1 small white sweet onion, coarsely diced

2 carrots, coarsely grated

½ cup finely chopped celery

¼ cup finely chopped fresh parsley

3 cups chicken broth

½ cup half-and-half

3 cups (12 ounces) shredded sharp Cheddar cheese

1 teaspoon dried tarragon

1 teaspoon salt

⅛ teaspoon freshly ground black pepper

1 tablespoon sweet sherry

6 slices French bread, toasted

Parsley sprigs

Cook bacon in a pressure cooker until almost crisp. Add onion, carrots, celery, and parsley and sauté 3 minutes. Add chicken broth and stir well. Secure lid. Over high heat, bring pressure up to medium. Reduce heat to medium to maintain pressure and cook 5 minutes.

Release pressure according to manufacturer's directions. Remove lid. Stir in half-and-half, cheese, tarragon, salt, pepper, and sherry. Cook over medium-high heat 3 minutes. Remove from heat. Stir well. Cover 2 minutes. Stir once again. Lay 1 slice of toasted bread into each soup bowl. Ladle soup over top. Garnish with parsley sprigs.

CAULIFLOWER AND RED PEPPER SOUP

A 2-pound head of trimmed cauliflower will yield about 4 cups of cut cauliflower. Always select a firm head, with florets tightly together. The white surface should be blemish-free, and the green leaves firm.

MAKES 6 SERVINGS

2 slices bacon, finely diced

1 medium white onion, coarsely diced

1 garlic clove, crushed

1 medium red bell pepper, coarsely diced

1 bay leaf

1 teaspoon dried tarragon

1 small cauliflower, leaves removed, stem trimmed, and cut into florets

1½ teaspoons salt

⅛ teaspoon freshly ground white pepper

3 cups chicken broth

⅓ cup half-and-half

¼ cup all-purpose flour or potato starch

½ cup (2 ounces) grated medium Cheddar cheese, plus extra for topping (optional)

Cook bacon in a pressure cooker until almost crisp. Add onion, garlic, and bell pepper. Stir well and sauté 3 minutes. Add remaining ingredients, except half-and-half, flour, and cheese. Secure lid. Over high heat, develop pressure to medium. Reduce heat to maintain pressure and cook 2 minutes.

Release pressure according to manufacturer's directions. Remove lid. Whisk together half-and-half with flour to form a paste. Stir in ½ cup of the hot broth. Blend mixture into the soup. Add cheese. Cook over medium-high heat, stirring, 3 minutes. Serve hot. Additional cheese may be grated over the top (if using).

◩ ◩ ◩

CHICKEN, BEAN, AND VEGETABLE SOUP

Bacon adds flavor to bean dishes. If concerned about the fat, substitute 2 tablespoons olive oil and a dash of smoke flavoring for the bacon.

MAKES 6 SERVINGS

3 slices bacon, finely diced

1 medium white sweet onion, coarsely diced

3 large carrots, cut into ½-inch pieces

2 garlic cloves, crushed

½ cup white beans, soaked

2 medium potatoes, peeled and cubed

2 stalks celery, coarsely chopped

4 cups chicken broth

1 large bay leaf

1 teaspoon dried tarragon

1½ teaspoons salt

⅛ teaspoon freshly ground black pepper

1 tablespoon fresh lemon juice

¼ cup tomato sauce

½ chicken breast, skinned

½ cup finely chopped fresh parsley

Cook bacon in a pressure cooker until almost crisp. Add onion, carrots, and garlic and sauté 2 minutes. Stir in remaining ingredients, except parsley. Secure lid. Over high heat, bring pressure up to high. Reduce heat to medium to maintain pressure and cook for 10 minutes.

Reduce pressure according to manufacturer's directions. Remove lid. Using a slotted spoon, transfer chicken breast to a cutting board and allow to cool enough to handle. Stir parsley into soup, reserving 2 tablespoons. Cook over medium heat 1 minute. Cut chicken breast into bite-size pieces and stir into the soup. Serve in soup bowls with reserved parsley sprinkled over tops.

CHICKEN SOUP WITH ORZO AND VEGETABLES

Orzo is shaped like a tiny pine nut. It is actually in the pasta family, yet many refer to it as a rice. It can easily be substituted in rice recipes and vice versa.

MAKES 6 SERVINGS

1 chicken breast half, skin removed

2 large leeks (white parts only), rinsed and chopped

2 garlic cloves, crushed

3 stalks celery, coarsely chopped

3 medium carrots, cut into ½-inch pieces

1 teaspoon dried tarragon

1 teaspoon salt

⅛ teaspoon freshly ground white pepper

1 cup orzo

4 cups chicken broth

½ cup finely chopped fresh parsley

½ pound asparagus, cut into 1-inch pieces

2 tablespoons fresh lemon juice

Place all ingredients in a pressure cooker, except parsley, asparagus, and lemon juice. Secure lid. Over high heat, bring pressure up to high. Reduce heat to medium to maintain pressure and cook 9 minutes.

Release pressure according to manufacturer's directions. Remove lid. Using a slotted spoon, transfer chicken breast to a cutting board and cool enough to handle. Set 6 asparagus tips aside. Stir parsley, remaining asparagus, and lemon juice into the soup. Cook over medium-high heat 4 minutes. Cut chicken breast into bite-size pieces and add to the soup. Serve in soup bowls, garnished with asparagus tips.

⬚ ⬚ ⬚

CHICKEN VEGETABLE SOUP

Elbow macaroni, mini pieces of curved tube macaroni, is generally made with semolina and water, without eggs.

MAKES 6 SERVINGS

2 tablespoons olive oil

1 large white sweet onion, coarsely chopped

3 garlic cloves, crushed

½ chicken breast, skinned

3 medium carrots, cut into ½-inch pieces

3 whole celery stalks, coarsely chopped

2 medium potatoes, peeled and cubed

1 large fresh fennel bulb, coarsely chopped

4 cups chicken broth

1½ teaspoons salt

⅛ teaspoon freshly ground black pepper

1 teaspoon dried basil

1 cup elbow macaroni

⅓ cup finely chopped fresh parsley

3 tablespoons grated fontinella cheese (optional)

Heat oil in a pressure cooker over medium heat. Add onion and garlic and sauté 3 minutes. Add chicken, and cook 2 minutes. Add remaining ingredients, except parsley and cheese.

Secure lid. Over high heat, bring pressure up to high. Reduce heat to medium to maintain pressure and cook for 8 minutes.

Release pressure according to manufacturer's directions. Remove lid. Using a slotted spoon, transfer chicken to a cutting board to cool enough to handle. Stir parsley into the soup and cook for 2 minutes. Cut chicken into bite-size pieces and add to soup. Serve in soup bowls with grated fontinella cheese sprinkled over top (optional).

CORN AND BROCCOLI SOUP WITH SAUSAGE

Fresh corn can be removed easily by simply securing the flat end of the corn on a cutting board and running a sharp knife from top to bottom, working around the cob.
MAKES 6 SERVINGS

2 tablespoons olive oil

1 small onion, diced

3 garlic cloves, crushed

¼ cup minced fresh parsley

3 carrots, cut into 1-inch pieces

3 cups chicken broth

1 teaspoon salt

Pinch crushed red pepper flakes

1 teaspoon dried tarragon

2 cups broccoli florets

4 cups fresh or frozen whole-kernel corn

8 ounces smoked cooked sausage, cut into 1-inch pieces

¾ cup half-and-half

3 tablespoons all-purpose flour

Seasoned Croutons (page 43)

Heat oil in a pressure cooker over medium heat. Add onion, garlic, and parsley and sauté until onion is softened. Add carrots, broth, seasonings, broccoli, and corn. Secure lid. Over high heat, bring pressure up to high. Reduce heat to medium to maintain pressure and cook 5 minutes.

Release pressure under cold running water. Remove lid. Stir in sausage. Blend half-and-half with flour. Stir into the soup and cook over high heat, stirring, 3 minutes. Serve with croutons.

CORN AND TOMATO CHOWDER WITH MEXICAN SAUSAGE

The corncobs add incredible flavor to the soup during the cooking process.

MAKES 6 SERVINGS

½ **small onion, thinly sliced**

1 **large ripe tomato, cut in quarters and seeded**

1 **tablespoon olive oil**

4 **large ears corn, husks and silks removed**

2 **slices bacon, cut into ½-inch pieces**

1 **medium onion, diced**

2 **garlic cloves, crushed**

½ **pound chorizo (Mexican sausage), cut into 1-inch pieces**

3 **cups chicken broth**

1 **medium potato, peeled and cut into ½-inch cubes**

1 **bay leaf**

⅛ **teaspoon dried sage**

Dash crushed red pepper flakes

1 **teaspoon salt**

⅓ **cup finely chopped fresh parsley**

½ **large red bell pepper, coarsely chopped**

2 **tablespoons sour cream**

½ **cup milk**

⅓ **cup all-purpose flour**

Tortilla chips

Preheat oven to 450 degrees F. Place onion slices in a single layer in a baking dish. Cut tomatoes into ¾-inch slices and place them over onion slices. Drizzle olive oil over top. Roast 10 minutes. Remove from oven and cover with foil. Set aside.

To slice off corn kernels, place corn flat end down on a cutting board and slice in a downward motion all around the corn. Set corn aside. Cut corncobs in half.

Cook bacon in a pressure cooker over medium heat until almost crisp. Add diced onion, garlic, and sausage. Sauté 2 minutes. Pour broth into the pressure cooker. Add corncobs, potato, bay leaf, sage, pepper flakes, salt, parsley, and bell pepper. Secure lid. Over high heat, bring pressure up to high. Reduce heat to medium to maintain pressure and cook 5 minutes.

Release pressure according to manufacturer's directions. Remove lid. Using tongs, remove corncobs. Whisk together sour cream, milk, and flour. Stir in ½ cup of hot broth. Pour mixture into the soup and cook over medium-high heat, stirring, 2 minutes. Taste and correct seasoning. Serve with tortilla chips.

CREAMY POTATO AND SPINACH SOUP

Fat-free half-and-half is readily available in the dairy section. It is a fine substitution for those on fat-free diets, and does not adversely affect the flavor.

MAKES 6 SERVINGS

2 slices bacon, finely diced

1 large white sweet onion, coarsely diced

2 garlic cloves, crushed

2 carrots, coarsely chopped

3 cups chicken broth

1½ teaspoons salt

⅛ teaspoon freshly ground black pepper

1 teaspoon dried tarragon

4 medium potatoes, peeled and cubed

1 (10-ounce) package spinach, rinsed

½ cup regular or fat-free half-and-half

3 tablespoons all-purpose flour

1 cup (4 ounces) grated mild Cheddar cheese

Cook bacon in a pressure cooker until almost crisp. Add onion, garlic, and carrots and sauté 2 minutes. Stir well. Add broth, salt, pepper, tarragon, and potatoes. Secure lid. Over high heat, bring pressure up to high. Reduce heat to medium to maintain pressure and cook 5 minutes.

Release pressure according to manufacturer's instructions, and remove lid. Add spinach. Secure lid. Over high heat, bring pressure up to medium. Reduce heat to maintain pressure and cook 3 minutes.

Release pressure under cold running water.

Remove lid. Blend half-and-half with flour. Stir in ½ cup of the hot broth and stir mixture into the soup. Stir in half of the cheese and cook 3 minutes. Serve in soup bowls with remaining cheese sprinkled over tops.

SWEET POTATO AND CARROT SOUP

The carrots are an important part of this soup, lending sweetness and color. Select firm, smooth carrots.

MAKES 6 SERVINGS

3 tablespoons butter

1 medium onion, finely diced

1 garlic clove, crushed

5 carrots, peeled and finely diced

1 large sweet potato, peeled and cubed

3 cups chicken broth

2 teaspoons brown sugar

1 teaspoon salt

⅛ teaspoon freshly ground white pepper

Dash freshly grated nutmeg

⅓ cup sour cream

3 tablespoons all-purpose flour or potato starch

Melt butter in a pressure cooker over medium heat. Add onion and garlic and sauté 3 minutes. Add remaining ingredients, except sour cream and flour. Over high heat, bring pressure up to high. Reduce heat to medium to maintain pressure and cook 5 minutes.

Release pressure under cold running water. Remove lid. Process soup through a food mill, blender, or food processor until smooth. Return to pan. Blend together sour cream and flour. Add ½ cup of the hot soup mixture and blend until smooth. Stir into the soup and cook over medium heat 4 minutes. Serve hot.

FRESH BROCCOLI SOUP

If the stalks of the broccoli are tough, peel away the surface of every stalk. Broccoli may be stored in the refrigerator, wrapped in wet paper towels, for up to 5 days.

MAKES 6 SERVINGS

2 slices bacon, finely chopped

1 large leek (white part only), rinsed and coarsely chopped

¼ cup finely chopped fresh parsley

1 teaspoon salt

Dash crushed red pepper flakes

1 large bay leaf

1 teaspoon dried tarragon

4 cups chicken broth

1 large potato, peeled and diced

4 cups 1-inch broccoli pieces

3 tablespoons butter, at room temperature

3 tablespoons sour cream

3 tablespoons all-purpose flour or potato starch

1 cup (4 ounces) grated Cheddar cheese

Cook bacon in a pressure cooker over medium heat until almost crisp. Add leek and parsley and sauté 2 minutes. Add salt, pepper flakes, bay leaf, tarragon, broth, and potato. Stir well. Secure lid. Over high heat, bring pressure up to high. Reduce heat to medium to maintain pressure and cook 5 minutes.

Release pressure under cold running water. Remove lid. Stir in broccoli. Secure lid. Over high heat, develop pressure to medium. Reduce heat to maintain pressure and cook 2 minutes.

Release pressure under cold running water. Remove lid. Stir well. Discard bay leaf. Blend butter, sour cream, and flour together. Add ½ cup of the hot broth and whisk until smooth. Stir into the soup along with the cheese. Cook, stirring, 3 minutes, or until cheese melts and soup thickens.

GREEK LEMON RICE SOUP

This traditional Greek soup is a favorite. The most important factor in its preparation is to temper the eggs with hot stock before adding them to the soup. This important technique will prevent curdling.

MAKES 6 SERVINGS

1 chicken breast half, skin removed

4 cups chicken broth

1 large carrot, coarsely chopped

2 stalks celery, coarsely chopped

¾ cup long-grain white rice

1½ teaspoons salt

⅛ teaspoon freshly ground white pepper

1 bay leaf

¼ cup fresh dill, finely chopped

½ cup fresh lemon juice

3 large eggs

1 tablespoon all-purpose flour

2 tablespoons finely chopped fresh parsley

Combine all ingredients in a pressure cooker, except eggs, flour, and parsley. Secure lid. Over high heat, bring pressure up to high. Reduce heat to medium to maintain pressure and cook 8 minutes.

Release pressure according to manufacturer's directions. Remove lid. Discard bay leaf. Using a slotted spoon, transfer chicken breast to a cutting board to cool enough to handle. With an electric hand mixer, beat eggs and flour on high speed until thick and creamy. Ladle ½ cup of the hot broth into the eggs and beat 1 minute longer. Pour into the hot soup, and stir until well incorporated. Heat until hot; do not boil. Stir in the parsley. Cut chicken into bite-size pieces and stir into soup. Serve hot.

❑ ❑ ❑

MEDITERRANEAN TOMATO-RED PEPPER SOUP

The seasoned bread crumbs add body to this lovely soup, and also enhance the flavor.

MAKES 6 SERVINGS

3 cups chicken broth

1 large leek (white part only), rinsed and coarsely diced

2 garlic cloves, crushed

1 large red bell pepper, coarsely chopped

1 teaspoon dried basil

1 teaspoon salt

Dash crushed red pepper flakes

1 teaspoon sugar

½ teaspoon ground fennel

1 (15-ounce) can diced tomatoes in sauce

¼ cup seasoned bread crumbs

6 thin slices Italian bread, toasted

¼ cup freshly grated Parmesan cheese

Combine all ingredients in a pressure cooker, except bread and cheese. Secure lid. Over high heat, bring pressure up to high. Reduce heat to medium to maintain pressure and cook 4 minutes.

Release pressure under cold running water. Remove lid. Using a food mill, blender, or food processor, process soup until smooth. Place a slice of bread in center of each soup bowl. Ladle soup over bread and sprinkle with Parmesan cheese.

MEXICAN TORTILLA SOUP

The jalapeño chile should be handled with great care. The juices are extremely hot and can cause a burning sensation. It is recommended that you wear plastic or rubber gloves when chopping it.

MAKES 6 SERVINGS

2 tablespoons olive or canola oil

1 medium sweet white onion, coarsely diced

4 garlic cloves, crushed

1 large red bell pepper, coarsely diced

1 large yellow bell pepper, finely diced

1 jalapeño chile, seeded and finely chopped

3 cups chicken broth

½ teaspoon ground cumin

1 teaspoon chili powder

½ teaspoon dried oregano

1½ teaspoons salt

⅛ teaspoon freshly ground black pepper

1 pound chorizo (Mexican sausage), cut into 1-inch pieces

2 tablespoons fresh lime juice

2 cups crushed tortilla chips

⅓ cup chopped fresh cilantro

1 whole ripe tomato, cubed

Heat oil in a pressure cooker over medium heat. Add onion and garlic and sauté 3 minutes. Combine all ingredients, except chips, cilantro, and tomato in a pressure cooker. Secure lid. Over high heat, bring pressure up to high. Reduce heat to medium to maintain pressure and cook 5 minutes.

Release pressure under cold running water. Remove lid. Using a hand blender, food mill, or food processor, process the soup until smooth. Scatter one-sixth of the chips into each of 6 soup bowls. Ladle hot soup over top and sprinkle with cilantro and tomato.

ONION SOUP

This hearty onion soup can be prepared with a light chicken broth or a rich beef stock. Either way, the flavors are incredible.

MAKES 6 SERVINGS

2 tablespoons olive or canola oil

4 large white onions, thickly sliced

2 garlic cloves, crushed

2 tablespoons minced fresh parsley

1 tablespoon sugar

3 cups chicken broth or beef stock

1 large bay leaf

1 teaspoon dried tarragon

1½ teaspoons salt

⅛ teaspoon freshly ground white pepper

2 tablespoons grated fontinella cheese

1½ cups (6 ounces) shredded mozzarella cheese

2 cups croutons

Heat oil in a pressure cooker over medium heat. Add onions, garlic, parsley, and sugar and sauté about 8 minutes. Transfer three-quarters of the onion mixture to a platter. Add remaining ingredients, except cheeses and croutons. Secure lid. Over high heat, bring pressure up to high. Reduce heat to medium to maintain pressure and cook 5 minutes.

Release pressure under cold running water. Remove lid. Stir well. Discard bay leaf. Stir in reserved onions. Preheat oven broiler. Place oven rack on second from top level. Combine cheeses. Place ⅓ cup of the croutons into each of 6 oven-proof bowls. Ladle onion soup over top of croutons. Sprinkle about ¼ cup of the cheese over each serving. Place bowls in a baking pan and slide under hot broiler. Broil until cheese is melted and golden brown.

▣ ▣ ▣

POTATO MUSHROOM SOUP

Portobello mushrooms are large meaty mushrooms, full of flavor. There are a variety of mushrooms in the marketplace, and any fresh mushroom will work in this recipe.

2 tablespoons butter

2 leeks (white parts only), coarsely diced

2 garlic cloves, crushed

¼ cup finely chopped fresh parsley

3 cups chicken broth

1 teaspoon salt

⅛ teaspoon freshly ground black pepper

⅛ teaspoon caraway seeds, crushed

1 teaspoon dried tarragon

3 medium potatoes, peeled and cubed

2 ounces fresh portobello mushrooms, rinsed well and cut into bite-size pieces

2 tablespoons sour cream

2 tablespoons all-purpose flour or potato starch

Parsley sprigs to garnish

Heat butter in a pressure cooker over medium heat. Add leeks, garlic, and parsley and sauté 3 minutes. Stir in broth, salt, pepper, caraway seeds, tarragon, and potatoes. Secure lid. Over high heat, bring pressure up to high. Reduce heat to medium to maintain pressure and cook 6 minutes.

Release pressure under cold running water. Remove lid. Stir in mushrooms. Cover and cook over medium heat 3 minutes. Blend sour cream and flour into a paste. Whisk in ½ cup of the hot broth. Stir into the soup and cook over medium-high heat 3 minutes. Ladle into bowls and garnish with a sprig of parsley.

COOK'S NOTE: If dried mushrooms are preferred for the soup, remember to reconstitute them in warm water for at least 30 minutes. The water will be sandy and the mushrooms should be rinsed very well before using.

PUERTO RICAN CHICKEN RICE SOUP

The jalapeño chile is a smooth, dark green hot chile that grows to approximately 2 inches long. They are easily seeded, but it is recommended to use rubber gloves for protection against the very hot seeds and veins. Jalapeño chiles are also available canned and seeded.

MAKES 6 SERVINGS

3 slices bacon, finely chopped

1 large onion, finely diced

3 garlic cloves, crushed

2 carrots, finely chopped

1 whole chicken breast, skinned and quartered

4 cups chicken broth

1 cup rice

1 cup canned diced tomatoes

1 fresh jalapeño chile, seeded and finely diced

1½ teaspoons salt

⅛ teaspoon freshly ground black pepper

1 cup frozen green peas

1 cup frozen whole-kernel corn

½ cup finely chopped fresh cilantro

2 cups crumbled corn chips

Cook bacon in a pressure cooker over medium heat until almost crisp. Add onion, garlic, and carrots and sauté 3 minutes. Add chicken and cook 1 minute. Stir in remaining ingredients except corn chips, reserving ¼ cup of the cilantro. Secure lid. Over high heat, bring pressure up to high. Reduce heat to medium to maintain pressure and cook 9 minutes.

Release pressure according to manufacturer's directions. Remove lid. Using a slotted spoon, transfer chicken to a cutting board to cool enough to handle. Tear chicken into bite-size pieces and add them to the soup. Stir well. Ladle soup into heated bowls. Top with corn chips and sprinkle with reserved cilantro.

◻ ◻ ◻

PUMPKIN SOUP IN SHELLS

This is a lovely autumn holiday soup. The individual pumpkins add charm to the presentation. Roasting the pumpkin adds remarkable fresh flavor to the soup. Canned pumpkin may be used instead of fresh. Merely substitute 1½ cups canned pumpkin for the fresh. Do not roast the canned pumpkin.

MAKES 6 SERVINGS

1 medium pumpkin

1 teaspoon dried tarragon

3 tablespoons butter, melted

1 teaspoon salt

2 tablespoons canola oil

3 leeks (white parts only), rinsed and finely diced

2 garlic cloves, crushed

4 cups chicken broth

1 teaspoon sherry

⅛ teaspoon freshly ground nutmeg

½ teaspoon salt

⅛ teaspoon freshly ground white pepper

1 cup (4 ounces) grated Swiss cheese

½ cup (2 ounces) grated fontinella cheese

1 cup half-and-half

6 (5- or 6-inch) pumpkins

1 cup Italian seasoned croutons

Preheat oven to 425 degrees F. Cut medium pumpkin into quarters. Remove seeds and membranes. Combine tarragon, butter, and salt in a small bowl. Brush over inner surface of pumpkin. Place pumpkin pieces on a baking sheet. Bake 20 minutes. Cool and cut into 2-inch pieces.

Heat the oil in a pressure cooker over medium heat. Add leeks and garlic and sauté 3 minutes. Add broth, sherry, nutmeg, salt, and pepper. Stir in pumpkin pieces. Secure lid. Over high heat, bring pressure up to high. Reduce heat to medium to maintain pressure and cook 7 minutes.

Release pressure under cold running water. Remove lid. Stir in cheeses and half-and-half. Using a hand blender, whisk, food processor, or standard blender, process soup until smooth.

Cut ½ inch off the top of each small pumpkin and remove seeds and membranes. Microwave until hot. Divide croutons among small pumpkins and pour soup over croutons. Serve hot.

SALMON AND VEGETABLE CHOWDER

It is best to use the fleshiest part of the salmon fillet in this recipe. To skin, simply run a sharp knife between the flesh and skin and carefully slide the knife, separating the skin from the flesh.

MAKES 6 SERVINGS

2 tablespoons canola oil

2 large leeks (white parts only), rinsed and coarsely chopped

2 cups chicken broth

1 (8-ounce) bottle clam juice

1 teaspoon dried thyme

1½ teaspoons salt

⅛ teaspoon freshly ground white pepper

2 large potatoes, peeled and cut into ½-inch cubes

2 medium carrots, cut into ½-inch pieces

1 (10-ounce) package fresh spinach, rinsed and shredded

1 cup frozen whole-kernel corn

½ pound salmon fillet, skinned and cut into 2-inch pieces

1 tablespoon fresh lemon juice

2 tablespoons sour cream

3 tablespoons all-purpose flour or potato starch

2 tablespoons chopped fresh chives

Heat oil in a pressure cooker over medium heat. Add leeks and sauté 2 minutes. Add broth, clam juice, thyme, salt, pepper, potatoes, and carrots. Stir well. Secure lid. Over high heat, bring pressure up to high. Reduce heat to medium to maintain pressure and cook 5 minutes.

Release pressure according to manufacturer's directions. Remove lid. Stir in spinach, corn, and salmon. Secure lid. Over high heat, bring pressure up to medium. Reduce heat to maintain pressure and cook 3 minutes.

Release pressure under cold running water. Remove lid. Stir in lemon juice. Blend together sour cream and flour. Add ½ cup of the hot broth and whisk until smooth. Stir into the soup. Cook over medium-high heat, stirring, 3 minutes. Serve in soup bowls with chives sprinkled over tops.

SHRIMP BISQUE

Shrimp is available in a variety of sizes. The jumbo size yields approximately 12 shrimp to a pound. The large size yields 25 to a pound, the medium size yields 32 per pound. Most shrimp sold in the United States are from bordering oceans. When cooked, a delicate pinkish-orange color develops.

MAKES 6 SERVINGS

3 cups water

1 (8-ounce) bottle clam juice

1½ pounds medium shrimp with shells

1 teaspoon salt

1 teaspoon dried thyme

3 tablespoons butter

2 leeks (white parts only), rinsed and finely diced

1 garlic clove, crushed

2 large carrots, finely diced

1 stalk celery, finely diced

1 cup canned diced tomatoes

1 teaspoon dried tarragon

½ teaspoon sweet paprika

1 large bay leaf

⅓ cup long-grain white rice

2 teaspoons fresh lemon juice

½ cup half-and-half

½ cup coarsely chopped fresh parsley

Place water, clam juice, shrimp, salt, and thyme in a pressure cooker. Secure lid. Over high heat, bring pressure up to high. Reduce heat to medium to maintain pressure and cook 2 minutes.

Release pressure under cold running water. Remove lid. Strain through a sieve into a heat-proof bowl or another pot. Set shrimp aside to cool.

Melt butter in the pressure cooker over medium heat. Add leeks, garlic, carrots, and celery and sauté 2 minutes. Add tomatoes, tarragon, paprika, bay leaf, rice, lemon juice, and strained stock. Secure lid. Over high heat, bring pressure up to high. Reduce heat to medium to maintain pressure and cook 8 minutes.

Release pressure under cold running water. Remove lid. Stir well. Peel shells from shrimp and devein. Coarsely chop shrimp. Stir into soup. Add half-and-half and ¼ cup of the parsley. Stir well. Taste for salt and correct seasoning. Serve in heated bowls and sprinkle with remaining parsley.

TOMATO SOUP

Beefsteak tomatoes are perfect for this soup. To remove the skins, score the tomatoes with a sharp knife and blanch in hot water for 2 minutes. Drain and run cold running water over the tomatoes. Cut the tomatoes into quarters and squeeze the seeds out.

MAKES 6 SERVINGS

3 tablespoons olive oil

1 medium white onion, finely diced

1 garlic clove, crushed

¼ cup finely chopped fresh parsley

1 large bay leaf

4 pounds ripe tomatoes, peeled, seeded, and
   coarsely chopped

1 teaspoon dried basil

1½ teaspoons salt

Dash crushed red pepper flakes

1 cup chicken broth

Croutons

Heat oil in a pressure cooker over medium heat. Add onion, garlic, and parsley and sauté 3 minutes. Add remaining ingredients except croutons and stir well. Secure lid. Over high heat, bring pressure up to high. Reduce heat to medium to maintain pressure and cook 5 minutes.

Release pressure under cold running water. Remove lid. Stir well. Process soup through a food mill into a soup pot. Serve hot with croutons.

BLACK-EYED PEA AND SAUSAGE SOUP

Serve soup with chunks of crusty bread.

MAKES 6 TO 8 SERVINGS

2 cups (12 ounces) dried black-eyed peas, (soaking
   instructions page 163)

½ pound bacon, cut into ½-inch pieces

1 large red onion, minced

3 garlic cloves, chopped

6 cups chicken broth

¼ cup tomato paste

2 teaspoons dried Greek oregano

1 bay leaf

1 teaspoon coarse sea salt or granulated salt

1 teaspoon crushed red pepper flakes

3 tablespoons light brown sugar

½ pound turkey kielbasa, cut into 1-inch pieces

⅓ cup green bell pepper, chopped

⅓ cup coarsely chopped fresh parsley

Drain black-eyed peas and set aside.

Sauté bacon in a pressure cooker, stirring, until crisp. Add onion and garlic and sauté until onion is softened, about 3 minutes. Add peas to bacon mixture and stir well. Add broth, tomato paste, oregano, bay leaf, salt, pepper flakes, and brown sugar. Stir until thoroughly mixed. Secure lid. Over high heat, bring pressure up to high. Reduce heat to maintain pressure and cook 5 minutes.

Release pressure according to manufacturer's directions. Remove lid. Add kielbasa, bell pepper, and parsley to soup. Bring to a boil over high heat and cook, uncovered, 3 minutes, stirring occasionally. Discard bay leaf.

COOK'S NOTES: Prepared soup may be frozen up to 3 months. Thaw in refrigerator.

To quickly presoak peas, combine peas and 4 cups water in a pressure cooker. Secure lid. Over high heat, bring pressure up to high. Turn off heat and allow pressure to slowly decrease. Remove lid. Drain peas and use in soup recipe.

RICH AND CREAMY BORSCHT

Try this soup both chilled and warm and decide which version is your favorite.

MAKES 6 SERVINGS

¼ cup olive oil

4 leeks (white parts only), rinsed and thinly sliced

2 carrots, diced

⅓ cup chopped parsley plus extra to garnish

2 large potatoes, peeled and quartered

6 large beets, peeled and quartered, and greens trimmed off

1 teaspoon salt

¼ teaspoon freshly ground white pepper

1 bay leaf

2 teaspoons dried basil, crushed between palms

½ teaspoon ground fennel

2 tablespoons prepared horseradish

5 cups chicken broth

2 tablespoons sherry

⅓ cup sour cream plus extra to serve

Heat oil in a pressure cooker over medium heat. Add leeks, carrots, and parsley and sauté 3 minutes. Add potatoes, beets, salt, pepper, bay leaf, basil, fennel, horseradish, broth, and sherry. Stir well. Secure lid. Over high heat, bring pressure up to high. Reduce heat to maintain pressure and cook 12 minutes.

Release pressure according to manufacturer's directions. Remove lid. Stir beet mixture. Discard bay leaf.

Pour beet mixture into a food processor or blender. Process until smooth. Blend in sour cream.

Refrigerate until chilled, or serve warm, topping individual servings with a dollop of sour cream and parsley.

VARIATION Drained yogurt or low-fat sour cream may be substituted for regular sour cream.

SEASONED CROUTONS

Keep these on hand to serve with your favorite soup.
MAKES 6 CUPS

1 cup butter, melted, or olive oil
½ cup grated Parmesan cheese
½ teaspoon dried tarragon
½ teaspoon dried basil
½ teaspoon dried oregano
¼ teaspoon dried thyme
1 loaf French or other good-quality bread, thinly
   sliced

Preheat oven to 350 degrees F.
Combine butter, cheese, and herbs in a small bowl. Using a pastry brush, cover both sides of each bread slice with seasoned butter and place slices on a baking sheet.

Bake 8 minutes, turn, and bake 8 minutes, or until golden brown. Cut slices into small cubes. Set aside to cool and dry. Store in a covered container.

▢ ▢ ▢

CABBAGE SOUP WITH KIELBASA

Green cabbage may be used in the recipe; however, the reddish-purple cabbage adds a beautiful color to the finished soup.
MAKES 6 SERVINGS

¼ cup olive oil
1 large onion, sliced
3 garlic cloves, crushed
¼ cup chopped fresh parsley plus extra to garnish
1 tablespoon minced fresh dill
3 cups chicken broth
1 small head red cabbage (4 cups), cored and
   sliced
1 bay leaf
3 medium potatoes, peeled and coarsely diced
1 tablespoon tomato paste
6 ounces smoked kielbasa, cut into bite-size pieces
1¼ teaspoons salt
¼ teaspoon freshly ground white pepper
1 tablespoon sugar
½ cup low-fat sour cream plus extra to garnish
Chopped fresh parsley to garnish

Heat oil in a pressure cooker. Add onion, garlic, parsley, and dill and sauté 2 minutes. Add broth, cabbage, bay leaf, potatoes, tomato paste, kielbasa, salt, pepper, and sugar. Stir well. Secure lid. Over high heat, bring pressure to medium-high. Reduce heat to maintain pressure and cook 4 minutes.

Release pressure according to manufacturer's directions. Remove lid. Stir vegetable mixture. Discard bay leaf. Gradually stir in sour cream. Serve hot; garnish individual servings with dollops of sour cream, and sprinkle with parsley.

CHILI

A taste of the West is made easy with your pressure cooker. If only the chuck-wagon cook had had such conveniences on the trail.

MAKES 6 TO 8 SERVINGS

½ **pound dried red kidney beans, soaked**

¼ **cup olive oil**

½ **pound bacon, cut into ½-inch pieces**

2 **large onions, chopped**

4 **garlic cloves, crushed**

2 **pounds coarsely ground beef**

½ **pound ground pork sausage**

4 **cups beef broth**

1 **(28-ounce) can crushed tomatoes**

½ **cup green bell pepper, chopped**

2 **tablespoons light brown sugar**

2½ **teaspoons salt**

1 **teaspoon freshly ground black pepper**

½ **teaspoon sweet paprika**

2 **tablespoons chili powder**

½ **teaspoon crushed red pepper flakes**

2 **teaspoons ground cumin**

2 **tablespoons Worcestershire sauce**

½ **teaspoon hot pepper sauce (optional)**

1 **(8-ounce) carton low-fat sour cream**

4 **green onions, chopped**

Drain beans and set aside.

Heat oil in a pressure cooker over medium-high heat. Add bacon, onions, and garlic and sauté 3 minutes. Stir in beef and sausage and cook 3 minutes, stirring to break up meat. Add beans, broth, tomatoes, bell pepper, brown sugar, salt, black pepper, paprika, chili powder, pepper flakes, cumin, Worcestershire sauce, and hot pepper sauce (if using). Stir well. Secure lid. Over high heat, bring pressure up to high and slide a heat diffuser under the pressure cooker. Reduce heat to maintain pressure and cook 13 minutes, shaking pan every 4 minutes to keep chili from sticking.

Release pressure according to manufacturer's directions. Remove lid. Stir chili; taste and correct seasoning as needed.

Serve hot; garnish each serving with a dollop of sour cream and green onions.

VARIATIONS Use turkey bacon, ground turkey, and turkey sausage instead of regular bacon, ground beef, and pork sausage if you want a chili without beef or pork.

If you prefer a hotter-flavored chili, add 2 tablespoons jalapeño salsa or ½ teaspoon hot pepper sauce.

CHICKEN NOODLE SOUP

A variety of noodles are available on the market. The vermicelli noodle works deliciously in this soup.

MAKES 6 SERVINGS

¼ **cup olive oil**

1 **small onion, minced**

2 **cups noodles, broken into pieces**

5 **cups chicken broth**

1 **chicken breast, skin removed**

2 tablespoons fresh lemon juice

1 cup chopped celery

¼ cup chopped fresh parsley plus extra to garnish

1 teaspoon coarse salt

¼ teaspoon freshly ground white pepper

1 bay leaf

1 teaspoon dried tarragon

Heat oil in a pressure cooker over medium heat. Add onion and sauté 2 minutes. Add noodles and cook, stirring often, 1 minute. Add broth, chicken, lemon juice, celery, parsley, salt, pepper, bay leaf, and tarragon. Secure lid. Over high heat, bring pressure up to high. Reduce heat to maintain pressure and cook 10 minutes.

Release pressure according to manufacturer's directions. Remove lid. Remove chicken to a cutting board to cool enough to handle. Remove chicken from bones, cut into 1-inch cubes, and add to soup. Serve hot; garnish each serving with parsley.

CREAM OF MUSHROOM SOUP

Porcini, chanterelles, morel, oyster, shiitake, and button mushrooms are all available in the supermarket at various times. Experiment with the varieties and enjoy the different flavors.

MAKES 6 SERVINGS

1½ pounds fresh mushrooms

¼ cup olive oil

4 leeks (white parts only), rinsed and minced

¼ cup minced fresh parsley

2 garlic cloves, crushed

4 cups chicken broth

2 tablespoons pale sherry

1 teaspoon salt

¼ teaspoon freshly ground white pepper

1 bay leaf

1 teaspoon dried tarragon

¼ cup butter, at room temperature

¼ cup all-purpose flour

½ cup sour cream

Clean mushrooms, removing all dirt. Cut stems from 1 pound, set stems aside, and slice caps vertically. Finely chop reserved stems with remaining ½ pound mushrooms.

Heat oil in a pressure cooker over high heat. Add leeks, parsley, garlic, and the finely chopped mushrooms and sauté 3 minutes, stirring frequently. Add sliced mushrooms, broth, sherry, salt, pepper, bay leaf, and tarragon. Secure lid. Over high heat, bring pressure up to medium. Reduce heat to medium and cook 3 minutes.

Release pressure according to manufacture's directions. Remove lid. Combine butter and flour, mixing to a paste consistency. Gradually stir sour cream into mushroom mixture. Add butter paste, 1 teaspoon at a time, stirring until paste is fully blended and soup is thickened and creamy. Serve hot.

POTATO-LEEK SOUP

Adding the flour to the vegetables while they are sautéing enhances the rich flavor of the soup.

MAKES 6 SERVINGS

2 tablespoons olive oil

¼ cup unsalted butter

4 leeks (white parts only), rinsed and thinly sliced

2 garlic cloves, crushed

1 large carrot, diced

4 large potatoes, peeled and thinly diced

¼ cup minced fresh parsley

3 tablespoons all-purpose flour

4 cups chicken broth

2 tablespoons bouquet garni in cheesecloth bag
   (page 205)

1 teaspoon coarse sea salt or granulated salt

¼ teaspoon freshly ground white pepper

⅓ cup sour cream (optional)

Heat oil and butter in a pressure cooker. Add leeks and garlic and sauté 2 minutes. Add carrot, potatoes, and parsley; sprinkle vegetables with flour. Sauté, stirring occasionally, 2 minutes. Stir in broth and add bouquet garni, salt, and pepper. Secure lid. Over high heat, bring pressure up to high. Reduce heat to maintain pressure and cook 8 minutes.

Release pressure according to manufacturer's directions. Remove lid. Stir in sour cream, a little at a time (if using). Bring almost to a boil, then simmer soup 5 minutes, stirring occasionally. Serve hot.

ITALIAN POTATO, RICE, AND SPINACH SOUP

Full-bodied, almost like a stew, this Italian soup is robust and a meal by itself.

MAKES 6 TO 8 SERVINGS

¼ cup olive oil

6 leeks (white parts only), rinsed and sliced

3 garlic cloves, crushed

2 carrots, coarsely diced

½ cup arborio rice

3 potatoes, peeled and cut into large bite-size
   cubes

5 cups chicken broth

½ cup chopped fresh parsley

½ cup chopped celery

1 bay leaf

1 teaspoon salt

¼ teaspoon freshly ground black pepper

2 teaspoons dried basil

2 tablespoons fresh lemon juice

3 tablespoons tomato paste

1 tablespoon light brown sugar

1 (10-ounce) package fresh spinach, rinsed and
   shredded

¼ cup grated Parmesan cheese

¼ cup grated fontinella cheese

Italian bread

Heat oil in a pressure cooker. Add leeks, garlic, and carrots and sauté 2 minutes. Add rice and potatoes. Stir well and cook 1 minute. Add broth, parsley, celery, bay leaf, salt, pepper, basil, lemon juice, tomato paste, and brown sugar. Stir well. Secure lid. Over high heat, bring pressure up to high. Reduce heat to maintain pressure and cook 8 minutes.

Release pressure according to manufacturer's directions. Remove lid. Stir soup. Lay spinach over soup. Secure lid. Over high heat, bring pressure up to high. Reduce heat to maintain pressure, slide a heat diffuser over burner, and cook 4 minutes.

Release pressure according to manufacturer's directions. Remove lid. Stir soup well. Ladle into bowls. Combine cheeses and sprinkle over soup. Serve with chunks of Italian bread.

COOK'S NOTE: Freeze soup in individual containers up to 3 months. Thaw in refrigerator or microwave oven.

MANHATTAN CLAM CHOWDER

This is a family favorite. Sometimes I introduce a new flavor to this soup by adding 1/2 cup canned smoked oysters, cut into small pieces.
MAKES 6 TO 8 SERVINGS

¼ cup all-purpose flour
¼ cup butter, at room temperature
¼ cup olive oil
1 slice bacon, cut into ½-inch pieces

1 large onion, diced
3 garlic cloves, crushed
2 carrots, diced
½ cup diced celery
¼ cup chopped fresh parsley
1 cup crushed canned tomatoes
3 tablespoons tomato paste
4 medium potatoes, peeled and diced
¼ cup green bell pepper, chopped
2 tablespoons light brown sugar
1 teaspoon salt
½ teaspoons dried thyme
½ teaspoon dried tarragon
2 bay leaves
½ teaspoon crushed red pepper flakes
2 dashes hot pepper sauce
¼ cup milk
2 (10-ounce) cans minced clams, liquid strained and reserved
2 cups Rich Fish Stock (page 143)

Make a paste by blending flour into butter; set aside.

Heat oil in a pressure cooker. Add bacon, onion, garlic, carrots, celery, and parsley and sauté 3 minutes. Add tomatoes, tomato paste, potatoes, bell pepper, brown sugar, salt, thyme, tarragon, bay leaves, pepper flakes, hot pepper sauce, milk, reserved clam liquid, and fish stock. Stir well. Secure lid. Over high heat, bring pressure up to high. Reduce heat to maintain pressure and cook 5 minutes.

Release pressure according to manufacturer's directions. Remove lid. Stir clams into vegetable mixture and cook over medium-high heat 3 minutes. Discard bay leaves. Stir flour paste into soup and cook 1 minute, stirring, or until soup is thickened and creamy. Serve hot.

⊡ ⊡ ⊡

NEW ENGLAND CLAM CHOWDER

Creamy and rich, this is the traditional clam chowder enhanced with herbs and sour cream.

MAKES 6 SERVINGS

¼ cup olive oil

3 leeks (white parts only), rinsed and sliced

2 garlic cloves, crushed

2 carrots, coarsely diced

½ cup coarsely diced celery

¼ cup chopped fresh parsley

2 (10-ounce) cans minced clams, liquid strained
   and reserved

2½ cups Rich Fish Stock (page 143)

4 potatoes, peeled and diced

1 teaspoon salt

¼ teaspoon freshly ground white pepper

2 tablespoons bouquet garni in cheesecloth bag
   (page 205)

2 bay leaves

¼ cup all-purpose flour

1 cup half-and-half or milk

¼ cup sour cream

¼ cup butter, at room temperature

Heat oil in a pressure cooker. Add leeks, garlic, carrots, celery, and parsley and sauté 3 minutes. Add reserved clam liquid, stock, potatoes, salt, pepper, bouquet garni, and bay leaves. Stir thoroughly. Secure lid. Over high heat, bring pressure up to high. Reduce heat to maintain pressure and cook 5 minutes.

Release pressure according to manufacturer's directions. Remove lid. Discard bouquet garni bag. Stir in clams. Cook over medium-high heat 2 minutes, stirring frequently. Remove from heat and discard bay leaves.

Combine flour, half-and-half, sour cream, and butter, whisking to combine. Gradually add paste to clam mixture and cook 1 minute, stirring, or until thickened and creamy. Serve hot.

VARIATION To reduce fat, add skim milk and low-fat sour cream at the end, substituting for half-and-half and regular sour cream. Simply make a paste with flour and blend into soup.

⊡ ⊡ ⊡

LENTIL SOUP

The white wine vinegar adds a zesty flavor. It is often added to Mediterranean legume dishes.

MAKES 6 SERVINGS

1 pound lentils, soaked

¼ cup olive oil

2 medium onions, minced

3 garlic cloves, crushed

6 cups chicken broth or water

2 carrots, finely diced

1 cup coarsely chopped celery

¼ cup tomato paste

1 tablespoon light brown sugar

1½ teaspoons salt

¾ teaspoon freshly ground white pepper

2 bay leaves

1 teaspoon dried tarragon

2 tablespoons white wine vinegar

Place lentils in a bowl. Add enough water to measure 2 inches above lentils. Soak 4 hours. Drain.

Heat oil in a pressure cooker over medium heat. Add onions and garlic and sauté 3 to 4 minutes. Stir in drained lentils. Add broth, carrots, celery, tomato paste, brown sugar, salt, pepper, bay leaves, and tarragon. Stir well. Secure lid. Over high heat, bring pressure up to high. Reduce heat to maintain pressure and cook 12 minutes.

Release pressure according to manufacturer's directions. Remove lid. Stir in vinegar. Discard bay leaves. Serve hot.

⬚ ⬚ ⬚

SPLIT PEA SOUP WITH HAM

Split pea soup is traditionally made with a ham bone.
MAKES 6 TO 8 SERVINGS

1 pound dried split green peas, soaked

¼ cup olive oil

1 large onion, diced

2 teaspoons minced or crushed garlic

1 ham bone or 4 slices smoked bacon, cut into
   ½-inch pieces

5 cups chicken broth

1 tablespoon fresh lemon juice

2 tablespoons bouquet garni in cheesecloth bag
   (page 205)

1 bay leaf

½ cup diced carrot

1 medium potato, peeled and diced

1 teaspoon sea salt

½ teaspoon freshly ground white pepper

½ cup diced smoked ham

Place peas in a bowl. Add enough water to measure 2 inches above peas. Soak 6 hours. Drain peas.

Heat oil in a pressure cooker over medium heat. Add onion and garlic and sauté 3 minutes. Add ham bone (if using bacon, cook 3 minutes before adding the next ingredients), broth, lemon juice, bouquet garni, and bay leaf. Secure lid. Over high heat, bring pressure up to high. Reduce heat to maintain pressure and cook 15 minutes.

Release pressure according to manufacturer's directions. Remove lid. Add carrot, potato, peas, salt, and pepper. Secure lid. Over high heat, bring pressure up to high. Reduce heat to maintain pressure and cook 8 minutes.

Release pressure according to manufacturer's directions. Remove lid. Remove bouquet garni bag. Stir soup with a wooden spoon. Add diced ham and mix well. Using a slotted spoon or large tongs, remove ham bone. Serve hot.

VARIATION If on a low-fat diet, substitute turkey bacon for ham bone and use nonfat chicken broth or vegetable stock.

COOK'S NOTE: Soup may be frozen up to 1 month. Thaw in refrigerator.

◻ ◻ ◻

VEGETABLE SOUP WITH SAUSAGE BITS

This family favorite is thick and hearty. To reduce calories and fat, use turkey sausage and turkey bacon. You'll love the flavors.

MAKES 6 TO 8 SERVINGS

⅓ cup olive oil

½ pound bacon, cut into 1-inch pieces

2 large onions, sliced

3 garlic cloves, crushed

2 carrots, cut into bite-size pieces

1 tablespoon all-purpose flour

½ pound breakfast sausage links, cut into 1-inch pieces

4 celery stalks, cut into 1-inch pieces

4 medium potatoes, peeled and cut into 1-inch cubes

6 cups beef broth

¼ pound vermicelli pasta, broken into small pieces

3 tablespoons tomato paste

2 tablespoons fresh lemon juice

1 tablespoon light brown sugar

2 teaspoons coarse salt

½ teaspoon freshly ground black pepper

2 teaspoons dried oregano

1 teaspoon dried basil

1 bay leaf

½ cup chopped fresh parsley

1 cup frozen green peas

1 cup cooked garbanzo beans (page 166)

Seasoned Croutons (page 43)

Heat oil in a pressure cooker over medium heat. Add bacon, onions, and garlic and sauté 4 minutes. Add carrots, sprinkle with flour, and cook, stirring, 2 minutes. Add sausage, celery, potatoes, broth, vermicelli, tomato paste, lemon juice, brown sugar, salt, pepper, oregano, basil, and bay leaf. Stir until thoroughly mixed. Secure lid. Over high heat, bring pressure up to high. Reduce heat to maintain pressure and cook 8 minutes.

Release pressure according to manufacturer's directions. Remove lid. Add parsley, peas, and beans to vegetable mixture. Cook over medium-high heat 4 minutes, stirring occasionally. Serve hot with croutons.

SALADS

The pressure cooker will indeed hasten recipe completion.

This chapter includes an assortment of ideas developed into tested recipes combining fresh vegetables, fruit, and pressure-cooked poultry along with pasta, rice, and legumes. The salads are light and garnished with flavor-filled dressings that will tantalize the palate of the most discriminating diner.

Using vegetables in their proper season will allow you to enjoy the ultimate in flavor and nutrient value, not to mention the lower cost.

Experiment with the new exotic greens such as red radicchio from Italy, lemon-tart arugula, or tender mâche, pressure cooked in combination with poached chicken or rice.

The recipes within this section will be the beginning of an adventure in using pressure cooking to prepare your favorite fruits and vegetables, leading to new and delicious salads.

CALABRIA BEAN AND PROSCIUTTO SALAD

This lovely southern Italian salad is a wonderful side dish for picnics, barbecues, or family dinners.

MAKES 6 SERVINGS

1 cup navy beans, soaked

2 tablespoons olive oil

⅓ pound prosciutto or ham, julienned

1 medium onion, coarsely diced

1 large bay leaf

3 cups chicken broth

1 teaspoon salt

Dash crushed red pepper flakes

2 garlic cloves, thinly sliced

2 medium carrots, cut into ½-inch pieces

½ medium red bell pepper, coarsely diced

¼ cup fresh coarsely chopped parsley

Dressing

3 tablespoons olive oil

1 teaspoon fresh lemon juice

½ teaspoon salt

¼ teaspoon dried tarragon

Dash freshly ground white pepper

Drain beans and set aside. Heat oil in a pressure cooker over medium heat. Add prosciutto and sauté 1 minute. Add onion and cook 2 minutes. Add beans, bay leaf, chicken broth, salt, and pepper flakes and stir well. Secure lid. Over high heat, bring pressure up to high. Reduce heat to medium to maintain pressure and cook 12 minutes.

Release pressure according to manufacturer's directions. Remove lid. Drain and transfer to a serving bowl. Toss together garlic, carrots, bell pepper, and parsley in a bowl. Spoon over beans.

To make the dressing: Whisk together olive oil, lemon juice, salt, tarragon, and pepper. Drizzle over vegetables and gently toss to combine.

◻ ◻ ◻

CHICKEN RICE SALAD WITH PINEAPPLE

Fresh pineapple is available generally year-round, and most available beginning in March through August. Select a pineapple that is free of soft spots or green on the skin. Canned pineapple can be substituted for fresh.

MAKES 6 SERVINGS

1 large pineapple

1 whole chicken breast, skinned

1 teaspoon dried thyme

1 teaspoon salt

⅛ teaspoon freshly ground white pepper

2½ cups pineapple juice

1 cup long-grain white rice

3 stalks celery, coarsely chopped

½ red bell pepper, coarsely chopped

4 green onions, finely diced

1 large carrot, coarsely diced

⅓ cup mayonnaise

1 teaspoon light brown sugar

Cut pineapple into lengthwise quarters and cut away along the skin, separating the pulp from the skin. Trim off the tough core and cut the pineapple into bite-size chunks. Set aside.

In a pressure cooker, combine chicken, thyme, salt, pepper, pineapple juice, and rice. Secure lid. Over high heat, bring pressure up to high. Reduce heat to medium to maintain pressure and cook 8 minutes.

Release pressure according to manufacturer's directions. Remove lid. Using a utility fork, remove chicken and set aside on cutting board to cool enough to handle. Combine rice, celery, bell pepper, onions, carrot, and pineapple, reserving 6 pieces to garnish, in a bowl. Cut chicken into bite-size pieces and add to bowl. Toss lightly. Whisk together mayonnaise and sugar; blend into salad. Garnish with reserved pineapple pieces.

* * *

GARDEN-FRESH LENTIL SALAD

Lentils are available in several varieties. They can be found with a brownish, yellow, black, or red exterior. Any one of the varieties will work very well in this delightful recipe.
MAKES 6 SERVINGS

1 cup dried lentils, soaked
2 cups water
1 teaspoon salt
⅓ cup minced fresh parsley
2 carrots, diced
1 large tomato, coarsely diced

3 tablespoons olive oil
1 large garlic clove, crushed
½ teaspoon dried mint flakes
1 teaspoon fresh lemon juice
¼ teaspoon salt
Dash freshly ground black pepper
Dash ground allspice

Soak lentils in 4 cups water at least 3 hours. Drain. Combine lentils, the 2 cups water, and salt in a pressure cooker. Secure lid. Over high heat, bring pressure up to high. Reduce heat to medium to maintain pressure and cook 8 minutes.

Release pressure according to manufacturer's directions. Remove lid. Drain and transfer to a serving bowl. Top with parsley and vegetables.

In a small bowl, whisk together olive oil, garlic, mint, lemon juice, salt, pepper, and allspice. Drizzle over top of vegetables. Toss gently until well coated.

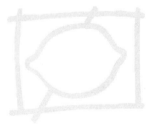

POTATO VEGETABLE SALAD WITH BACON BITS

Potato salad is always a welcome side dish for barbecues, family gatherings, or any meal. It should remain refrigerated until serving time, because the salad could pose a health risk if left at room temperature for more than an hour.

MAKES 6 SERVINGS

4 slices bacon, cut into ½-inch pieces

5 large potatoes, peeled and cut into thirds

1 cup water

1 large carrot, diced medium

2 stalks celery, diced medium

1 small red bell pepper, diced medium

⅓ cup finely chopped fresh parsley

3 large hard-boiled eggs, coarsely chopped

2 teaspoons apple cider vinegar

½ teaspoon prepared mustard

½ cup mayonnaise

1 teaspoon salt

⅛ teaspoon freshly ground white pepper

¼ teaspoon dried tarragon

Fry bacon in a skillet until crisp. Drain on paper towels and set aside.

Combine potatoes and water in a pressure cooker and secure lid. Over high heat, bring pressure up to high. Reduce heat to medium to maintain pressure and cook 4 minutes.

Release pressure under cold running water. Remove lid. Drain potatoes in a colander and cool under cold running water. Cut into bite-size pieces. Combine potatoes, vegetables, parsley, bacon bits, and eggs in a bowl. Toss gently.

Whisk together vinegar, mustard, mayonnaise, salt, pepper, and tarragon. Add to salad and toss gently to combine. Cover and refrigerate.

❑ ❑ ❑

POTATO-GREEN BEAN-CHICKEN SALAD

This lovely vegetable salad is perfect for lunches, family barbecues, and picnics.

MAKES 6 SERVINGS

3 chicken breast halves, cut into quarters

1 cup chicken broth

1 teaspoon salt

Pinch crushed red pepper flakes

1 teaspoon dried tarragon

12 small red-skinned potatoes, cut into halves

1 pound green beans, ends removed and cut into
   2-inch pieces

2 large tomatoes, cut into small wedges

½ yellow bell pepper, finely sliced

1 cup kalamata olives, pitted and chopped

1 large leek (white part only), rinsed well and thinly
   sliced

¼ cup olive oil or canola oil

1 tablespoon apple cider vinegar

1 teaspoon dried basil

2 garlic cloves, crushed

Place chicken breasts, broth, salt, pepper flakes, tarragon, potatoes, and green beans in a pressure cooker. Secure lid. Over high heat, bring pressure up to high. Reduce heat to medium to maintain pressure and cook 7 minutes.

Release pressure under cold running water. Remove lid. Transfer chicken to a cutting board and drain vegetables. Place vegetables in a large serving bowl. Cool. Tear chicken into large chunks and place in the bowl with the vegetables along with the tomatoes, bell pepper, olives, and leek.

Combine olive oil, vinegar, basil, and garlic in a bowl. Whisk together until well blended. Toss into vegetable salad. Cover and chill.

⊡ ⊡ ⊡

WARM SPINACH SALAD WITH BACON DRESSING

Spinach is a nutritious vegetable and offers a rich source of iron as well as vitamins A and C. Select a package of firm spinach. Since spinach is very gritty, it must be rinsed thoroughly in warm water. The warm water wilts the leaves just enough to release the sand and grit.

MAKES 6 SERVINGS

1 (10-ounce) package fresh spinach, rinsed well

5 cups water

1 teaspoon salt

4 slices bacon, cut into 1-inch pieces

1 medium onion, thinly sliced

1 garlic clove, crushed

2 tablespoons freshly grated Parmesan cheese

Combine spinach, water, and salt in a pressure cooker. Secure lid. Over high heat, bring pressure up to medium. Reduce heat to medium to maintain pressure and cook 3 minutes.

Release pressure under cold running water. Remove lid. Drain well, and transfer to a serving bowl.

Cook bacon in a skillet until crisp. Add onion and garlic. Stir well and sauté 3 minutes. Spoon bacon, onion, garlic, and some bacon fat over spinach and gently toss. Sprinkle with Parmesan cheese.

ZESTY RICE SALAD WITH CHICKEN BITS AND MUSTARD DRESSING

The zesty mustard dressing on this salad may also be used for any green salad. This particular combination is a wonderful treat for barbecues and may be served hot or cold for all family gatherings.

MAKES 8 SERVINGS

2 cups long-grain white rice

4½ cups chicken broth

1 whole chicken breast, skinned

1½ teaspoons salt

3 green onions, finely diced

2 medium carrots, coarsely chopped

½ large red bell pepper, finely diced

⅓ cup Honey Mustard Dressing (opposite)

2 tablespoons finely chopped fresh parsley

Combine rice, broth, chicken, and salt in a pressure cooker. Secure lid. Over high heat, bring pressure up to high. Reduce heat to medium to maintain pressure, slide a heat diffuser under pressure cooker, and cook 9 minutes.

Release pressure under cold running water. Remove lid. Transfer chicken breast to a cutting board to cool enough to handle.

Combine rice, onions, carrots, and bell pepper in a salad bowl. Toss gently. Cut chicken into bite-size pieces and toss into rice salad along with mustard dressing. Sprinkle parsley over top.

HONEY MUSTARD DRESSING

Egg coddlers work well for this recipe; however, they are not a common utensil in most kitchens. Simply boil the eggs for 3 minutes. The same results will be accomplished. It's a nice dressing for salads, chicken wings, or vegetables.

MAKES 10 SERVINGS

2 eggs, boiled 3 minutes (see Egg Safety, page 16)

3 tablespoons mayonnaise

1 teaspoon honey mustard

2 tablespoons butter, melted

2 tablespoons apple cider vinegar

½ teaspoon salt

Dash freshly ground white pepper

½ cup olive oil

Whisk together egg yolks, mayonnaise, mustard, butter, vinegar, salt, and pepper. Slowly drizzle olive oil into the mixture, whisking as you pour. Store in airtight container and refrigerate up to 2 days.

CARROT-GARBANZO
BEAN SALAD

The garlic-laced dressing accents a cooked carrot and garbanzo bean salad. You'll find lots of uses for this dressing.
MAKES 6 SERVINGS

1 cup water

6 carrots, cut into julienne strips

Dash of salt

1 cup cooked garbanzo beans (page 166)

3 green onions, minced

Greek Salad Dressing

1½ cups extra-virgin olive oil

½ cup vegetable oil

½ cup white wine vinegar

¼ cup fresh lemon juice

¼ cup mayonnaise

5 garlic cloves, crushed

1 teaspoon salt

½ teaspoon freshly ground black pepper

1 tablespoon dried oregano

1 teaspoon dried rosemary

1 teaspoon prepared mustard

Pour water into a pressure cooker. Layer carrots in a steam basket and insert basket into cooker. Sprinkle with salt. Secure lid. Over high heat, bring pressure up to medium. Reduce heat to maintain pressure and cook 2 minutes.

Release pressure according to manufacturer's directions. Remove lid. Drain carrots in a colander, rinsing under cold running water. Drain well. Combine carrots, beans, and green onions in a serving bowl.

Prepare dressing: Combine oils, vinegar, lemon juice, mayonnaise, garlic, salt, pepper, oregano, rosemary, and mustard in a food processor or blender. Process until smooth. Pour dressing into a jar with a tight-fitting lid. Shake well before using. Makes about 3 cups.

Pour ¼ cup dressing over vegetables and toss to coat. Refrigerate remaining dressing for another use.

COOK'S NOTE: Scrub carrots under cool running water using a vegetable brush. Unless the skin is thick there is no need to peel carrots.

GERMAN POTATO SALAD WITH SAUSAGE

The smoky taste from the bacon, whether pork or turkey, is an important factor in the flavor of the salad.

MAKES 6 TO 8 SERVINGS

3 slices regular or turkey bacon, cut into 1-inch pieces

1 medium onion, cut into ⅛-inch slices

2 garlic cloves, crushed

⅓ cup chicken broth

⅓ cup white wine vinegar

¾ teaspoon salt

¼ teaspoon freshly ground white pepper

¼ teaspoon dried dill weed

5 medium potatoes, peeled and cut into ½-inch slices

1 pound cooked bratwurst or turkey sausage, cut into 1-inch pieces

½ cup regular or light sour cream

½ teaspoon dry mustard

1 green bell pepper, diced

4 radishes, thinly sliced

⅓ cup minced fresh parsley

Cook bacon in a pressure cooker, stirring, until crisp. Stir in onion and garlic and sauté 2 minutes. Add broth, vinegar, salt, white pepper, and dill; mix thoroughly. Add potatoes and sausage and stir well. Secure lid. Over high heat, bring pressure up to medium-high. Reduce heat to maintain pressure and cook 4 minutes.

Release pressure according to manufacturer's directions. Remove lid. Stir potato-sausage mixture carefully but thoroughly. Add sour cream, mustard, bell pepper, radishes, and parsley, tossing gently to mix. Transfer salad to a serving bowl and serve warm or chilled.

▢ ▢ ▢

MIDDLE EASTERN BEET SALAD

Beautiful and delicious, the spearmint dressing adds a cooling touch.

MAKES 6 SERVINGS

Dressing

⅓ cup extra-virgin olive oil

2 tablespoons fresh lemon juice

½ teaspoon salt

⅛ teaspoon freshly ground white pepper

2 garlic cloves, crushed

1 teaspoon dried spearmint, crushed between palms

6 large beets, pressure-cooked (page 153)

1 green bell pepper, thinly sliced lengthwise

1 small onion, cut crosswise into thin slices and separated into rings

½ cup coarsely chopped fresh parsley

1 small cucumber, peeled, seeds removed, and cut into bite-size pieces

2 ripe tomatoes, halved, seeds removed, and diced

2 pita bread rounds, toasted and cut into bite-size squares (see Cook's Note, page 59)

Prepare dressing: Combine oil, lemon juice, salt, pepper, garlic, and spearmint in a measuring cup with a spout. Whisk until thoroughly blended and set aside.

Peel beets and cut each into 8 wedges. Combine with bell pepper, onion, parsley, cucumber, tomatoes, and bread pieces in a salad bowl; toss gently to combine.

Drizzle dressing over salad and toss gently to coat with dressing.

COOK'S NOTE: Pita bread is a flat Arabic bread and is very low in fat. Place bread on a baking sheet, brush with a little olive oil, and bake in a 375 degree F oven 8 minutes. Cut into squares.

CHINESE CHICKEN SALAD WITH SESAME DRESSING

Be adventurous and try cooked basmati or arborio rice for the salad.

MAKES 4 SERVINGS

2 cups Pressure-Steamed Rice (page 180)

2 cups cubed cooked chicken (page 118)

1 (6-ounce) can water chestnuts, drained and thinly sliced

1 pound snow peas, ends and any strings removed

2 celery stalks, diced

2 green onions, diced

Sesame Dressing

1/3 cup vegetable oil

1 tablespoon sesame oil

1 teaspoon soy sauce

1 teaspoon white wine vinegar

1 garlic clove, crushed

1/2 teaspoon salt

Combine rice, chicken, and vegetables in a salad bowl, gently tossing to combine.

Prepare dressing: Combine oils, soy sauce, vinegar, garlic, and salt in a measuring cup with a spout. Wisk until well blended.

Pour dressing over salad, tossing to thoroughly coat.

WARM GARBANZO BEAN SALAD

Great for parties, garbanzo bean salad originated in Italy. The salad is also delicious served chilled, eliminating the baking.

MAKES 6 SERVINGS

3 cups cooked garbanzo beans (page 166)

3 green onions, chopped

1 small red onion, sliced into rings

½ cup green bell pepper, chopped

½ cup minced fresh parsley

1 carrot, coarsely grated

Dressing

¼ cup extra-virgin olive oil

2 teaspoons fresh lemon juice

2 teaspoons white wine vinegar

1 tablespoon mayonnaise

2 garlic cloves, crushed

¼ teaspoon salt

Dash of freshly ground white pepper

½ teaspoon dried oregano

¼ cup freshly grated Parmesan or Romano
   cheese

Preheat oven to 375 degrees F. Combine beans, green onions, red onion, bell pepper, parsley, and carrot in an ovenproof bowl. Toss gently to mix thoroughly.

Prepare dressing: Combine oil, lemon juice, vinegar, mayonnaise, garlic, salt, pepper, and oregano in a measuring cup with a spout. Whisk until thoroughly blended.

Add dressing to bean mixture, a little at a time, tossing gently to coat vegetables, until reaching your preferred taste. Sprinkle salad with cheese and toss gently.

Bake 6 minutes, or until warmed. Stir and serve.

◻ ◻ ◻

WARM LAMB SALAD WITH PEPPERS AND FETA CHEESE

Made with lamb, this main dish salad is perfect for a summer luncheon.

MAKES 6 SERVINGS

¼ cup olive oil

1½ pounds (1-inch-thick) lamb steaks

1 small onion, minced

2 garlic cloves, crushed

1 cup chicken broth or stock

1 tablespoon fresh lemon juice

1 tablespoon sugar

1½ teaspoons salt

½ teaspoon freshly ground black pepper

1 teaspoon dried dill weed

1 teaspoon dried oregano

2 green bell peppers, sliced

⅓ cup chopped fresh parsley

2 cups (8 ounces) crumbled feta cheese or shaved fontinella or Parmesan cheese

Yogurt Dressing

¼ cup extra-virgin olive oil

¼ cup plain yogurt

1 tablespoon fresh lemon juice

1 garlic clove, crushed

½ teaspoon salt

½ teaspoon dried dill weed

Lettuce leaves

Heat oil in a pressure cooker over medium-high heat. Add steaks and sauté, turning to brown on both sides. Transfer steaks to a platter. Add onion and garlic and sauté 2 minutes. Add steaks, broth, lemon juice, sugar, salt, pepper, dill, and oregano. Stir well. Secure lid. Over high heat, bring pressure up to high. Reduce heat to maintain pressure and cook 10 minutes.

Release pressure according to manufacturer's directions. Remove lid. Remove steaks and place on a cutting board. Add bell pepper to cooking liquid. Secure lid. Over high heat, bring pressure up to medium. Reduce heat to maintain pressure at low and cook 2 minutes.

Release pressure according to manufacturer's directions. Remove lid. Drain bell pepper in a colander. Cut lamb into 2-inch slices. Combine lamb, bell pepper, parsley, and cheese in a salad bowl. Toss gently.

Prepare dressing: Combine oil, yogurt, lemon juice, garlic, salt, and dill in a jar with a tight-fitting lid. Shake until thoroughly blended. Store in refrigerator.

Arrange lettuce leaves on a serving platter and top with lamb mixture. Drizzle 2 tablespoons of the dressing over salad. Serve remaining dressing on the side.

MEATS

You'll forget about expensive cuts of meats, heavily marbled with fat, when you use the pressure cooker. Pressure cooking transforms the leaner, tougher cuts of meat into tender morsels that can be cut with a fork. This method is also perfect for game meat such as venison. You can be assured that nutrients are retained, along with wonderful, pronounced flavors.

As the liquid comes to a boil and the steam trapped beneath the tight lid begins to penetrate the meat, it begins to break down the muscle and protein, gradually tenderizing the meat. Following the recommended guidelines for preparation will assure ultimate flavor and retain nutrients.

SELECTING MEAT

The U.S. Department of Agriculture (USDA) grading system of meat is based on maturity and the amount of fat.

• **U.S. Prime:** Well-marbled with fat and therefore usually very tender. Save your money, as this grade does not require pressure cooking to tenderize.

- **U.S. Choice:** Grade most available in all grocery chains. It works extremely well in a pressure cooker.

- **U.S. Good:** Less expensive than prime and choice grades, it contains more muscle and is much leaner, with lower fat content. It works very well in pressure-cooked recipes but does require a longer cooking time to tenderize.

- **U.S. Select:** A new rating, this grade of meat is lean, low in fat, and tender.

BUYING MEAT

- **Beef:** Look for a red, firm surface. Fat marbling should be evenly distributed and excess fat trimmed from edges.

- **Pork:** Make sure it is USDA graded. Look for a light pink color. Fat marbling should be evenly distributed and excess fat trimmed from edges.

- **Lamb:** Look for dark pink to red moist surface, avoiding dark red meat. Lamb has less fat marbling than beef and pork; fat should be trimmed from edges.

- **Veal:** Look for delicate whitish pink surface, finely marbled with very little fat at edges.

TIMING CHART FOR MEAT

BEEF	PORK	LAMB	VEAL	VENISON
12 to 15 minutes per inch	**15 minutes per inch**	**10 minutes per inch**	**8 minutes per inch**	**20 minutes per inch**
Oxtail (for stocks)	Hocks	Neck	Breast	Steak
Short ribs	Shoulder	Shanks	Rump	Saddle (for stew)
Stewing beef	Riblets	Riblets	Steak	Rump (for ground venison)
Blade roast	Chops	Shoulder	Shoulder	Neck (for stew)
Chuck roast			Stew	Shoulder (for stew)
Flank steak				Shank (for stew)
Corned beef				Flank (for stew)
Shanks				
20 minutes per inch				
Brisket				

COOKING TIPS

- Make sure meat is cut into uniform pieces to ensure even cooking.

- Brown meat to seal in the natural juices and add rich color and flavor.

- Reduce the steam slowly at the end of the cooking cycle.

- When cooking venison or deer it is best to trim all fat from the meat since it causes a strong taste that will permeate the dish.

(BEEF)

BARBECUED BEEF SANDWICHES

Use your favorite bottled barbecue sauce in this easy recipe, which will become a family favorite. It can be made ahead of time and refrigerated, allowing the flavors to blend. It also freezes well.

MAKES 8 SERVINGS

2 slices bacon, finely diced

1 tablespoon olive oil

1 medium onion, finely diced

2 garlic cloves, crushed

¼ cup finely chopped fresh parsley

1 (1-pound) boneless beef chuck roast

1 cup bottled barbecue sauce

¼ cup beef broth or water

½ teaspoon sweet paprika

1½ teaspoons salt

¼ teaspoon freshly ground black pepper

¼ cup seasoned bread crumbs

8 crusty buns, toasted

½ cup (2 ounces) shredded Monterey Jack cheese

Sauté bacon with oil in a pressure cooker over medium heat until almost crisp. Add onion and sauté 1 minute. Add garlic, parsley, beef, barbecue sauce, beef broth, paprika, salt, and pepper. Secure lid. Over high heat, bring pressure up to high. Reduce heat to medium to maintain pressure and cook 1 hour and 10 minutes.

Release pressure according to manufacturer's directions. Remove lid. Transfer beef to a cutting board. Stir bread crumbs into the pan juices. Using a knife and fork, tear beef into small pieces. Return the beef to the pressure cooker and stir well. Serve on buns. Sprinkle cheese over top.

⊡ ⊡ ⊡

BOLOGNESE SAUCE

Bolognese Sauce is a rich tomato sauce featuring traditional ingredients found in the Mediterranean area. Often pancetta is used instead of bacon. If it is available, 2 ounces pancetta can be substituted for the bacon in this recipe. This recipe is perfect for a pasta dinner or ladled over noodles, rice, or baked potatoes. The sauce freezes well for up to 3 months.

MAKES 6 SERVINGS

3 slices bacon, finely diced

¼ cup olive oil

2 medium carrots, coarsely chopped

1 large onion, coarsely chopped

4 garlic cloves, crushed

½ pound ground pork

½ pound ground beef chuck

½ cup chicken broth

1 (15-ounce) can diced tomatoes in sauce

1 teaspoon dried basil

1 teaspoon ground fennel

⅓ cup half-and-half or skim evaporated milk

¼ cup seasoned bread crumbs

Cook bacon with oil in a pressure cooker over medium heat until almost crisp. Add carrots, onion, and garlic and sauté 2 minutes. Crumble pork and beef into the onion mixture and cook, stirring to break up meat, until browned. Add chicken broth, tomatoes, basil, and fennel. Stir well. Secure lid. Over high heat, bring pressure up to high. Reduce heat to medium to maintain pressure and cook 8 minutes.

Release pressure according to manufacturer's directions. Remove lid. Stir well. Pour half-and-half into the sauce and stir once again. Sprinkle bread crumbs into sauce and stir 1 minute. Cover and let stand at least 5 minutes before serving.

⊡ ⊡ ⊡

FRENCH BURGUNDY STEW

Burgundy, the most tantalizing region in eastern France, produces superb red and white wines. This recipe calls for a cup of French Burgundy; however, any rich wine may be substituted. Vermouth also makes a great substitute.

MAKES 6 SERVINGS

2 tablespoons olive or canola oil

2 pounds beef round or chuck, trimmed and cut into 2-inch pieces

1 large onion, sliced

4 large carrots, cut into 1-inch-thick slices

4 large potatoes, cut into eighths

1 teaspoon dried basil

1 teaspoon dried thyme

1/8 teaspoon freshly ground black pepper

1½ teaspoons salt

1 cup canned beef broth

3 tablespoons tomato paste

1 cup French Burgundy wine or 2 tablespoons
vermouth

2 tablespoons all-purpose flour or potato starch
mixed with 2 tablespoons water

Crusty French bread to serve

Heat oil in a pressure cooker over medium-high heat. Add beef, in batches, and brown on all sides. With a slotted spoon, transfer beef as it cooks to a platter. Add onion and cook, scraping bottom of pan to loosen any browned bits. Add remaining ingredients, except flour and bread. Stir well. Secure lid. Over high heat, bring pressure up to high. Reduce heat to medium to maintain pressure and cook 10 minutes.

Release pressure according to manufacturer's directions. Shake pan, stabilizing pressure under lid. Remove lid. Stir well. Stir ½ cup of the cooking juices into the flour mixture. Whisk until smooth. Stir into the stew and cook over medium-high heat 4 minutes. Cover and let stand 5 minutes. Serve hot with bread.

ROUND STEAK WITH ONION SAUCE

This dish is what comfort food is all about. It is perfect for a chilly evening meal. Serve with a side dish of mashed potatoes, rice, noodles, or pasta. It freezes well for up to three months; thaw in the refrigerator.

MAKES 6 SERVINGS

3 tablespoons olive oil

1 (1½-pound) beef round steak, cut into
6 portions

4 large onions, thickly sliced

4 garlic cloves, thinly sliced

1/3 cup parsley, finely chopped

1 cup beef broth

1 teaspoon dried thyme

½ teaspoon dried rosemary

Dash crushed red pepper flakes

1 teaspoon salt

¼ cup milk

2 tablespoons all-purpose flour or potato starch

Heat oil in a pressure cooker over medium-high heat. Add beef, in batches, and brown on all sides. With tongs, transfer beef as it cooks to a platter. Add onions, garlic, and parsley and sauté 2 minutes, scraping bottom of pan to loosen any browned bits. Add beef broth, herbs, pepper flakes, and salt. Secure lid. Over high heat, bring pressure up to high. Reduce heat to medium to maintain pressure and cook 14 minutes.

Release pressure according to manufacturer's

directions. Remove lid. Mix milk and flour into a smooth paste, and stir into the stew. Cook, stirring, over medium-high heat a few minutes, or until sauce begins to thicken.

⊡ ⊡ ⊡

SAUCY SHORT RIBS

Short ribs are traditionally cut into 3-inch pieces and come from the beef chuck. Because they are a tough cut, the meat requires a longer cooking time, and the pressure cooker reduces this time by 60 percent, offering a quick and tender meal. The addition of shallots in this recipe adds a delicate onion flavor to the finished sauce.

MAKES 6 SERVINGS

3 tablespoons olive oil

6 portions short ribs, cut and trimmed by butcher

2 large onions

3 garlic cloves, sliced

½ cup red wine

1 (28-ounce) can diced tomatoes in sauce

½ cup beef broth

1 teaspoon dried tarragon

1 teaspoon dried basil

1½ teaspoons salt

Pinch crushed red pepper flakes

12 shallots, peeled

16 baby carrots

6 red-skinned potatoes

¼ cup seasoned bread crumbs

Crusty bread

Heat oil in a pressure cooker over medium-high heat. Add short ribs, in 2 or 3 batches, and brown on all sides. Using tongs, transfer ribs to a platter. Add onions and garlic and cook 3 minutes, scraping bottom of pan to loosen any browned bits. Add wine, tomatoes, beef broth, tarragon, basil, salt, and pepper flakes. Return ribs to pressure cooker. Secure lid. Over high heat, bring pressure up to high. Reduce heat to medium to maintain pressure and cook 35 minutes.

Release pressure according to manufacturer's directions. Remove lid. Stir. Add shallots, carrots, and potatoes. Over high heat, bring pressure up to high. Reduce heat to medium to maintain pressure and cook 9 minutes.

Release pressure according to manufacturer's directions. Remove lid. Sprinkle bread crumbs into sauce, and stir well. Cover and let stand 5 minutes. Stir and serve hot with bread.

⊡ ⊡ ⊡

TRADITIONAL BEEF STEW

Many varieties of mushrooms are available in the market. They all differ in flavor. The button mushroom is most commonly used in the American kitchen; however, it is fun to experiment with exotic wild mushrooms such as cepe, chanterelle, morel, or shiitake. If dried mushrooms are used, soak in warm water for 2 hours, drain through a tight cheesecloth to eliminate the sand, and utilize the water used for soaking in the stew. It will add another dimension of flavor.

MAKES 6 SERVINGS

2 tablespoons canola oil

2 large onions, sliced

3 garlic cloves, sliced

1 pound beef round or chuck, trimmed and cut into
  2-inch pieces

1 cup beef broth

½ cup coarsely chopped fresh parsley

½ teaspoon dried thyme

1 teaspoon dried marjoram

1 bay leaf

1 teaspoon salt

⅛ teaspoon freshly ground black pepper

1 (15-ounce) can diced tomatoes

4 large potatoes, peeled and cut into 2-inch pieces

3 large carrots, cut into 2-inch pieces

1 pound mushrooms, halved if large

1 large red bell pepper, cut into strips

¼ cup seasoned bread crumbs

Crusty bread

Heat oil in a pressure cooker. Add onions and garlic and sauté 1 minute. Add beef, broth, herbs, salt, and pepper. Secure lid. Over high heat, bring pressure up to high. Reduce heat to medium to maintain pressure and cook 15 minutes.

Release pressure according to manufacturer's directions. Remove lid. Stir in tomatoes, potatoes, carrots, mushrooms, and bell pepper. Secure lid. Over high heat, bring pressure up to medium. Reduce heat to medium to maintain pressure and cook 8 minutes.

Release pressure according to manufacturer's directions. Swirl pot to stabilize pressure. Remove lid. Discard bay leaf. Stir bread crumbs into the stew. Cover and let stand 5 minutes. Serve with bread.

BEEF STROGANOFF

This lovely combination of thinly sliced beef in a rich sauce is named after a Russian, Count Stroganoff. It is traditionally served with rice or buttered noodles.

MAKES 6 SERVINGS

¼ cup olive oil

1 large onion, sliced

2 garlic cloves, crushed

1½ pounds stewing beef, thinly sliced

½ cup beef broth

2 tablespoons sherry

⅓ cup chopped fresh parsley

1 teaspoon salt

⅛ teaspoon freshly ground black pepper

1 teaspoon dried tarragon

1 pound mushrooms, sliced

2 medium tomatoes, cut into eighths and seeds
  removed

½ cup sour cream

½ teaspoon prepared mustard

2 tablespoons potato starch or all-purpose flour

Cooked noodles (page 166) or rice (page 175)

Heat oil in a pressure cooker. Add onion and garlic and sauté 3 minutes. Add beef, stir, and cook 2 minutes. Stir in broth, sherry, parsley, salt, pepper, and tarragon. Secure lid. Over high heat, bring pressure up to high. Reduce heat to maintain pressure and cook 18 minutes.

Release pressure according to manufacturer's directions. Remove lid. Stir mushrooms and tomatoes into beef mixture. Secure lid. Over high heat, bring pressure up to medium. Reduce heat to maintain pressure and cook 1 minute.

Release pressure according to manufacturer's directions. Remove lid. Cook beef and vegetable mixture over high heat 1 minute. Combine sour cream, mustard, and potato starch in a small bowl. Gradually add to beef and vegetable mixture and cook, stirring, until slightly thickened. Serve with noodles.

CORNED BEEF BRISKET WITH VEGETABLES AND HORSERADISH SAUCE

The point on the brisket indicates it has more fat and cooks up to be more tender than the flat cut. Thinly sliced, it makes lovely corned beef sandwiches.

MAKES 6 SERVINGS

4 cups water
1 (2½-pounds) corned beef brisket, uniformly shaped with point at one end
3 garlic cloves, quartered

2 bay leaves
4 carrots, cut into 3-inch pieces
1 head cabbage, cut into 6 wedges
6 potatoes, peeled and quartered
3 turnips, peeled and quartered

Horseradish Sauce
⅓ cup prepared horseradish
1 teaspoon prepared mustard
¼ cup sour cream
1 tablespoon fresh lemon juice
2 garlic cloves, crushed
2 tablespoons green onions (green part only), minced
1 teaspoon sugar
½ teaspoon salt
⅛ teaspoon freshly ground white pepper

Pour water into a pressure cooker. Add brisket. Over high heat, bring water to a rolling boil. Skim residue from surface. Add garlic and bay leaves. Secure lid. Over high heat, bring pressure up to high. Reduce heat to maintain pressure and cook 1 hour and 15 minutes.

Release pressure according to manufacturer's directions. Remove lid. Add vegetables to brisket and liquid, stirring gently. Secure lid. Over high heat, bring pressure up to high. Reduce heat to maintain pressure and cook 6 minutes.

Meanwhile, prepare Horseradish Sauce: Combine horseradish, mustard, sour cream, and lemon juice in a bowl; blend thoroughly. Add garlic, green onions, sugar, salt, and white pepper and mix well.

Release pressure according to manufacturer's directions. Remove lid. Transfer vegetables to a platter. Slice brisket across the grain and arrange slices on a platter. Serve with Horseradish Sauce.

▢ ▢ ▢

FAR EAST PEPPER STEAK

The pepper flakes in this dish with a hint of Asia may be a little hot to the palate. If you prefer a less spicy flavor, omit the red pepper flakes.

MAKES 6 SERVINGS

1 tablespoon sesame oil

2 tablespoons olive oil

1 large onion, sliced

3 garlic cloves, sliced

1 pound beef round steak, cut into 3- × ½-inch strips

½ cup beef broth or stock

1 tablespoon sherry

1 teaspoon light brown sugar

½ teaspoon salt

1 teaspoon grated fresh ginger

½ teaspoon crushed red pepper flakes

2 tomatoes, cut into eighths and seeds removed

1 green bell pepper, sliced lengthwise

4 green onions, coarsely chopped

¼ cup soy sauce

2 tablespoons water

2 tablespoons potato starch or cornstarch

Steamed basmati rice (page 175) to serve

Heat oils in a pressure cooker over medium-high heat. Add onion and garlic and sauté 2 minutes. Add beef strips, stir well, and cook over high heat 1 minute. Stir in broth, sherry, brown sugar, salt, ginger, and pepper flakes. Secure lid. Over high heat, bring pressure up to high. Reduce heat to maintain pressure and cook 10 minutes.

Release pressure according to manufacturer's directions. Remove lid. Stir in tomatoes, bell pepper, and green onions. Secure lid. Over high heat, bring pressure up to medium–high. Reduce heat to maintain pressure and cook 2 minutes.

Release pressure according to manufacturer's directions. Remove lid. Combine soy sauce, water, and potato starch in a small bowl. Blend until smooth. Gradually add to beef and vegetables, and cook, stirring gently, until thickened and creamy. Serve beef and vegetables over steamed rice.

COOK'S NOTE: Partially freeze beef before cutting for more uniform strips.

HEARTY ITALIAN MEAT SAUCE

It's versatile, it's hearty, and it's delicious on pasta, rice, or vegetables.

MAKES ABOUT 10 SERVINGS

¼ cup olive oil

1 large onion, diced

4 garlic cloves, crushed

1 carrot, finely diced

¼ pound prosciutto, diced

1½ pounds ground beef chuck or ground turkey

1 pound Italian sausage with fennel, cut into
  2-inch pieces

2 cups beef broth

1 (29-ounce) can tomato sauce

2 tablespoons Marsala wine

½ cup diced green bell pepper

½ cup minced fresh Italian parsley

2 tablespoons light brown sugar

1½ teaspoons salt

½ teaspoon crushed red pepper flakes

1 tablespoon dried oregano

2 teaspoons dried basil

1 teaspoon dried rosemary

2 bay leaves

Heat oil in a pressure cooker over medium heat. Add onion, garlic, carrot, and prosciutto and sauté 3 minutes, stirring well. Add beef and cook 2 minutes, stirring to break up meat. Stir in sausage, broth, tomato sauce, wine, bell pepper, parsley, brown sugar, salt, pepper flakes, oregano, basil, rosemary, and bay leaves. Secure lid. Over high heat, bring pressure up to high. Reduce heat to maintain pressure and cook 10 minutes.

Release pressure according to manufacturer's directions. Remove lid. Stir sauce well. Discard bay leaves. Cook over medium-high heat, uncovered, 5 minutes to reduce liquid and intensify flavor. Let stand 5 minutes, then skim fat from surface.

COOK'S NOTES: I have layered this sauce with cooked ziti, fontinella and Parmesan cheeses, and grilled eggplant, and baked it as a casserole. It's great.

Sauce may be frozen in airtight containers up to 2 months. Thaw in refrigerator.

HUNTER'S BEEF ONION STEW

A well-seasoned, robust peasant dish, this is juicy and satisfying on cold winter evenings.

MAKES 6 SERVINGS

¼ cup olive oil

2 large onions, diced

4 garlic cloves, crushed

2 carrots, thinly sliced

2 slices bacon, diced

1½ pounds beef round steak, cut into 2-inch cubes

1 (29-ounce) can Italian tomatoes

1 cup beef broth

½ cup chopped fresh parsley

2 tablespoons light brown sugar

2 teaspoons salt

½ teaspoon freshly ground black pepper

3 tablespoons whole allspice in cheesecloth bag

4 medium potatoes, peeled and cut into eighths

2½ pounds small pearl onions, peeled

2 tablespoons white wine vinegar

Crusty bread to serve

Heat oil in a pressure cooker over medium heat. Add diced onions, garlic, carrots, and bacon and sauté 3 minutes. Add beef, stir, and cook 1 minute. Stir in tomatoes, broth, parsley, brown sugar, salt, pepper, and allspice. Secure lid. Over high heat, bring pressure up to high. Reduce heat to maintain pressure and cook 12 minutes.

Release pressure according to manufacturer's directions. Remove lid. Add potatoes, pearl onions, and vinegar. Stir gently to mix with beef. Secure lid. Over high heat, bring pressure up to high. Reduce heat to maintain pressure and cook 6 minutes.

Release pressure according to manufacturer's directions. Remove lid. Stir stew gently. Remove allspice bag. Serve with chunks of bread.

VARIATION Rabbit, cut into serving pieces, is frequently used in this stew instead of beef.

SAUERBRATEN

The rich sauce makes the dish.
MAKES ABOUT 10 SERVINGS

¼ cup olive oil

1 (3-pound) beef sirloin roast

2 large onions, coarsely chopped

2 garlic cloves, crushed

1 carrot, coarsely chopped

1 celery stalk, coarsely chopped

2 cups beef broth

1 cup sweet red wine

1½ teaspoons salt

½ teaspoon freshly ground black pepper

2 tablespoons bouquet garni (page 205) plus
    4 whole cloves in cheesecloth bag

2 bay leaves, broken in halves

6 potatoes, peeled and quartered

½ cup sour cream

¼ cup butter, at room temperature

¼ cup tomato sauce

¼ cup all-purpose flour

Heat oil in a pressure cooker over medium heat. Add roast and brown, turning to brown all sides. Remove and set aside.

Add onions, garlic, carrot, and celery and sauté 3 minutes, scraping bottom of cooker with a wooden spoon to loosen any browned bits. Stir in broth, wine, salt, pepper, bouquet garni, and bay leaves. Add roast. Secure lid. Over high heat, bring pressure up to high. Reduce heat to maintain pressure and cook 1 hour.

Release pressure according to manufacturer's directions. Remove lid. Transfer roast to a cutting board. Cover with foil to retain heat.

Strain cooking liquid, measure 2 cups, and pour into pressure cooker. Discard vegetables and herbs. Add potatoes. Secure lid. Over high heat, bring pressure up to high. Reduce heat to maintain pressure and cook 5 minutes.

Release pressure according to manufacturer's directions. Remove lid. Using a slotted spoon, transfer potatoes to a platter. Combine sour cream, butter, tomato sauce, and flour in a small bowl, blending to paste consistency. Gradually add to cooking liquid and cook, stirring, 1 minute, or until mixture is slightly thickened. Slice beef and arrange on platter with potatoes. Serve with sauce.

COOK'S NOTE: Leftover beef makes marvelous hot sandwiches. It can be sliced and frozen up to 3 months. Thaw in refrigerator.

◻◻◻

SWISS STEAK AND ONIONS

Traditional in taste, but its cooking method is up-to-date. It's prepared in a fraction of the time the original took. Now you can even have this hearty dish midweek.
MAKES 6 TO 8 SERVINGS

2 pounds (1½-inch-thick) beef round steak
½ cup seasoned bread crumbs
¼ cup olive oil
1 medium onion, diced
2 garlic cloves, crushed
1 carrot, diced
¼ cup minced fresh parsley
½ teaspoon dried tarragon
1 bay leaf
⅔ cup beef broth
2 tablespoons light sherry
2 tablespoons tomato paste
5 large onions, sliced into rings
1 teaspoon salt
¼ teaspoon freshly ground black pepper
Buttered noodles or steamed potatoes to serve

Cut steak into serving pieces, slitting edges to prevent curling. Place bread crumbs into a shallow dish. Coat steak pieces with bread crumbs, shaking to remove excess crumbs.

Heat oil in a pressure cooker over high heat. Add steak and sauté, 2 pieces at a time to avoid crowding. Use long-handled tongs to turn steak to brown on both sides. Remove and set aside.

Add diced onion, garlic, carrot, parsley, tarragon, and bay leaf to hot oil and cook 3 minutes, stirring with a wooden spoon to loosen browned bits on bottom of cooker. Stir in broth, sherry, and tomato paste. Mix well. Place steak pieces in sauce. Secure lid. Over high heat, bring pressure up to high. Reduce heat to maintain pressure and cook 18 minutes.

Release pressure according to manufacturer's directions. Remove lid. Add sliced onions to steak and sauce. Season with salt and pepper, and stir well. Secure lid. Over high heat, bring pressure up to high. Reduce heat to maintain pressure and cook 2 minutes.

Release pressure according to manufacturer's directions. Remove lid. Gently stir beef and sauce with a wooden spoon. Discard bay leaf. Serve with noodles or potatoes.

COOK'S NOTE: Buy bottom round steak. It is firm, lean, and well flavored. The pressure cooker tenderizes this cut very nicely.

▢ ▢ ▢

STUFFED HEAD OF CABBAGE

What a beautiful presentation this dish makes. Everyone oohs and aahs when served.

MAKES 6 TO 8 SERVINGS

1 (2½-pound) head green cabbage

¼ cup olive oil or butter

2 large onions, diced

2 garlic cloves, crushed

⅓ cup minced fresh parsley

1 carrot, diced

2 celery stalks, chopped

1 pound ground beef, lamb, or turkey

1 cup long-grain white rice

2 cups beef or chicken broth

⅓ cup canned chopped tomatoes

1 teaspoon sugar

1 teaspoon salt

½ teaspoon freshly ground black pepper

2 tablespoons dried dill weed

1 teaspoon dried thyme

Tomato Sauce

¼ cup olive oil

1 onion, sliced

2 garlic cloves, crushed

½ green bell pepper, diced

2 cups beef or chicken broth

1 cup canned chopped tomatoes

1 tablespoon light brown sugar

1 teaspoon salt

½ teaspoon freshly ground black pepper

2 teaspoons dried oregano

Using a grapefruit knife or paring knife, hollow out center of cabbage head. Begin by cutting out core, removing center leaves as they are loosened. Remove leaves until outer leaves form a 2-inch-thick shell. Set aside.

Heat oil in a pressure cooker. Add onions, garlic, parsley, carrot, and celery and sauté 3 minutes. Crumble meat into mixture and stir well. Stir in rice, broth, tomatoes, sugar, salt, pepper, dill, and thyme. Mix thoroughly. Secure lid. Over high heat, bring pressure up to high. Reduce heat to maintain pressure and cook 6 minutes.

Release pressure according to manufacturer's directions. Remove lid. Stir meat and rice mixture thoroughly. Spoon into cabbage shell, mounding at top. Wrap a 24-inch length of cheesecloth around cabbage, overlapping at top. Set aside.

Rinse the pressure cooker and wipe dry. Prepare sauce: In pressure cooker, heat oil. Add onion, garlic, and bell pepper and sauté 2 minutes. Stir in broth, tomatoes, brown sugar, salt, black pepper, and oregano. Stir well.

Place steamer basket over sauce in cooker. Place cabbage in steamer basket. Secure lid. Over high heat, bring pressure up to high. Reduce heat to maintain pressure and cook 10 minutes.

Release pressure according to manufacturer's directions. Remove lid. Carefully transfer stuffed cabbage to a serving platter. Unwrap cheesecloth and slip from beneath cabbage. Ladle sauce over top of cabbage and on platter. Cut cabbage into wedges to serve.

SLOPPY JOES WITH PEPPERS

Fun-time recipe! These juicy, lightly spiced sloppy joes will be a favorite with everyone young at heart.
MAKES 6 SERVINGS

2 slices bacon, diced

2 tablespoons olive oil

1 large onion, diced

2 garlic cloves, crushed

1 pound lean ground beef or ground turkey

1 green bell pepper, sliced

½ cup beef broth

¼ cup tomato paste

2 tablespoons light brown sugar

1 teaspoon salt

¼ teaspoon crushed red pepper flakes

½ teaspoon chili powder

2 teaspoons prepared mustard

1 tablespoon Worcestershire sauce

8 crusty rolls or hamburger buns, warmed, to serve

Sauté bacon with oil in a pressure cooker over medium heat until crisp. Add onion and garlic and sauté 3 minutes. Add beef and cook 2 minutes, stirring to break up meat.

Add bell pepper, broth, tomato paste, brown sugar, salt, pepper flakes, chili powder, mustard, and Worcestershire sauce. Stir well. Secure lid. Over medium-high heat, bring pressure up to medium. Reduce heat to maintain pressure and cook 6 minutes.

Release pressure according to manufacturer's directions. Remove lid. Stir beef mixture thoroughly. Serve on rolls.

(VEAL)

ITALIAN VEAL STEW

Veal is from a young calf. It is generally very tender and low in fat.

MAKES 6 SERVINGS

3 tablespoons olive oil

1 large onion, coarsely diced

3 garlic cloves, crushed

2 pounds boneless veal shoulder, cut into 2-inch
    pieces

1 medium red bell pepper, thickly sliced

1 medium yellow or orange bell pepper, thickly
    sliced

1 cup chicken broth

1½ teaspoons salt

Dash crushed red pepper flakes

1 cup canned diced tomatoes

1 teaspoon dried basil

¼ cup half-and-half

¼ cup grated fontinella cheese

Steamed rice, noodles, or potatoes to serve

Heat oil in a pressure cooker. Add onion and sauté 3 minutes. Add garlic and veal. Cook 1 minute. Stir in remaining ingredients, except half-and-half, cheese, and rice. Secure lid. Over high heat, bring pressure up to high. Reduce heat to medium to maintain pressure and cook 10 minutes.

Release pressure according to manufacturer's directions. Remove lid. Stir in half-and-half. Transfer to serving platter and sprinkle with cheese. Serve with rice.

❑ ❑ ❑

PEARL ONION VEAL STEW

Pearl onions are available in most produce stores and are packaged in mesh bags. This tiny morsel of the onion family is a mild, sweet-flavored vegetable.

MAKES 6 SERVINGS

2 slices bacon, finely diced

2 medium sweet onions, sliced

3 garlic cloves, crushed

1½ pounds veal shoulder, cut into 2-inch cubes

1 cup chicken broth

1 teaspoon dried thyme

1 bay leaf

2 tablespoons fresh lemon juice

1 teaspoon salt

⅛ teaspoon freshly ground white pepper

4 cups pearl onions, peeled and scored

18 whole fresh mushrooms

2 tablespoons all-purpose flour or potato starch
    mixed with 2 tablespoons cold water

¼ cup minced fresh parsley

Crusty French bread to serve

Sauté bacon in a pressure cooker until crisp. Add sliced onions and sauté, stirring and scraping bottom of pan. Stir in garlic, veal, broth, herbs, lemon juice, salt, and pepper. Secure lid. Over high heat, bring pressure up to high. Reduce heat to medium to maintain pressure and cook 12 minutes.

Release pressure according to manufacturer's directions. Remove lid. Stir in pearl onions and mushrooms. Secure lid. Over high heat, bring pressure up to medium. Reduce heat to medium and cook 2 minutes.

Release pressure under cold running water. Remove lid. Blend ½ cup of hot liquid from stew into flour mixture and stir into stew. Cook, stirring, over medium-high heat 2 to 3 minutes, or until broth thickens. Stir in parsley and serve hot with bread.

⊡ ⊡ ⊡

OSSO BUCO IN RICH SAUCE

Rich in tradition, this Italian dish has been a long-time favorite. The veal shanks are perfect for pressure-cooked dishes, tender and succulent, a favorite for all. Serve with a side of risotto or buttered noodles.

MAKES 6 SERVINGS

¼ cup all-purpose flour

1 teaspoon sweet paprika

6 veal shanks, split into halves

2 slices bacon, finely diced

3 tablespoons canola oil

1 large onion, sliced

3 large carrots, cut into 1-inch pieces

4 stalks celery, large strings removed and cut into 2-inch pieces

5 garlic cloves, crushed

½ cup dry red wine

1 cup chicken broth

1 cup canned diced tomatoes

1 teaspoon dried thyme

1 teaspoon dried tarragon

1½ teaspoons salt

Pinch crushed red pepper flakes

½ cup chopped fresh parsley

Combine flour and paprika in a bowl. Coat veal with flour mixture, patting into meat.

Sauté bacon with oil in a pressure cooker over medium heat until almost crisp. Brown veal, 3 pieces at a time. Set aside. Add onion and sauté 2 minutes, scraping bottom of cooker with a wooden spoon to loosen any browned bits. Add carrots, celery, garlic, wine, broth, tomatoes, herbs, salt, and pepper flakes. Stir well. Secure lid. Over high heat, bring pressure up to high. Reduce heat to medium to maintain pressure and cook 25 minutes.

Release pressure according to manufacturer's directions. Remove lid. Stir in parsley. Serve in a large shallow bowl.

⊡ ⊡ ⊡

VEAL CASSOULET

The French cassoulets are perfect for the pressure cooker. Traditionally the stew is cooked very slowly for hours.

The pressure-cooker method reduces the cooking time by 70 percent and offers unbelievable flavors.

MAKES 6 SERVINGS

2 tablespoons olive or canola oil

2 medium onions, coarsely diced

3 garlic cloves, crushed

3 large carrots, cut into ½-inch pieces

½ cup minced fresh parsley

1½-pound veal shoulder, cut into 2-inch pieces

2 cups white beans, soaked

1 cup chicken broth

1 (15-ounce) can diced tomatoes

1 teaspoon ground fennel

½ teaspoon dried sage

1 teaspoon dried tarragon

1½ teaspoons salt

⅛ teaspoon freshly ground white pepper

½ pound bratwurst or any pork sausage, cut into 2-inch pieces

Crusty bread to serve

Heat oil in pressure cooker over medium heat. Add onions, garlic, carrots, and parsley and sauté 4 to 5 minutes. Add veal and cook 2 minutes, browning on all sides. Drain beans and stir into the veal mixture, along with the remaining ingredients, except sausage and bread. Secure lid. Over high heat, bring pressure up to high. Reduce heat to medium to maintain pressure and cook 10 minutes.

Release pressure according to manufacturer's directions. Remove lid. Stir in sausage. Secure lid. Over high heat, bring pressure up to high. Re-duce heat to medium and slide heat diffuser between pressure cooker and heat. Cook 3 minutes.

Release pressure under cold running water. Remove lid. Stir well. Serve hot with bread.

VEAL WITH SAUSAGE AND CORN SALSA

Salsa is a Mexican word for "sauce" and is usually a combination of fresh vegetables seasoned with chiles. Rice would be a wonderful side dish.

MAKES 6 SERVINGS

2 tablespoons olive or canola oil

6 (1-inch-thick) veal chops, trimmed

4 green onions, coarsely diced

3 garlic cloves, crushed

1 pound chorizo (Mexican sausage), cut into 2-inch pieces

1 cup chicken broth

1 teaspoon salt

⅛ teaspoon freshly ground black pepper

½ teaspoon dried chili powder

½ teaspoon dried ground cumin

1 small red bell pepper, coarsely diced

2 cups frozen whole-kernel corn

2 medium tomatoes, seeded and cut into ½-inch pieces

Heat oil in a pressure cooker over medium-high heat. Add veal chops and brown. Add remaining ingredients, except corn and tomatoes. Secure lid. Over high heat, bring pressure up to high. Reduce heat to medium to maintain pressure and cook 8 minutes.

Release pressure according to manufacturer's directions. Remove lid. Stir in corn and tomatoes. Cover and cook over medium heat 2 minutes. Using a slotted spoon, transfer veal and sausage to a deep platter. Cover with corn, tomato, and some of the cooking juices.

◻ ◻ ◻

VEAL FLORENTINE WITH PARMESAN

This Venetian recipe is full of great, healthy flavors.
MAKES 6 SERVINGS

2 pounds veal steak

⅓ cup dry bread crumbs

2 tablespoons butter

¼ cup corn oil or olive oil

3 tablespoons thinly sliced shallots

1 tablespoon sherry

1 cup chicken broth

2 tablespoons fresh lemon juice

1 teaspoon dried tarragon

1 bay leaf

2 (10-ounce) packages fresh spinach, rinsed well

⅓ cup freshly grated Parmesan cheese

Pressure Steamed Rice (page 180)

Cut veal into 6 pieces. Using a meat mallet, flatten cutlets between two sheets of waxed paper or plastic wrap to ¼-inch thickness. Press bread crumbs on both sides of veal, shaking to remove excess crumbs.

Heat butter and oil in a pressure cooker over medium heat. Add veal and sauté until lightly browned on both sides, turning with long-handled tongs. Remove and set aside. Add shallots and sauté 1 minute, scraping the bottom of the cooker with a wooden spoon to loosen any browned bits. Stir in sherry. Add broth, lemon juice, tarragon, and bay leaf. Stir well. Return veal to pressure cooker. Secure lid. Over high heat, bring pressure up to high. Reduce heat to maintain pressure and cook 10 minutes.

Release pressure according to manufacturer's directions. Remove lid. With tongs, transfer veal to a platter and cover to retain heat. Add spinach to cooking liquid. Over high heat, bring pressure up to medium. Reduce heat to maintain pressure and cook 3 minutes.

Release pressure according to manufacturer's directions. Remove lid. Stir spinach thoroughly. Drain through a colander, using a large, flat spatula to press excess moisture from spinach. Discard bay leaf. Spoon a serving of spinach on each serving plate and top with a veal cutlet. Sprinkle with cheese. Serve with rice.

COOK'S NOTE: Veal refers to a young calf up to 3 months old that is milk-fed. The flesh is generally pinkish white and very tender when prepared properly.

VEAL PAPRIKA
WITH SPAETZLE

The butcher will cut the veal into pieces upon request. Ask for a blade cut or arm steak. The bone will add extra flavor to this Hungarian favorite.

MAKES 6 SERVINGS

¼ cup olive oil

2 onions, sliced

1 garlic clove, crushed

¼ cup finely diced carrot

1½ pounds stewing veal, cut into 1-inch cubes

2 cups chicken broth

2 tablespoons sherry

2 tablespoons tomato paste

¼ cup chopped fresh parsley

1 teaspoon salt

¼ teaspoon freshly ground white pepper

1 tablespoon sweet paprika

1 teaspoon dried thyme

1 teaspoon caraway seeds in cheesecloth bag

1 bay leaf

½ cup sour cream

2 tablespoons butter, at room temperature

2 tablespoons all-purpose flour

Cooked spaetzle or cavatelli pasta to serve

Heat oil in a pressure cooker over medium-high heat. Add onions, garlic, and carrot and sauté 3 minutes. Add veal and cook over high heat 1 minute, stirring frequently. Stir in broth, sherry, tomato paste, parsley, salt, pepper, paprika, thyme, caraway seeds, and bay leaf. Secure lid. Over high heat, bring pressure up to high. Reduce heat to maintain pressure and cook 10 minutes.

Release pressure according to manufacturer's directions. Remove lid. Discard bay leaf and caraway seeds. Stir veal mixture well. Combine sour cream, butter, and flour in a small bowl, blending to paste consistency. Add, 1 tablespoon at a time, to veal mixture and cook, stirring, until thoroughly blended and mixture begins to thicken.

Serve over spaetzle.

VEAL PICCATA WITH SHRIMP

Veal steak comes from the leg of the animal. It is generally pink in color with some marbling. Your butcher will be happy to slice this into pieces for you.

MAKES 6 SERVINGS

1½ pounds veal steak, trimmed of fat and bone removed

⅓ cup seasoned bread crumbs

2 tablespoons butter

2 tablespoons olive oil

4 shallots, finely diced

3 garlic cloves, crushed

1 teaspoon dried basil

¾ cup chicken broth

⅓ cup fresh lemon juice

1 tablespoon sherry

2 teaspoons salt

¼ teaspoon freshly ground white pepper

12 large shrimp, peeled and deveined

1 cup pitted ripe olives, coarsely chopped

¼ cup sour cream

1 tablespoon potato starch or all-purpose flour

¼ cup freshly grated Parmesan cheese

Steamed rice and a green vegetable to serve

Cut veal into 6 serving pieces. Using a meat mallet, flatten between two pieces of waxed paper or plastic wrap to ½-inch thickness. Press bread crumbs into both sides of veal, shaking to remove excess crumbs.

Heat butter and oil in a pressure cooker over medium-high heat. Add veal and sauté, using long-handled tongs to turn to brown on both sides. Remove and set aside. Add shallots and garlic and sauté 1 minute, stirring with a wooden spoon to loosen any browned bits. Sprinkle with basil and stir. Add broth, lemon juice, sherry, salt, and pepper. Mix well. Return veal to cooker. Secure lid. Over high heat, bring pressure up to high. Reduce heat to maintain pressure and cook 10 minutes.

Release pressure according to manufacturer's directions. Remove lid. Add shrimp and olives to veal. Cook over high heat 3 minutes. Transfer veal to a platter. Top each portion with 2 shrimp.

Combine sour cream and potato starch in a small bowl. Stir into cooking liquid. Cook, stirring, over medium heat 1 minute. Spoon sauce over veal and shrimp. Sprinkle with cheese. Serve with rice and a vegetable.

(LAMB)

CURRIED LAMB WITH BASMATI RICE

Curry powder usually consists of a variety of spices such as cardamom, chiles, cinnamon, cloves, coriander, cumin, fennel seed, fenugreek, mace, nutmeg, red pepper, saffron, and turmeric. The turmeric gives it the yellow color.

MAKES 6 SERVINGS

3 tablespoons olive or canola oil

1 large onion, diced

4 garlic cloves, crushed

1½ pounds lamb shoulder, cut into 2-inch cubes

⅛ teaspoon mustard seed, crushed

½ teaspoon ground cumin

2 teaspoons curry powder

1 cup water

1⅛ teaspoons salt

Pinch crushed red pepper flakes

1 cup plain yogurt

1 cup canned chopped tomatoes

3 tablespoons all-purpose flour

3 cups steamed basmati rice (page 175) to serve

Heat oil in a pressure cooker over medium heat. Add onion and garlic and sauté 3 minutes. Add lamb and stir into the onion. Add spices, water, 1 teaspoon of the salt, and pepper flakes. Stir well. Secure lid. Over high heat, bring pressure up to high. Reduce heat to medium to maintain pressure and cook 15 minutes.

In the meantime, combine yogurt, remaining ⅛ teaspoon salt, tomatoes, and flour. Release pressure according to manufacturer's directions. Remove lid. Stir. Blend yogurt mixture into the lamb dish and cook over high heat 4 minutes, or until it begins to thicken. Serve with rice.

LAMB IN TOMATO SAUCE

Allspice is native to very warm climates. It is pea-size and can be readily found whole or ground. The flavor is a combination of cinnamon, cloves, and nutmeg. The spice is used in savory stews and also some desserts.

MAKES 6 SERVINGS

3 tablespoons olive oil

2 large white onions, coarsely diced

4 garlic cloves, crushed

1½ pounds lamb shoulder, cut into 2-inch cubes

1 (15-ounce) can diced tomatoes

1 cup canned tomato sauce

½ teaspoon salt

⅛ teaspoon ground black pepper

Dash crushed red pepper flakes

1 teaspoon ground allspice

¼ cup seasoned bread crumbs

Rice, pasta, noodles, or vegetables to serve

Heat oil in a pressure cooker over medium heat. Add onions and garlic and sauté 3 minutes. Add lamb and brown on all sides. Add remaining ingredients, except bread crumbs and rice. Stir well. Secure lid. Over high heat, bring pressure up to high. Reduce heat to medium to maintain pressure and cook 15 minutes.

Release pressure under cold running water. Remove lid. Stir in bread crumbs. Cover and cook 2 minutes. Serve sauce over rice with lamb on the side.

❑❑❑

LAMB AND LEEK STEW WITH POTATOES

Feathery dill leaves are available in both fresh and dried form. It is a delicate herb most frequently used in salads, vegetables, meats, and sauces. The dill seed is often used in the brine of pickled cucumbers and beets.

MAKES 6 SERVINGS

2 tablespoons olive or canola oil

3 large leeks (white parts only), rinsed and thinly
   sliced

3 garlic cloves, crushed

4 carrots, cut into 2-inch pieces

2 pounds lamb shoulder, cut into 2-inch cubes

2 teaspoons salt

⅛ teaspoon freshly ground black pepper

¼ cup fresh dill, minced, or 1 tablespoon dried

½ cup water

1 (15-ounce) can tomato sauce

4 large potatoes, peeled and cut into eighths

¼ cup seasoned bread crumbs

Crusty bread to serve

Heat oil in a pressure cooker over medium heat. Add leeks, garlic, and carrots and sauté 2 minutes. Add lamb and brown on all sides. Add seasonings, water, and tomato sauce. Stir well. Secure lid. Over high heat, bring pressure up to high. Reduce heat to medium to maintain pressure and cook 8 minutes.

Release pressure according to manufacturer's directions. Remove lid. Stir in potatoes. Secure lid. Over high heat, bring pressure up to high. Reduce heat to medium and cook 9 minutes.

Release pressure. Remove lid. Stir in bread crumbs. Cover and cook over medium heat 3 minutes. Stir well and serve with bread.

❑❑❑

LAMB MEATBALLS IN TOMATO SAUCE

Fennel is cultivated in the Mediterranean area. Used frequently in Greek and Italian dishes, fennel has a delicate sweet anise flavor; however, it is sweeter and much more delicate-flavored than anise.

MAKES 6 SERVINGS

Meatballs

1 pound ground lamb

2 tablespoons seasoned bread crumbs

1 small onion, finely diced

3 garlic cloves, crushed

¼ cup finely chopped fresh parsley

½ teaspoon dried oregano

1 teaspoon dried mint

½ teaspoon salt

⅛ teaspoon freshly ground black pepper

1 large egg, beaten

1 (15-ounce) can tomato sauce

½ cup beef broth

1 teaspoon dried basil

1 bay leaf

1 teaspoon ground fennel

½ teaspoon salt

Pinch crushed red pepper flakes

¼ cup seasoned bread crumbs

Spaghetti, rice, potatoes, or steamed green beans
    to serve

Shape the meatballs: Combine lamb, bread crumbs, onion, garlic, parsley, oregano, mint, salt, pepper, and egg in a large bowl. Blend well. Shape mixture into 2-inch meatballs.

In a pressure cooker, combine tomato sauce, beef broth, herbs, salt, and pepper flakes. Add meatballs. Secure lid. Over high heat, bring pressure up to high. Reduce heat to medium to maintain pressure and cook 5 minutes.

Reduce pressure according to manufacturer's directions. Remove lid. Discard bay leaf. Stir in bread crumbs. Serve meatballs and sauce over spaghetti.

LAMB SHANKS IN TOMATO SAUCE

The sauce developed in this dish is thick enough to use as a spaghetti sauce. The flavors are traditional Mediterranean. Don't forget the crusty bread for the delicious juices.

MAKES 6 SERVINGS

3 tablespoons olive or canola oil

3 large lamb shanks, split into halves

2 large onions, coarsely chopped

4 garlic cloves, crushed

½ cup chopped fresh parsley

4 medium carrots, cut into 3-inch pieces

1 teaspoon dried basil

1 teaspoon dried oregano

1 cup chicken broth or water

1 cup canned tomato sauce

1 teaspoon salt

¼ teaspoon freshly ground black pepper

1 bay leaf

2 large tomatoes, seeded and cut into eighths

3 tablespoons seasoned bread crumbs

Pasta, rice, potatoes, or vegetables to serve

Heat oil in a pressure cooker over medium-high heat. Add lamb shanks and brown on all sides. Transfer to a platter. Add onions, garlic, and parsley and sauté 3 minutes, stirring and scraping bottom of pan to loosen any brown bits. Add the shanks and remaining ingredients, except fresh tomatoes, bread crumbs, and pasta. Secure lid. Over high heat, bring pressure up to high. Reduce heat to medium to maintain pressure and cook 25 minutes.

Release pressure according to manufacturer's directions. Remove lid. Stir in tomatoes and bread crumbs. Cover and allow to stand 5 minutes. Transfer to a large shallow bowl. Serve with pasta.

COOK'S NOTE: Have the butcher cut the lamb shanks in half for you.

◪ ◪ ◪

LAMB SHANKS AND ARTICHOKE HEARTS WITH LEMON SAUCE

The artichoke is grown mainly in California and is referred to as the "globe" artichoke. Purchase deep green artichokes with tight leaves.

MAKES 6 SERVINGS

1 quart water

Juice of 1 large lemon

12 artichokes

3 tablespoons olive or canola oil

3 lamb shanks, split into halves

2 large onions, coarsely diced

4 garlic cloves, crushed

1 cup water

½ cup chopped fresh dill, or 2 tablespoons dried

2 teaspoons salt

⅛ teaspoon freshly ground black pepper

⅓ cup fresh lemon juice

2 large eggs

2 tablespoons all-purpose flour

⅓ cup chopped fresh parsley

Combine water with juice of 1 lemon in a large bowl. Prepare artichokes by removing and discarding coarse outer leaves until the pale green leaves are reached. Cut off about 1 inch from the tops. Cut the artichokes in half and remove the immature prickly leaves and fuzzy centers or chokes. Soak in lemon water until used to prevent discoloration.

Heat oil in a pressure cooker over medium-high heat. Add lamb shanks and brown on all sides. Transfer to a platter. Add onions and garlic and sauté 3 minutes, stirring and scraping bottom of pan to loosen any brown bits. Add water and dill. Stir well. Secure lid. Over high heat, bring pressure up to high. Reduce heat to medium to maintain pressure and cook 25 minutes.

Release pressure under cold running water and shake pan to stabilize pressure under lid. Remove lid. Drain artichokes and stir into lamb mixture along with salt, pepper, and ⅓ cup lemon juice. Secure lid. Over high heat, bring pressure up to medium. Reduce heat to medium and cook 4 minutes.

Release pressure under cold running water and remove lid. Whisk together eggs and flour. Whisk in 1 cup of broth from stew. Gently stir egg mixture into stew and cook 1 minute. Stir in parsley. Serve hot.

MEDITERRANEAN LAMB

When purchasing lamb, color should be your determining factor. Spring lamb is pink in color and under a year old. Lamb more than a year old is generally red in color, and mutton, or old lamb, is very dark in color. If mutton is purchased, more spices are necessary and cooking time should be increased.

MAKES 6 SERVINGS

3 tablespoons all-purpose flour

½ teaspoon salt

⅛ teaspoon freshly ground black pepper

3 lamb shanks, split into halves, or 1½ pounds
   lamb shoulder, cut into 2-inch pieces

3 tablespoons olive oil

1 large onion, coarsely diced

4 garlic cloves, crushed

4 carrots, cut into 2-inch pieces

8 celery stalks, veined and cut into 3-inch pieces

2 lemons, cut into eighths and seeds removed

1 teaspoon dried tarragon

1 teaspoon ground rosemary

½ teaspoon dried oregano

1 cup water

1 teaspoon salt

¼ teaspoon freshly ground black pepper

1 cup coarsely chopped fresh parsley

Steamed rice or potatoes to serve

Combine flour, salt, and pepper in a large plastic bag. Place lamb in the bag and toss until well coated. Remove from bag and toss in a colander to remove excess flour.

Heat oil in a pressure cooker over medium-high heat. Add lamb and brown on all sides. Transfer to a platter. Add onion, garlic, and carrots and sauté 3 minutes, scraping bottom to loosen any browned bits. Add lamb and remaining ingredients, except parsley and rice. Secure lid. Over high heat, bring pressure up to high. Reduce heat to medium to maintain pressure and cook 20 minutes (if using lamb shoulder, cook 15 minutes).

Release pressure according to manufacturer's directions. Remove lid. Stir parsley into the stew. Serve with rice.

LAMB–PINE NUT MEATBALLS WITH YOGURT SAUCE

Ground lamb is not always available. You can grind it at home by processing chilled, trimmed, and boned lamb shoulder in a food processor or through a meat grinder.

MAKES 6 SERVINGS

Meatballs

1 pound ground lamb

1 small onion, diced

2 garlic cloves, crushed

1 teaspoon dried mint

1 teaspoon salt

⅛ teaspoon freshly ground black pepper

1 large egg

3 tablespoons olive oil

¼ cup pine nuts

2 tablespoons fresh lemon juice

¾ cup water

1 pound baby carrots

1 cup plain yogurt

½ teaspoon dried mint

2 teaspoons chopped fresh parsley

Steamed rice and a vegetable to serve

Shape the meatballs: Mix lamb, onion, garlic, mint, salt, pepper, and egg in a bowl. Heat oil in a pressure cooker over medium heat. Add pine nuts, and cook, tossing, until golden. Remove pine nuts with a slotted spoon and stir into the lamb mixture until incorporated. Form mixture into 2-inch meatballs.

Add meatballs to pressure cooker and brown over high heat. Add lemon juice, water, and carrots. Secure lid. Over high heat, bring pressure up to medium. Reduce heat to medium to maintain pressure and cook 4 minutes.

Release pressure according to manufacturer's directions. Remove lid. Using a slotted spoon, transfer meatballs to a large shallow bowl. Combine ¼ cup of the liquid from the pressure cooker with yogurt, mint, and parsley. Drizzle sauce over meatballs. Serve with rice and a vegetable.

GREEK SPAGHETTI SAUCE

Serve the sauce over spaghetti, noodles, rice, or vegetables. It freezes well in airtight freezer containers for up to three months.

MAKES 6 SERVINGS

3 tablespoons olive oil

1 pound lean ground lamb or beef

1 large onion, coarsely diced

4 garlic cloves, crushed

½ cup chopped fresh parsley

1 teaspoon dried basil

1 bay leaf

1 teaspoon ground fennel

1½ teaspoons salt

⅛ teaspoon freshly ground black pepper

1 (15-ounce) can tomato sauce

½ cup beef broth

Pinch crushed red pepper flakes

1 tablespoon light brown sugar

¼ cup seasoned bread crumbs

Heat oil in a pressure cooker over medium-high heat. Add meat and cook, stirring to break up meat, until browned. Add onion, garlic, herbs, salt, and pepper. Stir well. Pour in tomato sauce and beef broth; add pepper flakes and sugar. Stir well. Secure lid. Over high heat, bring pressure up to high. Reduce heat to medium to maintain pressure and cook 8 minutes.

Release pressure according to manufacturer's directions. Remove lid. Discard bay leaf. Stir in bread crumbs. Cover and let stand 5 minutes before serving.

COOK'S NOTE: Seasoned dried bread crumbs act as a flavorful thickener for any soup or stew. More or less may be added depending on the desired consistency.

GREEK LAMB AND BEAN STEW

A favorite dish in Greek restaurants and homes, this fresh bean stew is robust in flavor. The beans are supposed to be well cooked, so don't expect crunchy beans!
MAKES 6 SERVINGS

¼ cup olive oil

2 large white onions, sliced

3 garlic cloves, crushed

2 pounds lamb shoulder, trimmed of fat and cut into 2-inch cubes

¼ cup all-purpose flour

1 (28-ounce) can Italian plum tomatoes

2 tablespoons tomato paste

¼ cup chopped fresh parsley

2 tablespoons light brown sugar

2 teaspoons sea salt or granulated salt

½ teaspoon freshly ground black pepper

2 tablespoons dried spearmint

2 tablespoons dried dill weed

1 teaspoon dried oregano

1½ pounds green beans, ends removed and cut into 2-inch pieces

3 potatoes, peeled and quartered

Crusty bread to serve

Heat oil in a large pressure cooker. Add onions and garlic and sauté 2 minutes. Dust lamb pieces with flour, add to onion and garlic, and sauté 2 minutes, stirring occasionally. Stir in tomatoes, tomato paste, parsley, brown sugar, salt, pepper, spearmint, dill, and oregano. Secure lid. Over high heat, bring pressure up to high. Reduce heat to maintain pressure and cook 8 minutes.

Release pressure according to manufacturer's directions. Remove lid. Stir lamb and sauce. Add green beans and potatoes. Stir well. Secure lid. Over high heat, bring pressure up to high. Reduce heat to maintain pressure and cook 8 minutes.

Release pressure according to manufacturer's directions. Remove lid. Stir stew. Cook, uncovered, over high heat 3 minutes to reduce liquid and intensify flavor, stirring occasionally. Serve with bread.

⬚ ⬚ ⬚

IRISH STEW

This traditional stew is always a composite of root vegetables and lamb or mutton. Since mutton is much stronger in flavor than the young lamb, most recipes use lamb. The flavors of the stew are fabulous, and it is traditionally served with dumplings.

¼ **cup corn oil or olive oil**

2 **pounds lamb shoulder, cut into 2-inch cubes**

3 **large onions, thinly sliced**

⅓ **cup minced fresh parsley**

2 **cups beef broth**

1 **tablespoon tomato paste**

1½ **teaspoons salt**

¼ **teaspoon freshly ground black pepper**

2 **bay leaves**

6 **celery stalks, cut into 2-inch pieces**

6 **small carrots, cut into 2-inch pieces**

6 **medium potatoes, peeled and cut into sixths**

2 **medium turnips, peeled and cut into ¼-inch slices**

¼ **cup butter, at room temperature**

1½ **tablespoons potato starch or all-purpose flour**

Dumplings to serve (optional)

Heat oil in a pressure cooker over medium-high heat. Add lamb pieces and sauté, turning with long-handled tongs to brown on both sides. Remove lamb and set aside. Add onions and parsley and sauté 2 minutes. Stir in broth, tomato paste, salt, pepper, and bay leaves. Stir well. Return lamb to cooker. Secure lid. Over high heat, bring pressure up to high. Reduce heat to maintain pressure and cook 8 minutes.

Release pressure according to manufacturer's directions. Remove lid. Stir lamb and liquid. Stir in celery, carrots, potatoes, and turnips. Secure lid. Over high heat, bring pressure up to medium. Reduce heat to maintain pressure and cook 6 minutes.

Release pressure according to manufacturer's directions. Remove lid. Remove bay leaf. Combine butter and potato starch, blending to paste consistency. Stir into lamb and vegetables and cook over medium-high heat 1 minute. Serve over dumplings (if desired).

ITALIAN COUNTRY LAMB AND WHITE BEAN STEW

This country stew, full of the flavors of old Italy, is a perfect meal for supper on a cold night.

MAKES 6 TO 8 SERVINGS

2 cups dried white beans, soaked

⅓ cup olive oil

¼ pound pancetta or bacon, diced

2 large onions, diced

2 carrots, cut into ½-inch slices

3 garlic cloves, crushed

½ cup minced fresh parsley

2 pounds lamb shoulder, trimmed of fat and cut into 2-inch cubes

1 (15-ounce) can crushed tomatoes

1 large green bell pepper, diced

3 cups chicken broth

2 tablespoons sherry

2 tablespoons light brown sugar

2 teaspoons salt

1 teaspoon crushed red pepper flakes

2 teaspoons dried basil

2 teaspoons dried oregano

2 bay leaves

½ cup (2 ounces) freshly grated Parmesan cheese

Italian bread to serve

Drain beans and set aside.

Heat oil in a pressure cooker. Add pancetta and sauté 1 minute. Stir in onions, carrots, garlic, and parsley. Sauté 2 minutes. Add lamb, tomatoes, bell pepper, beans, broth, sherry, brown sugar, salt, pepper flakes, basil, oregano, and bay leaves. Stir well. Secure lid. Over high heat, bring pressure up to high. Reduce heat to maintain pressure and cook 18 minutes.

Release pressure according to manufacturer's directions. Remove lid. Stir stew and discard bay leaves. Transfer to a deep platter and sprinkle with cheese. Serve with Italian bread.

COOK'S NOTE: Lamb is readily available in the meat department of supermarkets. Baby lamb is 6 to 8 weeks old, spring lamb 3 to 5 months old, and beyond that up to 1 year old, it is referred to as lamb. Mutton is more than 1 year old.

LAMB SHANKS WITH ORZO, GREEK VILLAGE STYLE

Orzo is a tiny pasta resembling rice in shape and with a satisfying, full-bodied texture.

MAKES 6 SERVINGS

¼ cup olive oil

4 lamb shanks, split into halves

2 large onions, diced

3 garlic cloves, crushed

½ cup chopped parsley

4½ cups beef broth

½ cup tomato sauce

2 tablespoons light sherry

2 tablespoons light brown sugar

1½ teaspoons salt

½ teaspoon crushed red pepper flakes

2 teaspoons dried oregano

1 teaspoon dried rosemary

½ teaspoon ground fennel

2 bay leaves

1½ cups orzo

Greek bread and feta cheese to serve

Heat oil in a pressure cooker over high heat. Add lamb pieces and sauté, using long-handled tongs to turn to brown on all sides. Transfer lamb to a platter; reserve.

Add onions, garlic, and parsley and sauté 3 minutes. Stir in broth, tomato sauce, sherry, brown sugar, salt, pepper flakes, oregano, rosemary, fennel, and bay leaves. Add lamb shanks. Secure lid. Over high heat, bring pressure up to high. Reduce heat to maintain pressure and cook 10 minutes.

Release pressure according to manufacturer's directions. Remove lid. Stir orzo into lamb and sauce. Secure lid. Over high heat, bring pressure up to high. Insert a heat diffuser between pan and heat. Reduce heat to maintain pressure and cook 10 minutes.

Release pressure according to manufacturer's directions. Remove lid. Stir lamb mixture thoroughly and discard bay leaves. Transfer to a large platter and serve with bread and feta cheese.

COOK'S NOTE: Have the butcher split the lamb shanks in half. This will allow the delicious marrow to be released during cooking, adding fabulous flavor to the dish.

SHEPHERD'S PIE

Shepherd's Pie was originally developed in England as an economical way to use leftovers. Therefore, if you have cooked lamb, substitute it for the ground lamb and cut the cooking time to 3 minutes.

MAKES 6 TO 8 SERVINGS

3 slices bacon, cut into 1-inch pieces

2 tablespoons olive oil

1 large onion, diced

3 garlic cloves, crushed

⅓ cup minced fresh parsley

1 pound ground lamb

½ cup beef broth

½ cup tomato sauce

3 carrots, cut into 1-inch pieces

1½ cups (1-inch pieces) celery

½ green bell pepper, diced

2 tablespoons sherry

1½ teaspoons salt

½ teaspoon freshly ground black pepper

1 teaspoon dried basil

1 teaspoon dried oregano

½ teaspoon dried rosemary

2 bay leaves

1 cup frozen green peas

Potato Topping

1 cup water

5 medium potatoes, peeled and cut into ½-inch
   cubes

¾ teaspoon salt

¼ teaspoon freshly ground white pepper

¼ cup sour cream

⅓ cup freshly grated Parmesan cheese

Sauté bacon with oil in a pressure cooker over medium heat until crisp. Add onion, garlic, and parsley and sauté 3 minutes. Crumble lamb into mixture and stir to break up meat. Add broth, tomato sauce, carrots, celery, bell pepper, sherry, salt, pepper, basil, oregano, rosemary, and bay leaves. Stir well. Secure lid. Over high heat, bring pressure up to high. Reduce heat to maintain pressure and cook 8 minutes.

Release pressure according to manufacturer's directions. Remove lid. Skim surface to remove excess grease. Stir in peas. Cook over high heat 2 minutes, stirring occasionally. Remove bay leaves. Ladle mixture into a 13 × 9-inch baking dish. Clean and dry pressure cooker.

Prepare Potato Topping: Pour water into pressure cooker. Place potatoes in steam basket and insert into cooker. Secure lid. Over high heat, bring pressure up to high. Reduce heat to maintain pressure and cook 5 minutes.

Release pressure according to manufacturer's directions. Remove lid. Remove basket and drain potatoes. Transfer to a bowl. Sprinkle with salt and pepper. Using an electric mixer, whip potatoes on low speed until mashed. Add sour cream, 1 tablespoon at a time, and continue to whip. Add ¼ cup of the cheese and whip until smooth and fluffy. Spoon potatoes into a 16-inch pastry bag fitted with a number 5 or 6 star pastry tube.

Preheat broiler. Press potatoes through pastry tube in an artistic pattern on top of lamb mixture. Sprinkle with remaining cheese. Broil 2 to 3 minutes, or until golden brown.

RICE MEATBALLS IN EGG-LEMON SAUCE

This lemon-sauced dish is traditionally made with ground lamb, but ground turkey can be used.

MAKES 6 SERVINGS

Meatballs

1½ pounds ground lamb

1 medium onion, diced

2 garlic cloves, crushed

1 cup long-grain white rice

1½ teaspoons salt

¼ teaspoon freshly ground black pepper

1 teaspoon dried oregano

⅓ cup olive oil

3 cups beef or chicken broth

1 teaspoon dried dill weed

Egg-Lemon Sauce

3 large eggs

1 tablespoon cornstarch or flour

⅓ cup fresh lemon juice

Steamed green beans or broccoli to serve

Shape the meatballs: Combine lamb, onion, garlic, rice, salt, pepper, and oregano in a bowl. Mix until thoroughly blended. Shape mixture into walnut-size balls.

Heat oil in a pressure cooker over medium-high heat. Add meatballs and sauté 2 minutes, using long-handled tongs to turn to brown on all sides. Stir in broth and dill. Secure lid. Over high heat, bring pressure up to high. Reduce heat to maintain pressure and cook 10 minutes.

Release pressure according to manufacturer's directions. Remove lid.

Prepare sauce: Using an electric mixer, beat eggs and cornstarch on medium-high speed 5 minutes. Gradually add lemon juice, continuing to beat. Gradually add ⅓ cup cooking liquid from meatballs.

Slowly pour sauce over meatballs, stirring gently to mix. Cook until hot, but do not boil. Serve with green beans.

(PORK)

BARBECUED PORK WITH GRITS

Today's pork is leaner and contains less fat than earlier pork cuts. Barbecued Pork may be served on crusty buns, on rice, or with potatoes.

MAKES 6 SERVINGS

3 slices bacon, finely diced

1 tablespoon olive oil

1 large onion, finely diced

2 garlic cloves, crushed

½ medium green bell pepper, finely diced

1½ pounds boneless pork loin, cut into 3-inch pieces

1 cup ketchup

2 tablespoons apple cider vinegar

⅓ cup light brown sugar

1 tablespoon molasses

1 tablespoon Dijon mustard

Dash Tabasco sauce

1 (3-inch) cinnamon stick

½ cup orange juice

½ cup water

¼ cup seasoned bread crumbs

Grits with Bacon (page 174) to serve

Sauté bacon with oil in a pressure cooker over medium heat until almost crisp. Add onion and sauté 1 minute, scraping bottom of the pan to loosen any browned bits. Add remaining ingredi-ents, except bread crumbs and Grits with Bacon. Stir well. Secure lid. Over high heat, bring pres-sure up to high. Reduce heat to medium to main-tain pressure and cook 15 minutes.

Release pressure according to manufacturer's directions. Remove lid. Using a slotted spoon, transfer meat to cutting board. Discard cinnamon stick. Stir in bread crumbs and cover. Shred meat into thin stringy pieces. Add to sauce and stir well. Serve with Grits.

▫ ▫ ▫

BASQUE STEW

Smoked ham hocks are cut from the shoulder and are great for pressure-cooked recipes. The smoked flavor adds depth to this traditional French stew. Hocks are also wonderful for bean soups and most bean dishes.

MAKES 6 SERVINGS

2 cups white beans, soaked

3 tablespoons olive or canola oil

1 large onion, coarsely diced

3 garlic cloves, crushed

2 dried whole cloves

1 cup chicken broth

1 teaspoon dried thyme

1 large bay leaf

2 smoked ham hocks

4 large potatoes, peeled and cut into eighths

3 cups cabbage, thinly sliced

⅓ cup chopped fresh parsley

¼ cup half-and-half

French bread, toasted and buttered, to serve

Drain beans and set aside. Heat oil in a pressure cooker over medium heat. Add onion and garlic and sauté 3 minutes. Add cloves, broth, herbs, ham hocks, and beans. Secure lid. Over high heat, bring pressure up to high. Reduce heat to medium to maintain pressure and cook 15 minutes.

Release pressure according to manufacturer's directions. Remove lid. Stir in potatoes. Secure lid. Over high heat, bring pressure up to high. Reduce heat to medium and cook 8 minutes.

Release pressure according to manufacturer's directions. Remove lid. Discard bay leaf and whole cloves. Remove ham hocks. Stir in cabbage and parsley. Cover and cook 5 minutes. Stir in half-and-half. Cut away the meaty part of the ham hock and add the meat to the stew. Stir well. Serve hot with bread.

ITALIAN BEAN STEW

Cannellini is a large white kidney bean. The beans must be soaked overnight in order to cook properly. The beans must be covered by at least 3 inches of water.

MAKES 6 SERVINGS

4 slices bacon, finely diced

1 tablespoon olive oil

2 large onions, coarsely diced

5 garlic cloves, crushed

1½ pounds pork shoulder, cut into 2-inch cubes

1 (28-ounce) can diced tomatoes in sauce

2 tablespoons sweet vermouth

1 cup beef broth

1 teaspoon dried basil

1 teaspoon dried crushed rosemary

1 bay leaf

2 cups dried cannellini beans, soaked overnight

4 large carrots

2 teaspoons salt

⅛ teaspoon crushed red pepper flakes

¼ cup finely chopped fresh parsley

¼ cup seasoned bread crumbs

Italian bread to serve

Sauté bacon with oil in a pressure cooker over medium heat until almost crisp. Add onions and garlic and sauté 2 minutes. Add pork and all remaining ingredients, except bread crumbs and bread. Secure lid. Over high heat, bring pressure up to high. Reduce heat to medium to maintain pressure and cook 15 minutes.

Release pressure according to manufacturer's directions. Remove lid. Stir in bread crumbs. Cook 2 minutes. Serve with bread.

KIELBASA SAUSAGE WITH CABBAGE AND POTATOES

Kielbasa is a Polish sausage readily found in most supermarkets. It is generally made of pork and a variety of spices. Kielbasa can be found precooked or fresh.

MAKES 6 SERVINGS

2 pounds fresh kielbasa sausage

3 tablespoons butter

1 medium onion, thickly sliced

1 (about 2-pound) head cabbage, cut into 1-inch
   slices

5 medium russet potatoes, peeled and quartered

1½ teaspoons salt

⅛ teaspoon freshly ground white pepper

1 teaspoon ground fennel

1 cup chicken broth

Using a very sharp knife, cut sausage into 2-inch pieces. Melt butter in a pressure cooker over medium heat. Add onion and sauté 3 minutes. Add sausage and cook on both sides 1 minute. Add cabbage, potatoes, salt, pepper, fennel, and broth. Stir well. Secure lid. Over high heat, bring pressure up to high. Reduce heat to medium to maintain pressure and cook 8 minutes.

Release pressure according to manufacturer's directions. Remove lid. Stir and transfer stew into a large serving bowl.

ASIAN MEATBALLS

Serve these meatballs and pineapple sauce with steamed rice.

MAKES 6 SERVINGS

Meatballs

2 tablespoons canola oil

4 green onions, finely diced

½ cup canned water chestnuts, finely chopped

½ red bell pepper, finely diced

1½ pounds ground pork

2 tablespoons soy sauce

¼ cup crushed pineapple, drained

1 large egg

2 tablespoons bread crumbs

¼ cup chicken broth

¼ cup crushed pineapple, drained

3 tablespoons light brown sugar

1 tablespoon apple cider vinegar

2 tablespoons cornstarch mixed with 2
   tablespoons pineapple juice or water

Shape the meatballs: Heat oil in a pressure cooker over medium heat. Add onions, water chestnuts, and bell pepper and sauté 2 minutes. In a large bowl, mix together pork, soy sauce, pineapple, egg, and bread crumbs. Add the onion mixture from the pressure cooker. Mix well. Form mixture into 2-inch balls.

Mix together broth, crushed pineapple, brown sugar, and vinegar. Place the meatballs into the pressure cooker and gently pour the broth mixture on top. Secure the lid. Over high heat, bring pressure up to high. Reduce heat to medium to maintain pressure and cook 7 minutes.

Release pressure according to manufacturer's directions. Remove lid. Stir ½ cup of the cooking juices into the cornstarch mixture. Stir into the pressure cooker and cook, stirring, over medium heat 1 minute, or until mixture thickens slightly.

VARIATION This recipe could also be an appetizer. Form the meatballs into small bite-size balls and reduce the time under pressure to 5 minutes. Serve in a chafing dish.

⊞ ⊞ ⊞

PORK CHOPS WITH CHILE VERDE SAUCE

Wearing rubber gloves is recommended when working with fresh jalapeño and Anaheim chiles to prevent burning the skin. Be careful not to touch your eyes.

MAKES 6 SERVINGS

Dash salt

Dash freshly ground black pepper

6 (1½-inch-thick) pork chops

3 tablespoons olive oil

1 large onion, coarsely diced

5 garlic cloves, crushed

1 cup chicken broth

4 large tomatillos, husks removed and chopped

2 small Anaheim chiles, finely chopped

1 large jalapeño chile, finely chopped

½ cup coarsely chopped fresh cilantro leaves

1 teaspoon fresh lemon juice

½ teaspoon salt

12 medium flour tortillas

½ cup sour cream

Sprinkle salt and pepper over pork chops. Heat oil in a pressure cooker over medium heat. Add pork chops, 2 at a time, and brown on each side. Set aside. Add onion and garlic and sauté 3

minutes. Add broth, tomatillos, chiles, cilantro, lemon juice, and salt. Stir well. Place pork chops into the mixture. Secure lid. Over high heat, bring pressure up to high. Reduce heat to medium to maintain pressure and cook 12 minutes.

Release pressure according to manufacturer's directions. Remove lid. Transfer pork chops to a cutting board. Cut into thin slices. Return pork to pressure cooker. Warm tortillas and spoon pork mixture into the centers. Roll the tortillas and serve with sour cream.

⊞ ⊞ ⊞

PORK CHOPS WITH BELL PEPPER SAUCE

This recipe is a good example of why interrupting the pressure cooking is a useful technique. First the pork chops are cooked to a tender consistency, then the bell peppers are added and cooked just long enough to soften them, allowing them to hold their shapes and colors, and develop delicious flavors. The addition of garlic at the end adds just a hint of garlic to the sauce.

The pork chops and sauce may be served with steamed rice, potatoes, or vegetables. Extra leftover juices may be used to steam the rice or noodles, or drizzled over the steamed rice.

MAKES 6 SERVINGS

6 (1-inch-thick) pork chops

2 tablespoons all-purpose flour

3 tablespoons olive oil

1 cup chicken broth

1 teaspoon salt

Pinch crushed red pepper flakes

1 teaspoon dried tarragon

1 *each* red, green, and yellow bell peppers, quartered

1 small onion, thickly sliced

1 garlic clove, crushed

1 tablespoon sour cream

Dust pork chops with flour. Heat oil in a pressure cooker over medium heat. Add pork chops, 2 at a time, and brown on each side. Set aside. Add broth to pressure cooker, and cook, stirring and scraping bottom to release any browned bits. Add salt, pepper flakes, and tarragon. Stir well. Add pork chops. Over high heat, bring pressure up to high. Reduce heat to medium to maintain pressure and cook 10 minutes.

Release pressure according to manufacturer's directions. Remove lid. Stir in bell peppers and onion. Secure lid. Over high heat, bring pressure up to medium. Reduce heat to medium to maintain pressure and cook 2 minutes.

Release pressure according to manufacturer's directions. Remove lid. Transfer pork chops to a platter. Using a slotted spoon, scoop the bell peppers and onion into a food processor or blender. Add garlic and sour cream. Blend until smooth. Pour sauce over pork chops.

PORK WITH APPLES AND SWEET POTATOES

The sweet potato is frequently confused with the yam, because it is often referred to as a "yam." Sweet potatoes are available in two colors, pale yellow and a darker orange. The orange version has more moisture and is generally sweeter. True yams are found in South and Central American cuisine and are less frequently available in U.S. supermarkets.

MAKES 6 SERVINGS

6 (1-inch-thick) pork chops, trimmed

2 tablespoons all-purpose flour

3 tablespoons olive oil

1 large onion, finely diced

1 cup apple juice or cider

¼ cup maple syrup

1 teaspoon salt

⅛ teaspoon freshly ground white pepper

3 large apples, peeled and quartered

2 large sweet potatoes, peeled and cut into 2-inch-thick slices

¼ cup packed light brown sugar

2 tablespoons cornstarch mixed with 2 tablespoons water

Steamed vegetables to serve

Dust pork chops with flour. Heat oil in a pressure cooker over medium heat. Add pork chops, 2 at a time, and brown on each side. Set aside. Add onion and cook 1 minute. Add apple juice, maple syrup, salt, and pepper. Stir well. Layer pork chops into juices. Secure lid. Over high heat, bring pressure up to high. Reduce heat to medium to maintain pressure and cook 7 minutes.

Reduce pressure according to manufacturer's directions. Remove lid. Stir in apples, sweet potatoes, and brown sugar. Secure lid. Over high heat, bring pressure up to medium. Reduce heat to medium to maintain pressure and cook 6 minutes.

Release pressure according to manufacturer's directions. Remove lid. Stir ½ cup of cooking juices into cornstarch mixture. Whisk until smooth and add to the pressure cooker. Cook, stirring, over medium heat 3 minutes. Serve with vegetables.

⬚ ⬚ ⬚

RICE WITH HAM AND CHEESE

Country-cured ham can be found in most meat counters along with the processed meats. Prosciutto, Italian cured ham, may be substituted in this recipe. Usually American country-cured ham comes from Kentucky, Tennessee, and Virginia.

MAKES 6 SERVINGS

2 tablespoons olive oil

1 small onion, finely diced

½ red bell pepper, coarsely diced

2 cups long-grain white rice

5 cups chicken broth

1½ teaspoons salt

⅛ teaspoon freshly ground white pepper

1 pound country-cured ham slices, cut into
    1 × 2-inch pieces

4 ounces (1 cup) grated medium Cheddar cheese

¼ cup half-and-half

Heat oil in a pressure cooker over medium heat. Add onion and sauté 3 minutes. Add bell pepper, rice, broth, salt, and pepper. Secure lid. Over high heat, bring pressure up to high. Reduce heat to medium to maintain pressure and cook 8 minutes.

Release pressure according to manufacturer's directions. Remove lid. Stir in ham, cheese, and half-and-half. Cover and cook over medium heat 2 minutes. Stir well. Serve hot in a shallow serving bowl.

⬚ ⬚ ⬚

SWEET AND SOUR PORK

Bean sprouts are often used in Asian cooking. There are a variety of sprouts available. Look for sprouts of mung beans, alfalfa seeds, soybeans, and wheat berries. Sprouts should not be cooked for more than a minute to retain their crispness.

MAKES 6 SERVINGS

1½ pounds pork shoulder, cut into 2-inch pieces

1 tablespoon all-purpose flour

2 tablespoons sesame oil

1 cup pineapple juice

1 tablespoon light brown sugar

Pinch mustard powder

½ teaspoon ground ginger

2 tablespoons apple cider vinegar

1 tablespoon low-sodium soy sauce

1 pound fresh snow peas

4 medium carrots, cut into 2-inch pieces

1 large red bell pepper, sliced thick

2 large onions, sliced thick

3 garlic cloves, thinly sliced

1½ teaspoons salt

¼ teaspoon freshly ground black pepper

2 tablespoons cornstarch mixed with

    2 tablespoons water

1 cup bean sprouts

Chinese noodles or rice to serve

Place pork in a plastic bag and add flour. Shake until coated. Heat sesame oil in a pressure cooker over medium-high heat. Add pork, in batches, and brown on all sides. Remove pork to a bowl. Add pineapple juice and scrape up any browned bits from pan. Add sugar, mustard, ginger, vinegar, soy sauce, snow peas, carrots, bell pepper, onion, garlic, salt, and black pepper. Stir well. Secure lid. Over high heat, bring pressure up to high. Reduce heat to medium to maintain pressure and cook 12 minutes.

Reduce pressure according to manufacturer's directions. Remove lid. Stir ½ cup of cooking juices into cornstarch mixture until smooth. Stir into pressure cooker. Add bean sprouts and stir well. Serve over noodles.

GERMAN PORK CHOPS AND SAUERKRAUT

Caraway seeds lend a wonderful nutty flavor to this traditional German dish. The caraway seeds are aromatic and come from a member of the parsley family.

MAKES 6 SERVINGS

6 (1-inch-thick) pork chops

⅓ cup all-purpose flour

3 slices bacon, cut into 1-inch pieces

¼ cup butter or olive oil

2 large onions, sliced

4 garlic cloves, crushed

3 carrots, cut into ½-inch slices

1 cup apple juice

1 cup chicken broth

1 tablespoon fresh lemon juice

1¼ teaspoons salt

½ teaspoon freshly ground black pepper

1 teaspoon dried thyme

2 bay leaves

8 juniper berries and 1 tablespoon caraway seeds

    in cheesecloth bag

2 (16-ounce) jars sauerkraut, drained and rinsed

2 teaspoons potato starch or all-purpose flour

    mixed with 2 tablespoons water

Steamed whole potatoes to serve

Dust pork chops with flour, shaking to remove excess.

Cook bacon in a pressure cooker over medium heat until crisp. Add butter and stir until melted and foaming. Add pork chops and sauté over medium heat until browned on both sides, turning with long-handled tongs. Transfer pork chops to a platter and reserve.

Add onions, garlic, and carrots and sauté 1 minute. Stir in apple juice, broth, lemon juice, salt, pepper, thyme, bay leaves, and bag with juniper berries and caraway seeds. Stir well. Return pork chops to cooker. Secure lid. Over high heat, bring pressure up to high. Reduce heat to maintain pressure and cook 15 minutes.

Release pressure according to manufacturer's directions. Remove lid. Stir sauerkraut into pork chop mixture and cook over high heat 3 minutes. Discard cheesecloth bag and bay leaves. Stir ¼ cup hot broth into flour mixture and stir into hot mixture. Cook, stirring, over medium heat 1 minute. Serve hot with potatoes.

(VENISON)

BARBECUED VENISON MEATBALLS

This luscious combination served in crusty buns makes a delicious sandwich, or it can be served with rice or potatoes.

MAKES 6 SERVINGS

Meatballs

1½ pounds ground venison

1 small onion, finely diced

2 garlic cloves, crushed

¼ cup minced fresh parsley

1 teaspoon salt

⅛ teaspoon freshly ground black pepper

1 small apple, grated

1 large egg

½ cup seasoned bread crumbs

2 slices bacon, finely diced

3 tablespoons canola oil

1 medium onion, finely diced

2 garlic cloves, crushed

1 cup ketchup

¼ cup water

½ teaspoon chili powder

Dash Tabasco sauce

1 tablespoon light brown sugar

Shape the meatballs: In a medium bowl, mix together venison, onion, garlic, parsley, salt, pepper, apple, and egg. Form mixture into 1½-inch meatballs. Coat each meatball with bread crumbs.

Sauté bacon with oil in a pressure cooker over medium heat until almost crisp. Add meatballs, 6 at a time, and brown on all sides. Set aside. Add onion and garlic. Sauté 2 minutes, stirring and scraping bottom of pan to loosen any browned bits. Stir in ketchup, water, chili powder, Tabasco sauce, and brown sugar. Add meatballs to the sauce, one at a time. Secure lid. Over high heat, bring pressure up to medium. Reduce heat to medium to maintain pressure and cook 15 minutes.

Release pressure according to manufacturer's directions. Remove lid. Gently stir and serve.

VENISON BORSCHT

Borscht is from Central Europe. It is always garnished with a dollop of sour cream and a dash of freshly chopped parsley.

MAKES 6 SERVINGS

¼ cup all-purpose flour

½ teaspoon salt

⅛ teaspoon freshly ground black pepper

1½ pounds venison shoulder, trimmed and cut into 2-inch pieces

3 tablespoons canola oil

2 large leeks (white parts only), rinsed and thinly sliced

3 carrots, cut into 1-inch pieces

¼ cup minced fresh parsley plus extra to garnish

2 cups beef broth

4 large beets, rinsed and cut in half

3 large potatoes, peeled and cut into 2-inch slices

1 teaspoon salt

Dash crushed red pepper flakes

1 large bay leaf

1 teaspoon dried basil

½ teaspoon ground fennel

2 tablespoons dry sherry

1 cup sour cream

Chopped parsley for garnish

Combine flour, salt, and pepper in a large plastic bag. Place venison in the bag and toss until well coated. Remove from bag and toss in a colander to remove excess flour.

Heat oil in a pressure cooker over medium-high heat. Add venison, in 3 batches, and brown on all sides. Transfer browned meat to a platter. Add leeks, carrots, and parsley and cook 2 minutes, scraping bottom of pan to loosen any browned bits. Return venison to pressure cooker and add broth and beets. Secure lid. Over high heat, bring pressure up to high. Reduce heat to medium to maintain pressure and cook 30 minutes.

Release pressure according to manufacturer's directions. Remove lid. Using a slotted spoon, transfer beets into a bowl of cold water. Slide skins off and cut into thin slices. Process beets in a blender or food processor until chunky smooth. Transfer back to the pressure cooker. Add potatoes, salt, pepper flakes, bay leaf, basil, fennel, and sherry. Secure lid. Over high heat, bring pressure up to high. Reduce heat to medium and cook 5 minutes.

Release pressure according to manufacturer's directions. Remove lid. Discard bay leaf. Ladle ½ cup of hot broth into ½ cup of the sour cream. Stir well. Stir sour cream mixture into the borscht. Serve with dollops of remaining sour cream and garnish with parsley.

⊡ ⊡ ⊡

VENISON CHILI SAUCE ON ENGLISH MUFFINS

This versatile dish may be served on a bun, on corn or regular muffins, or as a soup topped with sour cream or cheddar cheese.

MAKES 6 SERVINGS

2 slices bacon, finely diced

2 tablespoons olive oil

1 medium onion, finely diced

3 garlic cloves, crushed

¼ cup finely chopped fresh cilantro

¾ pound ground venison

1 cup beef broth

1 cup tomato sauce

½ green bell pepper, chopped

1 teaspoon salt

⅛ teaspoon freshly ground black pepper

1 teaspoon chili powder

½ teaspoon sweet paprika

½ teaspoon ground cumin

Dash Tabasco sauce

6 English muffins, split

1 cup (4 ounces) grated Cheddar cheese

Sauté bacon with oil in a pressure cooker over medium heat until almost crisp. Add onion, garlic, and cilantro. Sauté 2 minutes. Add venison and cook 2 minutes, stirring to break up meat. Add beef broth, tomato sauce, bell pepper, salt, black pepper, chili powder, paprika, cumin, and Tabasco sauce. Stir well. Secure lid. Over high heat, bring pressure up to high. Reduce heat to medium to maintain pressure and cook 14 minutes.

Release pressure according to manufacturer's directions. Remove lid. Stir well. Toast muffins. Place on a serving dish and spoon venison chili over top of each muffin. Sprinkle cheese over top.

⊡ ⊡ ⊡

VENISON IN CHILE SAUCE

Serve with hot steamed rice or steamed potatoes and vegetables.

MAKES 6 SERVINGS

1½ pounds venison, leg or loin, cut into
    4 1-inch-thick slices

¼ cup all-purpose flour

3 tablespoons olive oil

1 small onion, finely diced

4 garlic cloves, crushed

¼ cup chopped fresh cilantro

2 tablespoons fresh lemon juice

½ cup beef broth

½ cup tomato sauce

1 teaspoon ground dried chiles

1 teaspoon ground cumin

Dash crushed red pepper flakes

2 teaspoons light brown sugar

1 teaspoon salt

¼ cup unseasoned bread crumbs

Dust each side of the venison pieces with flour. Heat oil in a pressure cooker over medium heat. Add venison, 2 slices at a time, and brown on both sides. Transfer to a platter. Add onion, garlic, and cilantro to the pressure cooker and sauté 2 minutes, scraping bottom of pan to loosen any browned bits. Add lemon juice, beef broth, tomato sauce, ground chile, cumin, pepper flakes, brown sugar, and salt. Stir well. Return venison to pressure cooker. Secure lid. Over high heat, bring pressure up to high. Reduce heat to medium to maintain pressure and cook 25 minutes.

Release pressure according to manufacturer's directions. Remove lid. Stir in bread crumbs. Cook 1 minute. Stir and serve.

COOK'S NOTE: The various venison cuts are similar to beef.

VENISON MARINADE

Marinade is generally used for tougher cuts of venison from the shoulder, neck, rump, or flank.

MAKES ABOUT 4 CUPS

2 cups apple cider vinegar

1 cup red wine vinegar

1 teaspoon salt

1 teaspoon ground mustard

Dash crushed red pepper flakes

1 teaspoon ground cloves

1 large onion, finely diced

4 garlic cloves, crushed

1 cup olive oil

Bring all ingredients to a boil. Remove from heat and cool. Place venison in a large stainless-steel or glass bowl and pour marinade over top. Refrigerate for at least 24 hours, turning meat every 6 hours. Drain. Prepare meat in desired recipe.

VENISON STEW WITH PEARL ONIONS

Trim as much of the fat off the meat as possible. If not, the fat will permeate the stew with a gamey flavor. The shoulder of the venison is a tougher part and requires a longer cooking period.

3 pounds pearl or tiny onions

Juice of 1 lemon

2 pounds venison shoulder, cut into 2-inch cubes

¼ cup all-purpose flour

3 slices bacon, finely diced

3 tablespoons olive oil

1 large onion, coarsely diced

5 garlic cloves, crushed

⅓ cup minced fresh parsley

4 carrots, cut into 1-inch pieces

½ cup beef broth

1 (15-ounce) can diced tomatoes in sauce

2 teaspoons salt

Dash crushed red pepper flakes

1½ teaspoons ground allspice

1 large bay leaf

1 tablespoon light brown sugar

12 red-skinned potatoes, rinsed and cut in half

2 tablespoons apple cider vinegar

¼ cup seasoned bread crumbs

Crusty bread to serve

Peel onions and place in a bowl with lemon juice and enough water to cover. Set aside.

Place venison and flour in a large plastic bag and shake, coating each piece. Place in a colander and toss to remove excess flour.

Sauté bacon with oil in a pressure cooker over medium heat until almost crisp. Add diced onion, garlic, parsley, and carrots. Stir and cook 2 minutes. Add venison and cook, stirring, 2 minutes. Add beef broth, tomatoes, salt, pepper flakes, allspice, bay leaf, and brown sugar. Stir well. Secure lid. Over high heat, bring pressure up to high. Reduce heat to medium to maintain pressure and cook 30 minutes.

Release pressure according to manufacturer's directions. Remove lid. Drain pearl onions. Stir potatoes and onions into stew. Secure lid. Over high heat, bring pressure up to high. Reduce heat to medium and cook 4 minutes.

Release pressure according to manufacturer's directions. Remove lid. Discard bay leaf. Stir in apple cider vinegar and bread crumbs. Cover and let stand 5 minutes. Serve hot with bread.

VENISON STROGANOFF

Count Stroganoff, of Russia, would be very pleased with this dish. The venison adds a rich dimension to the flavor.

MAKES 6 SERVINGS

¼ cup all-purpose flour

½ teaspoon salt

⅛ teaspoon freshly ground black pepper

1½ pounds venison steak, trimmed and cut into
   2 × ½-inch strips

3 tablespoons canola oil

1 small onion, finely diced

⅓ cup finely chopped fresh parsley

1 teaspoon dried tarragon

½ teaspoon dried thyme

1 large bay leaf

½ cup canned diced tomatoes in sauce

½ cup beef broth

1 teaspoon salt

⅛ teaspoon freshly ground black pepper

1½ pounds fresh mushrooms, thinly sliced

½ cup sour cream

¼ cup crumbled blue cheese

2 tablespoons dry sherry

2 tablespoons all-purpose flour or potato starch

Cooked noodles to serve

Combine ¼ cup flour, salt, and pepper in a large plastic bag. Place venison in the bag and toss until well coated. Remove from bag and toss in a colander to remove excess flour.

Heat the oil in a pressure cooker over medium-high heat. Add venison, in 3 batches, and brown on all sides. With a slotted spoon, transfer venison to a platter. Add onion and parsley and cook 2 minutes, scraping bottom of pan to loosen any browned bits. Return venison to pressure cooker and add tarragon, thyme, and bay leaf. Stir well. Pour in tomatoes and beef broth. Stir. Add salt and pepper. Secure lid. Over high heat, bring pressure up to high. Reduce heat to medium to maintain pressure and cook 30 minutes.

Release pressure according to manufacturer's directions. Remove lid. Discard bay leaf. Add mushrooms. Cover and simmer 3 minutes.

In a small bowl, whisk together sour cream, blue cheese, sherry, and 2 tablespoons flour. Ladle some of the juices from the stew into the sour cream mixture and mix well. Slowly incorporate the mixture into the stew and stir well. Cook 2 minutes, stirring occasionally. Serve over noodles.

VENISON VEGETABLE STEW

It is very important to brown the venison in small portions. This will prevent steaming the meat rather than browning it.

MAKES 6 SERVINGS

2 pounds venison shoulder, cut into 2-inch
    pieces

¼ cup all-purpose flour

2 slices bacon, finely diced

3 tablespoons olive oil

1 large onion, sliced

4 garlic cloves, crushed

⅓ cup chopped fresh parsley

½ cup beef broth

1 (15-ounce) can diced tomatoes in sauce

2 teaspoons salt

⅛ teaspoon freshly ground black pepper

1 teaspoon dried basil

1 medium red bell pepper, sliced

3 large potatoes, peeled and cut into 2-inch pieces

4 medium carrots, cut into 2-inch pieces

2 cups fresh or frozen whole-kernel corn

¼ cup seasoned bread crumbs

Crusty bread to serve

Place venison and flour in a large plastic bag and shake, coating each piece. Place in a colander and toss to remove excess flour.

Sauté bacon with oil in a pressure cooker over medium-high heat until almost crisp. Add venison, in batches to prevent overcrowding, and brown on each side. Transfer to a platter. Add onion, garlic, and parsley and cook 3 minutes, scraping bottom of pan to loosen any browned bits. Return venison to pressure cooker and add broth, tomatoes, salt, pepper, and basil. Stir well. Secure lid. Over high heat, bring pressure up to high. Reduce heat to medium to maintain pressure and cook 35 minutes.

Release pressure according to manufacturer's directions. Remove lid. Stir in bell pepper, potatoes, carrots, and corn. Secure lid. Over high heat, bring pressure up to high. Reduce heat to medium and cook 5 minutes.

Release pressure according to manufacturer's directions. Remove lid. Stir in bread crumbs. Cover and let stand 5 minutes. Serve with bread.

▢ ▢ ▢

VENISON WITH RICH PESTO SAUCE

Cutting the venison in little pieces will decrease cooking time needed to tenderize it and allow it to absorb some of the rich, succulent sauce. Serve over rice, pasta, potatoes, polenta, or vegetables.

MAKES 6 SERVINGS

¼ cup all-purpose flour

½ teaspoon salt

⅛ teaspoon freshly ground black pepper

6 (1-inch-thick) steaks sliced from venison leg, cut
    into 2 × 1-inch strips

3 tablespoons olive oil

1 large onion, coarsely diced

3 garlic cloves, crushed

¼ cup finely chopped fresh parsley

2 medium carrots, coarsely chopped

½ cup beef broth

½ cup tomato sauce

1 teaspoon dried basil

¼ cup freshly grated Parmesan cheese

Combine flour, salt, and pepper in a large plastic bag. Add venison and toss until well coated. Remove from bag and toss in a colander to remove excess flour.

Heat oil in a pressure cooker over medium-high heat. Add venison, in batches to prevent overcrowding, and brown on all sides. With a slotted spoon, transfer venison to a platter. Add onion, garlic, parsley, and carrots and sauté 3 minutes, scraping bottom of pan to loosen any browned bits. Add beef broth, tomato sauce, and basil. Stir and return venison to pressure cooker. Secure lid. Over high heat, bring pressure up to high. Reduce heat to medium to maintain pressure and cook 30 minutes.

Release pressure according to manufacturer's directions. Remove lid. Stir in Parmesan cheese.

(POULTRY)

Poultry blends well with other ingredients when cooked. It is excellent when prepared in a pressure cooker.

It is very economical to purchase a whole chicken, duck, or turkey and cut it into pieces. The skin can be removed, if desired. The pieces may be used in stocks, stews, or any favorite recipe. Any remaining pieces may be wrapped airtight in freezer paper, marked with the item and date, and frozen for future use.

Some people prefer free-range poultry because of its richer, purer flavor. It can be found in most butcher shops. If you live in an area where kosher or Amish birds are available, they are excellent in quality and flavor.

BUYING POULTRY

When buying poultry, be selective. Look for a fresh, moist surface with a rich pink and yellow hue. Dark gray dry marks on the bird indicate it was improperly frozen and handled and that bacteria may be present. Look for a meaty bird without skin tears or bruises.

Poultry is available in these categories.

• **Fryer:** Tender and great for any kind of preparation, including barbecuing.

• **Broiler:** Firmer than a fryer but still tender.

- **Roaster:** A more mature, tougher bird best used for stuffing and roasting.

COOKING TIME FOR POULTRY

Cut poultry into uniform pieces before cooking in a pressure cooker to ensure even cooking.

Cook poultry 10 minutes for each 2 inches of thickness.

▣ ▣ ▣

STEWED CHICKEN

The leeks and shallots add a delightful natural sweetness to this stewed chicken dish. For a more natural chicken flavor, omit the basil and oregano. Served with steamed noodles, rice, potatoes, or pasta, this dish will become a healthy favorite.

MAKES 6 SERVINGS

1 whole chicken, cut into sixths

¼ cup all-purpose flour

3 tablespoons olive or canola oil

1 large leek (white part only), rinsed and sliced

4 garlic cloves, crushed

¼ cup minced fresh parsley

1 bay leaf

1 teaspoon dried basil

½ teaspoon dried oregano

1 cup chicken broth

1 cup canned plum tomatoes, crushed

1½ teaspoons salt

⅛ teaspoon freshly ground black pepper

12 whole shallots, peeled

12 baby carrots

4 large potatoes, peeled and cut into eighths

¼ cup seasoned bread crumbs

Lightly dust chicken pieces with flour and shake off excess. Heat oil in a pressure cooker over medium-high heat. Add chicken, in batches, and brown on all sides. Transfer to a platter. Add leek, garlic, and parsley and sauté 3 minutes, scraping bottom of cooker with a wooden spoon to loosen any browned bits. Add the chicken and remaining ingredients, except bread crumbs. Stir well. Secure lid. Over high heat, bring pressure up to high. Reduce heat to medium to maintain pressure and cook 9 minutes.

Release pressure according to manufacturer's directions. Remove lid. Stir well. Sprinkle bread crumbs over top and stir. Cook 3 minutes over medium heat.

▣ ▣ ▣

STUFFED CHICKEN WITH GRAVY

The flavors in these bundles of pure delicious joy will be reminiscent of the holidays. Serve with creamy mashed potatoes covered with the rich gravy juices.

MAKES 6 SERVINGS

6 boneless, skinless chicken breast halves

⅛ teaspoon salt

⅛ teaspoon freshly ground white pepper

¾ teaspoon dried tarragon

3 slices bread, cubed

1 small onion, finely diced

2 tablespoons minced fresh parsley

½ teaspoon dried sage

1½ cups chicken broth

1 teaspoon fresh lemon juice

1 teaspoon salt

⅛ teaspoon freshly ground white pepper

3 tablespoons potato starch or all-purpose flour

¼ cup canned tomato sauce

2 tablespoons sour cream

Using a meat mallet, flatten chicken between two sheets of waxed paper or plastic wrap to ⅛-inch thickness. Combine salt, pepper, and ¼ teaspoon of the tarragon. Rub both sides of chicken with the seasonings.

In a bowl, mix bread, onion, parsley, sage, and ⅛ cup of the chicken broth. Divide mixture into 6 equal parts and place a portion on each chicken piece. Fold chicken over stuffing. Secure with kitchen twine. Pour remaining broth, lemon juice, salt, pepper, and remaining ½ teaspoon tarragon into a pressure cooker. Lay chicken bundles into the broth. Secure lid. Over high heat, bring pressure up to high. Reduce heat to medium to maintain pressure and cook 9 minutes.

Release pressure under cold running water. Combine potato starch, tomato sauce, and sour cream until smooth. Stir in ¼ cup of the hot broth, stir the mixture into the chicken, and cook, stirring, over medium-high heat for several minutes, or until the juices thicken.

ASIAN CHICKEN BREASTS

The five-spice powder adds authentic flavors to this lovely recipe. To prepare the spice for home use simply mix ½ teaspoon each ground cinnamon, ground cloves, ground fennel seeds, ground star anise, and ground Szechwan pepper. The spice is also available packaged in Asian markets and some supermarkets.

MAKES 6 SERVINGS

6 chicken breast halves, skin removed

¼ teaspoon salt

¼ teaspoon freshly ground white pepper

½ teaspoon five-spice powder

¼ teaspoon ground ginger

2 tablespoons sesame oil

4 green onions, finely diced

2 garlic cloves, crushed

½ cup chicken broth

½ cup pineapple juice

2 tablespoons cornstarch mixed with
    2 tablespoons water

Steamed rice to serve

Rinse chicken breasts. Mix salt, pepper, five-spice powder, and ginger in a bowl. Pat each side of the chicken with the spice mix. Heat sesame oil in a pressure cooker over medium heat. Add chicken, in batches, and brown on both sides. Add green onions, garlic, broth, and pineapple juice. Stir. Secure lid. Over high heat, bring pressure up to high. Reduce heat to medium to maintain pressure and cook 8 minutes.

Release pressure according to manufacturer's directions. Remove lid. Stir ¼ cup of the hot juices into cornstarch mixture. Stir into cooking juices. Cook, stirring, over medium heat 2 minutes, or until thickened. Serve with steamed rice.

⊞ ⊟ ⊞

CHICKEN BREASTS STUFFED WITH FRESH VEGETABLES

Cotton kitchen twine can be found in most cooking utensil departments. Make sure the twine is not a synthetic blend.

MAKES 6 SERVINGS

6 boneless, skinless chicken breasts halves

⅛ teaspoon plus ¾ teaspoon salt

¼ teaspoon freshly ground white pepper

¼ teaspoon dried tarragon

3 tablespoons olive oil

1 medium onion, finely diced

2 garlic cloves, crushed

¼ cup finely chopped fresh parsley

1 large carrot, finely diced

½ cup chicken broth

½ teaspoon dried basil

½ cup canned diced tomatoes

1 tablespoon all-purpose flour mixed with

2 tablespoons water

Steamed noodles, rice, or mashed potatoes to serve

Using a meat mallet, flatten chicken between two sheets of waxed paper or plastic wrap to ⅛-inch thickness. Combine ⅛ teaspoon salt, ⅛ teaspoon pepper, and tarragon. Remove waxed paper and rub salt mixture all over breasts

Heat oil in a pressure cooker over medium heat. Add onion, garlic, parsley, and carrot and sauté 3 minutes. Remove mixture and divide into 6 portions. Place in the center of each chicken piece. Fold the chicken over the filling.

Secure with kitchen twine. Pour the chicken broth, ¾ teaspoon salt, remaining ⅛ teaspoon pepper, basil, and tomatoes into the pressure cooker. Lay stuffed chicken into the juices. Secure the lid. Over high heat, bring pressure up to high. Reduce heat to medium to maintain pressure and cook 9 minutes.

Release pressure according to manufacturer's directions. Remove lid. Using a slotted spatula, remove the chicken bundles to a platter and set aside. Stir ½ cup of the hot juices into flour mixture. Blend until smooth. Stir into the cooking juices and cook over medium heat, stirring, 2 minutes, or until thickened. Add chicken and baste with sauce. Serve with noodles.

⊞ ⊟ ⊞

CHICKEN BREASTS WITH CARIBBEAN SAUCE

Caribbean flavors have become extremely popular in recent years, due to island travel. The spices—mixtures or

variations of nutmeg, ginger, allspice, chiles, and garlic—are the identifying flavor. Packages of Caribbean spices are available in specialty food markets. It is always fun to experiment with different amounts and combinations.

MAKES 6 SERVINGS

6 chicken breast halves, skin removed

1 large onion, sliced

1 medium red bell pepper, sliced

3 garlic cloves, sliced

½ cup chicken broth

¼ cup bottled medium-hot salsa

2 teaspoons light brown sugar

1 teaspoon salt

1 tablespoon fresh lime juice

Dash of freshly grated nutmeg

¼ teaspoon ground ginger

2 tablespoons cornstarch

½ cup pineapple chunks, in juice

Steamed rice to serve

Combine all the ingredients in a pressure cooker, except cornstarch, pineapple, and rice. Stir well. Secure lid. Over high heat, bring pressure up to high. Reduce heat to medium to maintain pressure and cook 9 minutes.

Release pressure according to manufacturer's directions. Remove lid. Combine cornstarch with juice from the pineapple, developing a smooth paste. Stir into the cooking juices. Cook, stirring, 1 minute, or until it begins to thicken. Add pineapple pieces. Stir well. Place a chicken breast on a plate and top off with saucy juices. Serve with rice.

CHICKEN BREASTS WITH ONIONS AND HERBS

Bread crumbs are an excellent thickening agent. If, however they are not handy, flour may be substituted by simply blending flour with ½ cup liquid and stirring into the pressure cooker juices. This dish is delicious served over pasta, noodles, rice, beans, or potatoes.

MAKES 6 SERVINGS

3 tablespoons olive oil

6 chicken breast halves, skin removed

3 large onions, sliced

2 garlic cloves, crushed

¼ cup chopped fresh parsley

2 bay leaves

1 teaspoon dried rosemary

1 cup chicken broth

1 teaspoon light brown sugar

1 teaspoon salt

⅛ teaspoon freshly ground white pepper

1 tablespoon tomato paste

2 tablespoons seasoned bread crumbs

Heat oil in a pressure cooker over medium heat. Add chicken and brown on each side. Transfer chicken to a platter. Add onions and garlic and sauté 1 minute, scraping bottom of cooker with a wooden spoon to loosen any browned bits. Add chicken with remaining ingredients, except bread crumbs, and stir well. Secure lid. Over high heat, bring pressure up to high. Reduce heat to medium to maintain pressure and cook 8 minutes.

Release pressure according to manufacturer's directions. Remove lid. Discard bay leaf. Stir in bread crumbs. Cover and let stand several minutes. Stir and serve.

CHICKEN AND GREEN BEAN STEW

Full of traditional Greek flavors, this stew will become a healthy favorite for the whole family. Dried mint has long been a symbol of hospitality. There are over 30 species of mint, the most available being peppermint and spearmint. Spearmint is used for cooking, and peppermint is traditionally used for baking and candy.

MAKES 6 SERVINGS

2 teaspoons olive oil

2 large onions, diced

4 garlic cloves, crushed

6 chicken breast halves, skin removed

12 baby carrots

2 pounds green beans, ends removed

3 medium potatoes, peeled and cut into 2-inch
  pieces

1 (15-ounce) can tomato sauce

1 cup chicken broth

1 tablespoon dried dill weed

1 teaspoon dried mint

2 teaspoons salt

1/8 teaspoon freshly ground white pepper

2 tablespoons seasoned bread crumbs

Greek bread and feta cheese

Heat oil in a pressure cooker over medium heat. Add onions and garlic and sauté 2 minutes. Add chicken and cook 1 minute on each side. Add carrots, green beans, potatoes, tomato sauce, chicken broth, herbs, salt, and pepper. Secure lid. Over high heat, bring pressure up to high. Reduce heat to medium to maintain pressure and cook 9 minutes.

Release pressure according to manufacturer's directions. Remove lid. Stir well. Sprinkle bread crumbs into the stew and stir. Cover and let stand 5 minutes. Serve hot with bread and feta cheese.

DILLY CHICKEN IN MUSTARD SAUCE

There are a variety of mustards from many countries on the market. Chinese mustard is packed full of zesty flavor. German prepared mustard can range from hot to sweet and mild. French Dijon is a popular tangy mustard and readily available. Read the labels for ingredients that may alter the mustard flavor.

MAKES 6 SERVINGS

3 tablespoons all-purpose flour

1/4 teaspoon salt

1/8 teaspoon freshly ground black pepper

3 tablespoons olive or canola oil

6 chicken legs

2 leeks (white parts only), rinsed and thinly sliced

2 garlic cloves, crushed

1 cup chicken broth

1 teaspoon prepared grainy mustard

⅓ cup chopped fresh dill, or 2 tablespoons dried

Steamed rice and vegetables to serve

Combine flour, salt, and pepper in a plastic bag. Place chicken in bag and shake until coated. Heat oil in a pressure cooker over medium-high heat. Add chicken legs, 2 at a time, and brown on all sides. Set aside. Add leeks and garlic and sauté 3 minutes, scraping bottom of cooker with a wooden spoon to loosen any browned bits. Add the broth and mustard. Stir well. Return chicken to cooker. Secure lid. Over high heat, bring pressure up to high. Reduce heat to medium to maintain pressure and cook 10 minutes.

Release pressure according to manufacturer's directions. Remove lid. Stir. Transfer chicken to a platter and add the dill. Cook over high heat 5 minutes, stirring. Spoon juices over chicken and serve hot with rice and vegetables.

LEMON CHICKEN WITH GARBANZO BEANS

Packed full of Middle Eastern flavors, this lemony dish goes well with steamed rice and vegetables. The thinly sliced lemons add eye appeal to the presentation.

MAKES 6 SERVINGS

1½ cups dried garbanzo beans, soaked

3 tablespoons olive oil

2 leeks (white parts only), rinsed and sliced

5 garlic cloves, crushed

6 chicken breast halves, skin removed

1½ teaspoons salt

⅛ teaspoon freshly ground white pepper

1 teaspoon dried mint

2 cups chicken broth

⅓ cup fresh lemon juice

3 tablespoons all-purpose flour or potato starch
    mixed with 3 tablespoons water

6 thin lemon slices

Drain garbanzo beans and set aside. Heat oil in a pressure cooker over medium heat. Add leeks and garlic and sauté 3 minutes. Add chicken. Sprinkle salt, pepper, and mint over chicken. Add broth, lemon juice, and garbanzo beans. Stir well. Secure lid. Over high heat, bring pressure up to high. Reduce heat to medium to maintain pressure and cook 12 minutes.

Release pressure according to manufacturer's directions. Remove lid. Stir ¼ cup of the hot cooking juices into flour mixture. Pour the mixture into the chicken and cook, stirring, until juices begin to thicken. Garnish with lemon slices.

MINI MEATBALLS IN TOMATO SAUCE

This Mediterranean-influenced meatball may be served over noodles or rice, or consider a flavor-filled meatball sandwich, served in a hearty bun.

MAKES 6 SERVINGS

Meatballs

1 teaspoon canola oil

1 small onion, finely diced

1 large garlic clove, crushed

1 large carrot, finely diced

2 tablespoons finely chopped fresh parsley

¼ teaspoon salt

⅛ teaspoon freshly ground white pepper

1 medium egg, beaten

¼ cup seasoned bread crumbs

⅛ teaspoon ground nutmeg

½ teaspoon ground allspice

½ pound ground turkey breast

½ pound turkey sausage, casings removed

½ cup chicken broth

½ cup canned diced tomatoes

1 tablespoon all-purpose flour or potato starch
  mixed with 1 tablespoon water

Heat oil in a pressure cooker over high heat. Add onion, garlic, carrot, and parsley and sauté 3 minutes. Transfer to a large bowl and add salt, pepper, egg, bread crumbs, spices, turkey, and sausage. Form mixture into 1½-inch meatballs and place in a pressure cooker. Combine chicken broth and tomatoes. Pour over meatballs. Secure lid. Over high heat, bring pressure up to medium-high. Reduce heat to medium to maintain pressure, and cook 7 minutes.

Release pressure according to manufacturer's directions. Remove lid. Stir gently. Stir ½ cup hot cooking juices into flour mixture. Return to pressure cooker and cook, stirring, over medium heat 1 minute, or until thickened. Serve warm.

▫ ▫ ▫

NORTH AFRICAN CHICKEN WITH GARBANZO BEANS

This recipe is traditionally cooked in a tagine, a cooking vessel frequently used in Africa. By using the pressure cooker at least 60 percent of the cooking time is reduced, and the flavors are incredible.

MAKES 6 SERVINGS

1 cup dried garbanzo beans, soaked

3 tablespoons olive oil

6 chicken breast halves without skin, cut into
  quarters

2 large onions, thickly sliced

4 garlic cloves, crushed

½ cup chicken broth

½ cup canned diced tomatoes

½ teaspoon ground ginger

½ teaspoon ground cinnamon

⅛ teaspoon ground allspice

½ cup chopped fresh parsley

1½ teaspoons salt

⅛ teaspoon freshly ground black pepper

1 cup toasted almond halves

Steamed rice or vegetables to serve

¼ cup olive oil

1 large onion, diced

2 garlic cloves, crushed

1 carrot, finely diced

⅓ cup chopped fresh parsley

3 pounds chicken, cut into 8 pieces (2 inches thick)

2 cups chicken broth or stock

1 tablespoon sherry

2 tablespoons tomato paste

1 teaspoon salt

¼ teaspoon freshly ground black pepper

2 tablespoons sweet paprika

1 teaspoon dried thyme

1 teaspoon caraway seeds, crushed and in a cheesecloth bag

1 bay leaf

½ cup sour cream

2 tablespoons butter, at room temperature

1½ tablespoons potato starch or all-purpose flour

Cooked noodles or spaetzle to serve

Drain garbanzo beans and set aside. Heat oil in a pressure cooker over medium heat. Add chicken and brown on each side. Transfer to a platter. Add onions and garlic and sauté 3 minutes, scraping bottom of cooker with a wooden spoon to loosen any browned bits. Add broth, tomatoes, ginger, cinnamon, allspice, parsley, salt, and pepper. Add garbanzo beans and chicken. Stir well. Secure lid. Over high heat, bring pressure up to high. Reduce heat to medium to maintain pressure and cook 12 minutes.

Release pressure according to manufacturer's directions. Remove lid and stir well. Over medium heat, cook, uncovered, 5 minutes, to reduce liquid. Meanwhile, toast almonds in a 375 degrees F oven 6 minutes, or until browned. Stir into the stew. Serve over rice.

◻ ◻ ◻

CHICKEN PAPRIKA

This Hungarian stew is a personal favorite. The spices have been chosen to balance the flavors perfectly.

MAKES 6 SERVINGS

Heat oil in a pressure cooker. Add onion, garlic, carrot, and parsley and sauté 3 minutes. Add chicken, stir well, and cook 1 minute. Stir in broth, sherry, tomato paste, salt, pepper, paprika, thyme, caraway seeds, and bay leaf. Secure lid. Over high heat, bring pressure up to high. Reduce heat to maintain pressure and cook 10 minutes.

Release pressure according to manufacturer's directions. Remove lid. Remove bay leaf and bag of caraway seeds. Cook chicken mixture over medium-high heat 1 minute.

Combine sour cream, butter, and potato starch. Blend into chicken mixture and cook, stirring, until mixture begins to thicken. Serve immediately over noodles.

COOK'S NOTE: Remember to first crush the caraway seeds in a mortar and pestle, then tie in a bag. If you skip the bag, count on having lots of seeds in the stew.

□ □ □

STEAMED CHICKEN

Steamed chicken can be enjoyed as is or used in other dishes calling for cooked chicken.
MAKES 6 SERVINGS

8 chicken pieces
½ teaspoon salt
¼ teaspoon freshly ground black pepper
1 cup water

Season chicken pieces with salt and pepper. Pour water into pressure cooker. Insert steam rack. Place chicken pieces on top of rack. Secure lid. Over high heat, bring pressure up to high. Reduce heat to maintain pressure and cook 10 minutes.

Release pressure according to manufacturer's directions. Remove lid. Using tongs, place steamed chicken on a platter.

CHICKEN PICCATA

Italian in origin, this is full of lemony flavor. Always use freshly squeezed lemon juice for the best results.
MAKES 6 SERVINGS

6 chicken breast halves
½ cup all-purpose flour
¼ cup olive oil
4 shallots, minced
3 garlic cloves, crushed
¾ cup chicken broth
⅓ cup fresh lemon juice
1 tablespoon sherry
2 teaspoons salt
¼ teaspoon freshly ground white pepper
1 teaspoon dried basil
1 cup pimento-stuffed green olives, minced
¼ cup sour cream
1 tablespoon potato starch or all-purpose flour
¼ cup grated fontinella cheese
1 lemon, thinly sliced, to garnish

Lightly dust chicken pieces with flour. Heat oil in a pressure cooker over medium-high heat. Add chicken breasts, 2 at a time, and sauté until brown on all sides, using long-handled tongs to turn. Set aside. Add shallots and garlic and sauté 2 minutes, scraping bottom of cooker with a wooden spoon to loosen any browned bits. Stir in broth, lemon juice, sherry, salt, pepper, basil, and olives. Mix well. Add chicken, placing pieces skin side down. Secure lid. Over medium-high heat, bring pressure up to high. Reduce heat to maintain pressure and cook 10 minutes.

Release pressure according to manufacturer's directions. Remove lid. Stir chicken mixture, then transfer chicken to a serving platter, and cover to retain heat. Whisk sour cream and potato starch together. Stir into cooking liquid and cook over medium heat 1 minute, stirring constantly.

Spoon sauce over chicken. Sprinkle with cheese and garnish with lemon slices.

COOK'S NOTE: To easily dust the chicken pieces with flour, place flour and chicken in a bag. Shake up and down several times, coating the chicken. Remove chicken pieces and shake off excess flour.

CHICKEN WITH ARBORIO RICE AND PEPPERS

The bacon in this robust Italian stew adds a traditional flavor. The red and green bell pepper strips give the dish flavor and eye appeal.

MAKES 6 SERVINGS

¼ cup olive oil

3 pounds chicken, cut into serving pieces (2 inches thick)

3 slices bacon, cut into 1-inch pieces

2 large onions, coarsely chopped

4 garlic cloves, crushed

½ cup chopped fresh parsley

1½ cups arborio rice

1 teaspoon dried rosemary, crushed between palms

1½ teaspoons dried basil, crushed between palms

2 bay leaves

4 cups chicken broth

1 cup tomato puree

1 tablespoon light brown sugar

1½ teaspoons salt

½ teaspoon freshly ground black pepper

1 red bell pepper, cut lengthwise into ⅛-inch strips

1 green bell pepper, cut lengthwise into ⅛-inch strips

½ cup (2 ounces) grated fontinella or Parmesan cheese

Heat oil in a pressure cooker over medium-high heat. Add chicken, in batches, and sauté in hot oil until brown on all sides, using long-handled tongs to turn. Transfer chicken to paper towels and reserve. Add bacon, onions, garlic, and parsley and sauté 3 minutes, scraping bottom of cooker to loosen any browned bits. Add rice, rosemary, basil, and bay leaves. Stir well and cook 1 minute. Add broth, tomato puree, brown sugar, salt, and black pepper. Stir in chicken pieces. Secure lid. Over high heat, bring pressure up to high. Reduce heat to maintain pressure and insert a heat diffuser between cooker and heat. Cook 9 minutes.

Release pressure according to manufacturer's directions. Remove lid. Stir chicken and rice mixture. Add bell peppers. Secure lid. Over high heat, bring pressure up to medium. Insert a heat diffuser between pan and heat, and cook 2 minutes.

Release pressure according to manufacturer's directions. Remove lid. Discard bay leaves. Stir half of cheese into chicken and rice mixture. Transfer to a serving platter and sprinkle with remaining cheese.

▢▢▢

CHICKEN POT PIE WITH PUFF PASTRY

This pot pie is done in two steps. First, the luscious filling is cooked in a pressure cooker, then it is baked to perfection.

MAKES 6 SERVINGS

¼ cup olive oil

1 large onion, sliced

2 garlic cloves, crushed

3 carrots, cut into ½-inch slices

1 cup (½-inch slices) celery

6 chicken breast halves, skin removed, boned, and
    cut into 1½- to 2-inch pieces

1½ cups chicken broth or stock

1 tablespoon fresh lemon juice

2 teaspoons sherry

½ pound mushrooms (stems and caps) thinly sliced

3 medium potatoes, peeled and diced

1½ teaspoons salt

¼ teaspoon freshly ground white pepper

1 teaspoon dried tarragon

½ teaspoon dried thyme

½ teaspoon ground fennel

1 bay leaf

1½ cups frozen green peas

½ cup half-and-half or milk

2 tablespoons butter, at room temperature

2 tablespoons potato starch or all-purpose flour

1 (17¼-ounce) package frozen puff pastry,
    thawed

Heat oil in a pressure cooker over medium-high heat. Add onion, garlic, carrots, and celery and sauté 2 minutes. Add chicken, stir, and cook 1 minute. Stir in broth, lemon juice, sherry, mushrooms, potatoes, salt, pepper, and herbs. Secure lid. Over high heat, bring pressure up to high. Reduce heat to maintain pressure and cook 6 minutes.

Release pressure according to manufacturer's directions. Remove lid. Stir in peas. Bring to a boil and cook 1 minute. Reduce heat to medium. Discard bay leaf.

Combine half-and-half, butter, and potato starch in a small bowl, blending until smooth. Stir into chicken mixture until thoroughly mixed. Pour into a 13 × 9-inch baking dish or 6 individual ovenproof dishes.

Preheat oven to 400 degrees F. On a lightly floured surface, roll puff pastry, overlapping pastry sheets, into a rectangle slightly larger than baking dish, or cut out rounds slightly larger than individual dishes. Brush away excess flour. Place pastry over chicken mixture. Using a paring knife, trim away excess dough around dish edges. Place dish on a baking sheet. Bake 12 minutes, or until golden brown.

COOK'S NOTE: Puff pastry is available in the frozen food section at most major grocery stores. Thaw in the refrigerator before using.

CHICKEN WITH TWO PEPPERS AND NOODLES

This tasty pasta dish is wonderful with any available noodle. The flavor is in the robust sauce!

MAKES 6 SERVINGS

¼ cup olive oil

1 large white onion, sliced

3 garlic cloves, crushed

4 chicken breast halves, each cut into halves
   (2 inches thick)

1 red bell pepper, sliced lengthwise into strips

1 green bell pepper, sliced lengthwise into strips

3 cups chicken broth or stock

1 (8-ounce) can tomato sauce

1 tablespoon fresh lemon juice

2 tablespoons light brown sugar

2 teaspoons salt

¼ teaspoon freshly ground black pepper

2 teaspoons dried basil

1½ teaspoons dried oregano

½ teaspoon ground fennel

1 bay leaf

1 (16-ounce) bag dried noodles

½ cup (2 ounces) grated fontinella cheese

½ cup freshly grated Parmesan cheese

Heat oil in a pressure cooker over medium-high heat. Add onion and sauté 3 minutes. Add garlic, chicken, and bell peppers. Sauté 3 minutes, stirring occasionally. Stir in broth, tomato sauce, lemon juice, brown sugar, salt, black pepper, and herbs. Add noodles and stir again. Secure lid. Over high heat, bring pressure up to high. Reduce heat to maintain pressure and insert a heat diffuser between cooker and heat. Cook 10 minutes.

Release pressure according to manufacturer's directions. Remove lid. Discard bay leaf. Stir chicken and noodle mixture and transfer to a serving bowl. Combine cheeses and sprinkle over chicken and noodles.

PARISIAN CHICKEN STEW

The delicate asparagus and snow peas are added to this tasty stew just before the last 2 minutes of cooking. The pressure-cooking process is interrupted to add the veggies. If they were added at the beginning, the vegetables would be overcooked and unrecognizable.

MAKES 6 SERVINGS

⅓ cup olive oil

1 large carrot, thinly sliced

4 leeks (white parts only), sliced

3 garlic cloves, crushed

1 (3-pound) chicken, cut into 8 pieces (1½ to
    2 inches thick)

½ cup chicken broth

¼ cup white wine

2 tablespoons fresh lemon juice

3 carrots, cut into 2-inch pieces

3 medium potatoes, peeled and quartered

2 teaspoons salt

½ teaspoon freshly ground white pepper

⅓ cup chopped fresh parsley

1½ tablespoons dried tarragon

1 teaspoon fresh rosemary or ½ teaspoon dried
    rosemary

2 medium tomatoes, quartered and seeds removed

3 tablespoons chopped fresh chives or 1½
    tablespoons dried

1 pound asparagus, trimmed and cut into 2-inch
    pieces

1 pound snow peas, ends removed

⅓ cup sour cream

3 tablespoons all-purpose flour

Heat oil in a pressure cooker over medium-high heat. Add sliced carrot, leeks, and garlic and sauté 2 minutes. Add chicken and cook 2 minutes, turning chicken once or twice. Stir in broth, wine, lemon juice, carrot pieces, potatoes, salt, pepper, parsley, tarragon, and rosemary. Secure lid. Over high heat, bring pressure up to medium-high. Reduce heat to maintain pressure and cook 8 minutes.

Release pressure according to manufacturer's directions. Remove lid. Stir chicken mixture. Add tomatoes, chives, asparagus, and peas. Stir gently. Secure lid. Over high heat, bring pressure up to medium-high. Reduce heat to maintain pressure and cook 2 minutes.

Release pressure according to manufacturer's directions. Remove lid. Stir chicken and vegetable mixture gently. Combine sour cream and flour in a small bowl; add by spoonfuls to stew and cook, stirring, until slightly thickened and creamy. Taste and correct seasoning if needed.

COOK'S NOTE: Individual servings of stew may be frozen up to 2 months. Thaw in refrigerator.

GREEK CHICKEN AND RICE PILAF

This is a Greek peasant dish. The oregano and dried fennel are traditional flavors.

MAKES 6 SERVINGS

⅓ cup olive oil

1 large onion, diced

2 garlic cloves, crushed

1 (2½- to 3-pound) chicken, cut into 8 pieces

4 cups chicken broth or stock

2 cups long-grain white rice

1 tablespoon light brown sugar

¼ cup tomato paste

2 teaspoons salt

½ teaspoon freshly ground white pepper

1 teaspoon dried oregano

½ teaspoon ground fennel

2 bay leaves

Heat oil in a pressure cooker over medium-high heat. Add onion and garlic and sauté 2 minutes. Add chicken pieces and cook 2 minutes, stirring occasionally. Stir in broth, rice, brown sugar, tomato paste, salt, pepper, oregano, fennel, and bay leaves. Secure lid. Over high heat, bring pressure up to high. Reduce heat to maintain pressure and insert a heat diffuser between cooker and heat. Cook 9 minutes.

Release pressure according to manufacturer's directions. Remove lid. Shake chicken and rice mixture well and stir to distribute cooking liquid. Discard bay leaves.

❑❑❑

TORTELLINI AND CHICKEN IN PARMESAN CREAM SAUCE

Tortellini is available both dried and fresh in most supermarkets. These tender bundles are deliciously wonderful.

MAKES 6 SERVINGS

3 slices bacon, cut into ½-inch pieces

¼ cup butter

4 shallots, minced

3 tablespoons minced fresh parsley

4 chicken breast halves, skin removed, boned

1 small carrot, thinly sliced

1 (8-ounce) package dried, cheese-filled tortellini

1 teaspoon dried tarragon

2 cups chicken broth

1 pound asparagus, trimmed and cut into 2-inch pieces

½ cup half-and-half or milk

3 tablespoons butter, at room temperature

⅓ cup freshly grated Parmesan cheese plus extra to serve

2 teaspoons potato starch or flour

Parsley sprigs to garnish

Cook bacon in a pressure cooker over medium heat until crisp. Add butter, shallots, and pars–

ley. Stir well and sauté 2 minutes. Stir in chicken, carrot, tortellini, and tarragon. Add broth and mix well. Secure lid. Over high heat, bring pressure up to high. Reduce heat to maintain pressure and insert a heat diffuser between cooker and heat. Cook 6 minutes.

Release pressure according to manufacturer's directions. Remove lid. Stir in asparagus. Remove diffuser. Secure lid. Over high heat, bring pressure up to medium-high. Insert heat diffuser between pan and heat. Reduce heat to maintain pressure and cook 2 minutes.

Release pressure according to manufacturer's directions. Remove lid. Combine half-and-half, butter, 1/3 cup cheese, and potato starch in a small bowl. Blend thoroughly. Gradually add to chicken and tortellini mixture, gently stirring over medium heat until sauce begins to thicken and becomes creamy. Transfer chicken and tortellini with sauce to a serving platter. Sprinkle with additional cheese and garnish with parsley sprigs.

◻ ◻ ◻

PAELLA

This saffron-flavored Spanish stew is full of fresh ingredients including shellfish, chicken, herbs, and vegetables.
MAKES 6 SERVINGS

1/4 pound bacon, cut into 1-inch pieces

2 large onions, sliced

1/4 cup olive oil

4 garlic cloves, crushed

1 3/4 cups long-grain white rice

6 chicken pieces (legs, thighs, breasts, wings)

5 cups chicken broth or stock

1/4 cup plus 2 tablespoons tomato paste

1/2 cup bottled clam juice

3 tablespoons fresh lemon juice

2 tablespoons sherry

1 tablespoon light brown sugar

1/4 cup chopped fresh parsley

2 1/2 teaspoons salt

1 pinch saffron threads

1/2 teaspoon sweet paprika

3/4 teaspoon crushed red pepper flakes

2 teaspoons dried oregano

2 bay leaves

1/2 cup sliced green bell pepper

1/2 pound sea scallops

1/2 pound shrimp in shells

1 cup frozen green peas

1 cup pitted ripe olives

6 lemon slices to garnish

Cook bacon in a pressure cooker until crisp. Add onions and oil and sauté over medium-high heat 2 minutes. Add garlic, rice, and chicken pieces. Cook, stirring frequently, 1 minute. Add broth, tomato paste, clam juice, lemon juice, sherry, brown sugar, parsley, salt, saffron, paprika, pepper flakes, oregano, and bay leaves. Stir well. Secure lid. Over high heat, bring pressure up to high. Reduce heat to maintain pressure and insert a heat diffuser between cooker and heat. Cook 8 minutes.

Release pressure according to manufacturer's directions. Remove lid. Add bell pepper, scallops, and shrimp to chicken mixture. Stir well. Secure lid. Cook over medium-low heat 3 minutes, shaking pan occasionally.

Release pressure according to manufacturer's directions. Stir mixture, add peas and olives, and stir again. Discard bay leaves. Taste and correct seasoning if needed. Spoon into a serving dish. Garnish with lemon slices.

COOK'S NOTE: Saffron is from the orange-yellow stigmas of the saffron crocus, and it is known as the world's most expensive spice. It takes about 12,000 to 14,000 stigmas to prepare an ounce of dried saffron.

⊡ ⊡ ⊡

ITALIAN MEATBALLS IN PASTA SAUCE

This robust tomato sauce is delicious with spaghetti, noodles, or rice.

MAKES 6 SERVINGS

Meatballs

2 tablespoons olive oil

1 medium onion, finely diced

4 garlic cloves, crushed

¼ cup finely chopped fresh parsley

¼ cup seasoned bread crumbs

1 egg, beaten

1 teaspoon salt

⅛ teaspoon freshly ground white pepper

1 pound ground turkey breast

1 (15-ounce) can tomato sauce

1 cup chicken broth

1 teaspoon dried basil, ground

1 teaspoon ground fennel

½ teaspoon dried oregano

Dash crushed red pepper flakes

½ large green bell pepper, finely diced

¼ cup seasoned bread crumbs

¼ cup freshly grated Parmesan cheese

Pasta, rice, noodles, or green beans to serve

Shape the meatballs: Heat oil in a pressure cooker over medium heat. Add onion, garlic, and parsley and sauté 2 minutes. Transfer to a large bowl. Stir in bread crumbs, egg, salt, and white pepper. Add turkey and thoroughly blend. Form mixture into 2-inch meatballs and place in a pressure cooker.

Add tomato sauce, broth, herbs, pepper flakes, and bell pepper. Secure lid. Over high heat, bring pressure up to high. Reduce heat to medium to maintain pressure and cook 8 minutes.

Release pressure under cold running water. Remove lid. Stir in bread crumbs and cheese. Cook, uncovered, over low heat 3 minutes. Serve with pasta.

PASTA BOW TIES WITH TURKEY SAUSAGE

The interesting bow tie–shaped pasta is found in all grocery stores. Any pasta or noodle may be substituted in this dish.

3 tablespoons olive oil

1 large onion, finely diced

3 garlic cloves, crushed

¼ cup finely chopped fresh parsley

3 cups pasta bow ties

1 pound turkey sausage, cut into 2-inch pieces

3 cups chicken broth

1 cup tomato sauce

½ teaspoon ground fennel

1 teaspoon dried basil

1½ teaspoons salt

Pinch crushed red pepper flakes

¼ cup nonfat half-and-half

⅓ cup freshly grated Parmesan cheese

Heat oil in a pressure cooker over medium heat. Add onion, garlic, and parsley and sauté 2 minutes. Add remaining ingredients, except half-and-half and cheese. Secure lid. Over high heat, bring pressure up to high. Reduce heat to medium to maintain pressure and insert a heat diffuser between cooker and heat. Cook 9 minutes.

Release pressure according to manufacturer's directions. Remove lid. Stir well. Stir in half-and-half and heat until hot. Transfer to a large pasta serving platter and sprinkle with cheese.

SMOKED TURKEY BREAST WITH NOODLES IN PEPPER SAUCE

Smoked turkey breast is found at all deli counters or with the packaged lunch meats.

MAKES 6 SERVINGS

2 tablespoons olive oil

1 large onion, coarsely diced

3 garlic cloves, crushed

¼ cup minced fresh parsley

3 medium carrots, cut into 1-inch-thick slices

1 small red bell pepper, thinly sliced

1 small green bell pepper, thinly sliced

1 teaspoon dried basil

1 teaspoon ground fennel

1 teaspoon salt

⅛ teaspoon freshly ground black pepper

3 cups chicken broth

3 cups dried egg noodles

1 pound smoked turkey breast, thinly sliced

½ cup half-and-half

⅓ cup grated fontinella cheese

Heat oil in a pressure cooker over medium heat. Add onion, garlic, parsley, and carrots and sauté 2 minutes. Add remaining ingredients, except turkey breast, half-and-half, and cheese. Stir well. Secure lid. Over high heat, bring pressure up to high. Reduce heat to medium to maintain pressure and insert a heat diffuser between pan and heat. Cook 8 minutes.

Release pressure according to manufacturer's directions. Remove lid. Stir in turkey breast and half-and-half and heat until hot. Transfer to a pasta serving platter and sprinkle cheese over top.

▣ ▣ ▣

SWEDISH MEATBALLS WITH CARROTS AND DILL SAUCE

This lovely meatball dish may be served hot for a buffet dinner party, or may be served over noodles for family dinner.

MAKES 6 SERVINGS

Meatballs

2 tablespoons olive oil or canola oil

1 small onion, finely chopped

2 pounds ground turkey breast

½ large apple, peeled, cored, and shredded

1 large egg, beaten

1 teaspoon salt

¼ teaspoon freshly ground black pepper

⅛ teaspoon ground nutmeg

1 teaspoon dried tarragon

1 cup chicken broth

1 pound baby carrots

½ cup sour cream

½ teaspoon prepared mustard

1 teaspoon prepared creamy horseradish

2 teaspoons dried dill weed

2 teaspoons salt

⅛ teaspoon freshly ground black pepper

2 tablespoons all-purpose flour or potato starch

Noodles or polenta to serve

Shape the meatballs: Heat oil in a pressure cooker and over medium heat. Add onion and sauté 2 minutes. Transfer into a bowl. Add turkey, apple, egg, salt, pepper, nutmeg, and tarragon to onion. Thoroughly mix. Form mixture into 1-inch meatballs and layer into the pressure cooker.

Pour chicken broth over meatballs and add carrots. Secure lid. Over high heat, bring pressure up to high. Reduce heat to medium to maintain pressure and cook 7 minutes.

Release pressure under cold running water. Remove lid. Combine sour cream, mustard, horseradish, dill, salt, and pepper with flour. Whisk in ½ cup of hot cooking juices and pour mixture into the meatball mixture, gently stirring. Cook over medium heat 3 minutes. Serve with noodles.

TURKEY SLOPPY JOES

This family favorite is perfect for cool autumn evenings, tailgate parties, or children's birthday celebrations. Serve with your favorite condiments.

MAKES 6 SERVINGS

2 tablespoons olive or canola oil

1 medium onion, finely diced

2 garlic cloves, crushed

1 pound ground turkey breast

¼ cup minced fresh parsley

½ red bell pepper, finely diced

1 cup canned tomato sauce

1 teaspoon ground chili powder

⅛ teaspoon ground cumin

1 teaspoon salt

⅛ teaspoon freshly ground black pepper

1 teaspoon sugar

½ teaspoon prepared mustard

6 onion rolls

½ cup (2 ounces) grated Cheddar cheese

Heat oil in a pressure cooker over medium heat. Add onion and garlic and sauté 2 minutes. Add turkey and sauté until browned, stirring to break up meat. Add remaining ingredients, except rolls and cheese. Stir well. Secure lid. Over high heat, bring pressure up to high. Reduce heat to medium to maintain pressure and cook 8 minutes.

Release pressure according to manufacturer's directions. Remove lid. Stir well. Split rolls and heat; place a spoonful of turkey mixture into each roll. Top with Cheddar cheese.

TURKEY-STUFFED BELL PEPPERS

Try a colorful assortment of bell peppers. A variety will add eye appeal to this healthy one-dish meal. The flavor of fresh dill is much more pronounced than that of dried dill and may be used when in season. Simply increase the amount to ¼ cup minced fresh dill.

MAKES 6 SERVINGS

3 green bell peppers

3 red bell peppers

3 tablespoons olive or canola oil

1 medium onion, diced

2 medium carrots, diced

¼ cup finely chopped fresh parsley

2 garlic cloves, crushed

1 pound ground turkey breast

½ teaspoon ground fennel

1 tablespoon dried dill weed

1 cup long-grain white rice

2½ cups chicken broth

1½ teaspoons salt

⅛ teaspoon freshly ground white pepper

½ cup canned diced tomatoes

3 tablespoons seasoned bread crumbs

¼ freshly grated Parmesan cheese

Crusty bread to serve

Rinse the bell peppers well. Using a sharp knife cut off ½ inch all around the top. Scoop out the seeds and veins from the inside. Rinse the inside of the peppers and set aside. Remove the large green stems from the tops and chop the pepper that was around the stems.

Heat oil in a pressure cooker over medium-high heat. Add onion, carrots, parsley, and garlic and sauté 3 minutes. Add the turkey and stir well. Add chopped bell peppers and herbs, rice, 2 cups of the chicken broth, salt, and pepper. Stir well. Secure lid. Over high heat, bring pressure up to medium. Reduce heat to medium to maintain pressure and insert a heat diffuser between cooker and heat. Cook 6 minutes.

Release pressure under cold running water. Remove lid. Stir well. Transfer rice mixture to a bowl. Spoon rice mixture into the bell peppers, filling to the top. Pour diced tomatoes and remaining ½ cup broth into pressure cooker. Place filled peppers into the sauce. Secure lid. Over high heat, bring pressure up to medium-high. Reduce heat to medium and cook 5 minutes.

Release pressure according to the manufacturer's directions and remove lid. Gently remove peppers to a platter. Sprinkle bread crumbs into sauce, stir, and cook 3 minutes over medium heat. Spoon sauce over the peppers. Sprinkle with Parmesan cheese. Serve hot with bread.

TURKEY TETRAZZINI

Tetrazzini is a rich dish usually made with strips of chicken and layered with spaghetti and creamy cheese sauce. Turkey has been substituted in this recipe and works very well.

MAKES 6 SERVINGS

2 tablespoons seasoned bread crumbs

1 pound turkey breast, cut into 2-inch strips

3 tablespoons olive oil or canola oil

2 large leeks (white parts only), rinsed and thinly sliced

4 garlic cloves, crushed

1 large yellow bell pepper, thinly sliced

1 teaspoon dried basil

1 teaspoon ground fennel

1½ teaspoons salt

Dash crushed red pepper flakes

1 cup canned tomato sauce

2 cups chicken broth

¾ pound dried spaghetti, broken into 3-inch pieces

½ cup half-and-half

½ cup grated fontinella cheese

1 cup (4 ounces) grated part-skim milk mozzarella

1 cup (3 ounces) freshly grated Parmesan cheese

Preheat oven to 375 degrees F. Butter a 12 × 9-inch baking dish; set aside.

Place bread crumbs and turkey in a large plastic bag. Toss until coated. Heat oil in a pressure cooker over medium-high heat. Add leeks and garlic and sauté 2 minutes. Add turkey and cook, stirring, 1 minute. Stir in remaining ingredients, except half-and-half and cheeses. Secure lid. Over high heat, bring pressure up to high. Reduce heat to medium to maintain pressure and insert a heat diffuser between cooker and heat. Cook 8 minutes.

Release pressure according to manufacturer's directions. Remove lid. Pour in half-and-half and stir well. Combine cheeses. Pour one-third of the turkey mixture into prepared baking dish and sprinkle with one-third of the cheeses. Repeat, ending with cheese. Bake 20 minutes, or until top is golden brown. Serve hot.

FISH AND SHELLFISH

Fish has very little fat or muscle and therefore will cook very quickly. Cook on low pressure 2 minutes per 1 inch of thickness. Always reduce the steam quickly under cold running water at the end of the cooking cycle. Select pieces of fish that are uniform in thickness for best results. For steaming, wrap the fish in cheesecloth or parchment paper. If a golden appearance is desired, sauté the fish in very hot oil before sealing the pressure cooker and cooking the fish.

Fish is an excellent alternative to red meat. If you're "fishing" for a change of taste, check the chart (page 324). Select seafood with a flavor and texture close to your usual "catch." Try the substitutes in your favorite recipes. Plan on 8 ounces of boned fish per serving.

Store fish in ice water or on ice until ready to use. Avoid fish that has a strong odor or hazy eyes. The flesh should be firm.

FISH BUYER'S GUIDE

Mild Flavor	Moderate Flavor	Full Flavor
Cod	Buffalo	Bluefish
Crab	Butterfish	Catfish
Grouper	Flounder	Haddock
Lake perch	Halibut	Mackerel
Lobster	Mahimahi	Marlin
Monkfish	Mullet	Salmon
Ocean catfish	Ocean perch	Smoked fish
Pollock	Orange roughy	Swordfish
Rockfish	Pompano	Tuna
Scrod	Red snapper	
Sheepshead	Sea bass	
Skate	Shad	
Trout	Shark	
Walleye pike	Smelt	
Whitefish	Sole	
	Sturgeon	
	Whiting	

FETTUCCINE WITH SCALLOPS AND VEGETABLES

Clam juice is found in bottles around the seafood counter in the grocery store. It adds a delicate seafood flavor to this pasta dish.

MAKES 6 SERVINGS

3 tablespoons olive oil

2 medium leeks (white parts only), rinsed and sliced

2 garlic cloves, crushed

1 large yellow or orange bell pepper, sliced lengthwise into medium strips

1 cup bottled clam juice

3 cups chicken broth

1 pound fettuccine

1 teaspoon salt

⅛ teaspoon freshly ground white pepper

1 tablespoon fresh lemon juice

1 teaspoon dried thyme

12 fresh asparagus spears, trimmed and cut into 2-inch pieces

1 pound scallops

¼ cup grated fontinella cheese

Heat oil in a pressure cooker over medium-high heat. Add leeks and garlic and sauté 2 minutes. Stir in bell pepper. Add remaining ingredients, except asparagus, scallops, and cheese. Secure lid. Over high heat, bring pressure up to high. Reduce heat to medium to maintain pressure and insert a heat diffuser between cooker and heat. Cook 8 minutes.

Release pressure according to manufacturer's directions. Remove lid. Stir in asparagus and scallops. Secure lid. Cook over high heat 1 minute.

Release pressure under cold running water. Remove lid. Stir well. Transfer to a serving platter and sprinkle cheese over top.

FISH CHOWDER

Trout or salmon may be substituted for the whitefish in this delicious chowder. Make sure the fishmonger includes the head along with the fish. It definitely adds flavor to the base.

MAKES 6 SERVINGS

1 (2-pound) whitefish

1 (8-ounce) bottle clam juice

2 cups water

2 leeks (white parts), rinsed and thinly sliced

2 garlic cloves, crushed

½ cup coarsely chopped fresh parsley

1 teaspoon dried thyme

2 large carrots, coarsely diced

3 medium potatoes, peeled and cut into 1-inch cubes

2 tablespoons fresh lemon juice

1½ teaspoons salt

⅛ teaspoon freshly ground white pepper

2 cups frozen whole-kernel corn

1 cup frozen green peas

½ cup half-and-half

3 tablespoons cornstarch

Rinse whitefish inside and out. Cut into thirds. Combine whitefish, clam juice, water, leeks, garlic, parsley, and thyme in a pressure cooker. Secure lid. Over high heat, bring pressure up to medium. Reduce heat to medium to maintain pressure and cook 5 minutes.

Release pressure according to manufacturer's directions. Remove lid. Using a slotted spoon, transfer fish to a platter. Add carrots, potatoes, lemon juice, salt, and pepper to the pressure cooker. Secure lid. Over high heat, bring pressure up to high. Reduce heat to medium and cook 6 minutes.

In the meantime, remove flesh from fish bones in large pieces and set aside.

Release pressure under cold running water. Remove lid. Stir in corn and peas. Make a paste by combining the half-and-half with the cornstarch. Stir into the soup and cook over high heat 3 minutes. Add the fish pieces and stir well. Serve hot.

ITALIAN FISH STEW

Plum tomatoes are also referred to as Italian or Roma tomatoes. They are sweet, flavorful, and egg-shaped. The tomatoes can be found in most produce markets and are most frequently red; however, yellow plum tomatoes are also available. For eye appeal, the red tomato is best for this recipe.

MAKES 6 SERVINGS

1½ pounds red snapper or whitefish

3 tablespoons olive oil

1 large sweet onion, sliced

4 garlic cloves, sliced

½ cup coarsely chopped fresh parsley

1 medium red bell pepper, sliced lengthwise into thin strips

8 plum tomatoes, quartered

1 (8-ounce) bottle clam juice

2 teaspoons fresh lemon juice

1 bay leaf

1 teaspoon dried basil

½ teaspoon dried thyme

Dash crushed red pepper flakes

1½ teaspoons salt

½ pound shrimp, peeled

¼ cup seasoned bread crumbs

6 slices Italian bread, toasted

Rinse fish inside and out. Cut into quarters. Set aside.

Heat oil in a pressure cooker over medium heat. Add onion and garlic and sauté 3 minutes. Add fish and remaining ingredients, except shrimp, bread crumbs, and bread. Secure lid. Over high heat, bring pressure up to medium. Reduce heat to maintain pressure and cook 5 minutes.

Release pressure under cold running water. Remove lid. Stir shrimp and bread crumbs into the stew. Cook over medium-high heat until shrimp turns pink. Place a slice of bread in each soup bowl and ladle fish and juices over top. Serve hot.

◾ ◾ ◾

SEAFOOD GUMBO WITH SAUSAGE

It's Creole and full of flavor! The gumbo has many varieties of shellfish, several vegetables, chicken, and sausage. The word gumbo derives from an African word for okra.

MAKES 6 SERVINGS

3 slices bacon, cut into ¼-inch pieces

1 large onion, diced

1 large red bell pepper, coarsely chopped

4 garlic cloves, crushed

3 stalks celery, coarsely chopped

2 carrots, cut into 1-inch pieces

1 cup chicken broth

1 (8-ounce) bottle clam juice

1 pound shrimp, peeled

1 pound bay scallops

½ pound lump crabmeat, drained

1 (12-ounce) container fresh oysters, drained

1½ teaspoon sweet paprika

1 teaspoon dried thyme

Dash crushed red pepper flakes

1½ teaspoons salt

½ pound smoked turkey sausage, cut into 2-inch pieces

1½ cups frozen sliced okra

1 cup canned diced tomatoes

½ cup finely chopped fresh parsley

3 tablespoons butter, melted

3 tablespoons all-purpose flour or potato starch

Steamed rice to serve

Cook bacon in a pressure cooker over medium heat until crisp. Add onion, bell pepper, garlic, celery, and carrots. Sauté 3 minutes. Add broth, clam juice, seafood, paprika, thyme, pepper flakes, and salt. Secure lid. Over high heat, bring pressure up to medium. Reduce heat to medium to maintain pressure and cook 4 minutes.

Release pressure under cold running water. Remove lid. Stir in okra, tomatoes, and parsley. Cover and cook 3 minutes. Whisk together melted butter and flour. Stir in ⅓ cup of hot broth and blend well. Stir into gumbo and cook over medium heat 2 minutes. Serve hot over rice.

SEASONED STEAMED MUSSELS

Look for mussels with tightly closed shells. Avoid purchasing those with broken or cracked shells. If the mussel feels light or loose, this signals the mussel is dead. Small mussels are more delicate and tender than the larger ones.

MAKES 6 SERVINGS

2 pounds mussels or clams or combination

¾ cup water

⅓ cup fresh lemon juice

1 large onion, finely diced

6 garlic cloves, thinly sliced

1 teaspoon dried thyme

½ cup finely chopped fresh parsley

1 teaspoon salt

3 lemons, cut into wedges

Using a stiff brush, scrub shellfish under warm water. Combine shellfish with all remaining ingredients, except lemon wedges, in a pressure cooker. Secure lid. Over high heat, bring pressure up to medium. Reduce heat to medium to maintain pressure and cook 2 minutes.

Release pressure under cold running water. Remove lid. Using a slotted spoon, lift shellfish out of the pot onto a large serving platter. Surround with lemon wedges.

BOUILLABAISSE

Bouillabaisse is traditionally served in deep soup bowls and topped with a dollop of a garlic-based sauce called rouille. The sauce gives the soup a pungent flavor and helps thicken the liquid when blended in.

MAKES 6 SERVINGS

Rouille

4 garlic cloves, peeled

3 slices bread, crumbled

⅓ cup olive oil

¼ cup Rich Fish Stock (page 143)

3 drops hot pepper sauce

¼ teaspoon salt

1 teaspoon dried basil

¼ cup olive oil

3 or 4 leeks (white parts only), rinsed and sliced

1 garlic clove, crushed

⅓ cup chopped fresh parsley

1 carrot, thinly sliced

1 cup tomato sauce

1 cup Rich Fish Stock (page 143)

1 teaspoon grated lemon zest

1 tablespoon sherry

2 teaspoons salt

⅛ teaspoon crushed red pepper flakes

¾ teaspoon dried thyme

½ teaspoon ground fennel

1 large pinch saffron

2 bay leaves

2 tomatoes, quartered and seeds removed

½ green bell pepper, sliced

2 celery stalks, cut into 1-inch pieces

1 lobster tail, cut into thirds

1 pound shrimp, peeled and deveined

1 pound flounder, cut into 2-inch pieces

1 pound scallops, rinsed well

Crusty bread to serve

Prepare Rouille: Combine garlic, bread, oil, stock, hot pepper sauce, salt, and basil in a food processor or blender. Process until smooth. Set aside.

Heat oil in a pressure cooker over medium heat. Add leeks, garlic, parsley, and carrot and sauté 3 minutes. Stir in tomato sauce, stock, lemon zest, sherry, salt, pepper flakes, thyme, fennel, saffron, and bay leaves. Stir well. Add tomatoes, bell pepper, celery, and lobster. Mix thoroughly. Secure lid. Over high heat, bring pressure up to medium-high. Reduce heat to maintain pressure and cook 3 minutes.

Release pressure as quickly as possible according to manufacturer's directions, usually under cold running water. Remove lid. Gently stir lobster and vegetable mixture. Add shrimp, flounder, and scallops. Secure lid. Over high heat, bring pressure up to high. Reduce heat to maintain pressure and cook 2 minutes.

Release pressure as quickly as possible according to manufacturer's directions, usually under cold running water. Remove lid. Pour Bouillabaisse into wide soup bowls and add a dollop of Rouille. Serve with bread.

COOK'S NOTE: When seafood is purchased for Bouillabaisse, reserve all trimmings for fish stock. The trimmings may be frozen for later use.

LOUISIANA SEAFOOD CREOLE

This Creole stew is rich in flavor and contains all the flavors we associate with Louisiana cuisine. There is just a hint of a spicy aftertaste.

MAKES 6 SERVINGS

⅓ cup olive oil

3 slices bacon, cut into ½-inch pieces

2 large onions, sliced

3 garlic cloves, crushed

1 cup (½-inch slices) celery

2 carrots, cut into ¼-inch slices

⅓ cup chopped fresh parsley

1 cup bottled clam juice

2 tablespoons fresh lemon juice

2 tablespoons sherry

1 cup canned crushed tomatoes

¼ cup jalapeño salsa

1 tablespcon light brown sugar

1½ teaspoons salt

½ teaspoon crushed red pepper flakes

½ teaspoon red (cayenne) pepper

2 teaspoons sweet paprika

1 teaspoon dried thyme

2 bay leaves

1 pound mushrooms, stems trimmed and caps
    thinly sliced

1 large green bell pepper, thinly sliced lengthwise

1 cup pimiento-stuffed green olives

1 pound bay scallops

1 pound shrimp, peeled and deveined

3 tablespoons butter, at room temperature

2 teaspoons potato starch or flour

Pressure Steamed Rice (page 180) to serve

Heat oil in a pressure cooker over medium heat. Add bacon, onions, and garlic and sauté 2 minutes. Add celery, carrots, and parsley. Cook 1 minute. Stir in clam juice, lemon juice, sherry, tomatoes, salsa, brown sugar, salt, pepper flakes, cayenne, paprika, thyme, and bay leaves. Stir well. Secure lid. Over high heat, bring pressure up to high. Reduce heat to maintain pressure and cook 2 minutes. Release pressure according to manufacturer's directions. Remove lid.

Stir mushrooms, bell pepper, olives, scallops, and shrimp into tomato mixture. Stir well. Secure lid. Over high heat, bring pressure up to medium. Reduce heat to maintain pressure and cook 2 minutes. Release pressure as quickly as possible according to manufacturer's directions, usually under cold running water. Remove lid.

Gently stir seafood mixture. Discard bay leaves. Combine butter and potato starch, blending to paste consistency. Add 1 tablespoon at a time to seafood mixture, stirring to blend, and cook over medium heat 1 minute. Serve over rice.

RED SNAPPER WITH POTATOES, GREEN PEPPER, AND TOMATOES

Red snapper is a delicious ocean fish found off the U.S. coast. This one-dish Italian meal is flavor-filled with seasonings blended for ultimate satisfaction.
MAKES 6 SERVINGS

¼ cup olive oil

1 large onion, sliced

2 garlic cloves, crushed

1 green bell pepper, sliced

6 tomatoes, cut into sixths and seeds removed

4 potatoes, cut into ½-inch slices

1 cup bottled clam juice

1 tablespoon fresh lemon juice

1½ teaspoons salt

¼ teaspoon crushed red pepper flakes

1½ teaspoons dried basil

1 teaspoon dried oregano

6 (6-ounce) red snapper fillets (1 inch thick)

1½ tablespoons potato starch or all-purpose flour
    mixed with 2 tablespoons water

¼ cup freshly grated Parmesan cheese

Heat oil in a pressure cooker over medium heat. Add onion and garlic and sauté 2 minutes. Add bell pepper and tomatoes. Stir well and cook 1 minute. Add potatoes, clam juice, lemon juice, salt, pepper flakes, and herbs. Stir well. Secure lid. Over high heat, bring pressure up to medium-high. Reduce heat to maintain pressure and cook 4 minutes.

Release pressure according to manufacturer's directions. Remove lid. Gently stir vegetable mixture. Place red snapper over vegetables. Secure lid. Over medium-high heat, bring pressure up to medium. Reduce heat to maintain pressure and cook 2½ minutes. Release pressure quickly according to manufacturer's directions, usually under cold running water. Remove lid.

Using a slotted spatula, carefully transfer red snapper and potatoes to a platter. Cover to retain heat. Stir ¼ cup of the cooking liquid into potato starch mixture, stir into remaining liquid, and cook, stirring, 1 minute, or until sauce thickens. Spoon sauce over red snapper and potatoes. Sprinkle with cheese.

□ □ □

SALMON STEAKS WITH LEEKS IN YOGURT DILL SAUCE

Salmon is commonly known as a saltwater fish; however, it has become landlocked in freshwater lakes during the spawning season. In general the lake salmon is less flavorful than the sea salmon. This fresh-flavored dish will be a low-fat favorite.
MAKES 6 SERVINGS

2 tablespoons olive oil

4 leeks (white parts only), rinsed and cut into
    ¼-inch slices

2 garlic cloves, crushed

2 tablespoons minced fresh parsley

1 cup bottled clam juice

2 tablespoons fresh lemon juice

1 teaspoon sherry

1½ teaspoons salt

¼ teaspoon freshly ground white pepper

2 teaspoons dried dill weed, or ⅓ cup chopped
   fresh dill

6 (1-inch-thick) salmon steaks

1 teaspoon prepared horseradish

¼ cup low-fat yogurt

2 teaspoons potato starch or all-purpose flour

Heat oil in a pressure cooker over medium heat. Add leeks, garlic, and parsley and sauté 2 minutes. Add clam juice, lemon juice, sherry, salt, pepper, and dill. Stir well. Place salmon steaks in cooking liquid. Secure lid. Over high heat, bring pressure up to medium–high. Reduce heat to maintain pressure and cook 3 minutes.

Release pressure quickly according to manufacturer's directions, usually under cold running water. Remove lid. Transfer salmon steaks to a platter. Cover to retain heat. Combine horseradish, yogurt, and potato starch in a small bowl. Whisk into cooking liquid and cook over medium heat, stirring, 1 minute, or until mixture thickens. Spoon sauce over salmon.

SEAFOOD IN CRUST

You'll want to lick the plate because the flavor combination of the seafood and the garlic bread container is so good. Serve with steamed fresh green peas.

MAKES 6 SERVINGS

6 hard-crust rolls

½ cup butter, melted

3 garlic cloves, crushed

¼ cup olive oil

5 tablespoons butter, at room temperature

6 shallots, sliced

¼ cup chopped fresh parsley

2 carrots, sliced

1 cup bottled clam juice

2 tablespoons fresh lemon juice

1 tablespoon sherry

1½ teaspoons salt

¼ teaspoon freshly ground white pepper

2 tablespoons bouquet garni in cheesecloth bag
   (page 205)

1 pound shrimp, peeled and deveined, or
   scallops

1½ pounds scrod or whitefish, boned and
   cut into 2-inch pieces

1 pound fresh mushrooms, sliced

¼ cup half-and-half

1 tablespoon potato starch or all-purpose
   flour

Using a bread knife, slice tops from rolls. Remove soft bread from inside rolls, leaving a shell. Blend melted butter and 2 of the garlic cloves in a small bowl. Brush inside of rolls with garlic butter. Set aside.

Heat oil and 3 tablespoons of the room-temperature butter in a pressure cooker over medium heat. Add shallots, remaining garlic, parsley, and carrots and sauté 2 minutes. Stir in clam juice, lemon juice, sherry, salt, pepper, and bouquet garni. Mix thoroughly. Fold in seafood and mushrooms. Secure lid. Over high heat, bring pressure up to medium. Reduce heat to maintain pressure and cook 3 minutes.

Release pressure quickly according to manufacturer's directions, usually under cold running water. Remove lid.

Combine remaining 2 tablespoons butter, half-and-half, and potato starch in a small bowl. Gradually stir into seafood mixture. Cook, stirring, over medium heat 2 minutes, or until mixture thickens. Place rolls on individual plates. Ladle seafood mixture with sauce into rolls, allowing it to overflow onto plates.

COOK'S NOTE: The bread from the center of the rolls may be processed in a food processor into crumbs for another use.

WHITEFISH FILLETS WITH VEGETABLES IN PARCHMENT

The whitefish is popular because of its lovely, sweet flavor. The fish and vegetables are wrapped in parchment paper.

MAKES 6 SERVINGS

¼ cup plus 2 tablespoons butter, at room temperature
¼ cup fresh lemon juice
3 shallots or green onions (white parts only), minced
2 garlic cloves, crushed
¼ cup minced fresh parsley
1 teaspoon salt
¼ teaspoon freshly ground white pepper
1 teaspoon dried thyme
3 pounds whitefish, cut into 6 pieces
2 medium potatoes, peeled and cut into ⅛-inch sticks
3 carrots, cut into 3-inch sticks
1 zucchini, cut into ½-inch slices
1½ cups water
Green salad to serve

Combine butter, lemon juice, shallots, garlic, parsley, salt, pepper, and thyme in a small bowl. Whisk until well mixed.

Cut 6 (8-inch) pieces of parchment paper. Butter one side of each piece. Lay a fillet on each piece of parchment. Rub or brush lemon butter mixture over fillets. Place several pieces of potato on each fillet, then carrots, then zucchini. Wrap parchment, envelope style, around each fillet to enclose. Place in steam basket, crisscross to fit. Pour the water into pressure cooker. Insert steam basket. Secure lid. Over high heat, bring pressure up to high. Reduce heat to maintain pressure and cook 5 minutes.

Release pressure according to manufacturer's directions. Remove lid. Remove steam basket. Using spatula, transfer bundles to a serving dish. Unwrap fish and vegetables and serve with salad.

COOK'S NOTE: Before preparing whitefish, rinse the fish thoroughly and look around the bottom area for a band of fat, usually grayish pearl in color. With a sharp knife, trim away this band or it will add a fishy flavor to the dish.

STUFFED FLOUNDER ROLLS WITH SAUCE AND ASPARAGUS

A member of the flat fish family, the flounder is a light-textured, delicately flavored fish. Combined with delicate spring asparagus, it makes a lovely one-dish presentation.
MAKES 6 SERVINGS

2 tablespoons butter

3 tablespoons olive oil

2 green onions, minced

2 tablespoons minced fresh parsley

½ teaspoon dried thyme

⅓ pound bay scallops

4 slices bread, crumbled

¼ cup bottled clam juice or water

1 tablespoon fresh lemon juice

¼ teaspoon salt

Dash freshly ground black pepper

2 tablespoons fresh lemon juice

1½ teaspoons salt

⅛ teaspoon freshly ground white pepper

6 (1-inch-thick) sole or flounder fillets, rinsed

1 cup bottled clam juice

½ teaspoon dried thyme

1½ pounds asparagus, trimmed

2 egg yolks

¼ cup half-and-half or milk

¼ cup butter, at room temperature

Prepare stuffing: Heat butter and oil in a large skillet. Add green onions and parsley and sauté 2 minutes. Add thyme and scallops, stir well, and cook over high heat 2 minutes. Stir in bread crumbs, clam juice, lemon juice, salt, and pepper. Place mixture in a food processor or blender. Process until a thick paste consistency. Set aside.

Combine lemon juice, 1 teaspoon of the salt, and pepper in a small bowl. Rub mixture over both sides of fillets. Place fillets on work surface, skin side up. Spoon 2 tablespoons of stuffing on widest end of each fillet and roll up.

Pour clam juice into pressure cooker. Add thyme, remaining ½ teaspoon salt, and remaining lemon juice mixture. Stir well. Place each fish roll in steam basket. Top with asparagus. Insert basket in cooker. Secure lid. Over high heat, bring pressure up to high. Reduce heat to maintain pressure and cook 3 minutes.

Release pressure according to manufacturer's directions. Remove lid. Remove basket from cooker. Transfer fish and asparagus to a serving platter. Cover to retain heat. Combine egg yolks, half-and-half, and butter in a small bowl. Whisk mixture into cooking liquid over medium-high heat. Cook, stirring, until thickened; do not boil. Spoon sauce over fish rolls and asparagus.

❑ ❑ ❑

SMOKED SALMON WITH FETTUCCINE IN CREAM SAUCE

This versatile pasta dish makes a great entrée, side dish, or first course. The pasta cooks in a thyme-flavored broth.
MAKES 6 SERVINGS

¼ **cup olive oil**

2 **cups fettuccine**

4 **cups chicken broth**

¾ **teaspoon salt**

¼ **teaspoon freshly ground white pepper**

1 **teaspoon dried thyme**

3 **tablespoons butter, cut into small pieces**

½ **cup sour cream or yogurt**

1 **pound smoked salmon, trout, or whitefish, separated into bite-size pieces**

2 **green onions, chopped**

⅓ **cup freshly grated Parmesan or fontinella cheese**

Heat oil in a pressure cooker. Add fettuccine, broth, salt, pepper, and thyme. Secure lid. Over high heat, bring pressure up to high. Reduce heat to maintain pressure and cook 8 minutes.

Release pressure according to manufacturer's directions. Remove lid. Drain fettuccine through a colander and place in a pasta bowl. Toss with butter and sour cream. Add fish and green onions, tossing gently until mixed. Sprinkle with cheese.

❑ ❑ ❑

STEAMED WHOLE FISH WITH LEMON-PARSLEY SAUCE

If you prefer the fish to remain straight during the pressure-cooking process, insert a wooden skewer through the entire fish, beginning at the head and ending at the tail. Otherwise, the fish will curve, which I think makes a lovely presentation.
MAKES 6 SERVINGS

1 **(12- to 14-inch) whole pickerel, trout, or whitefish with head and tail, ready to cook**

2 **tablespoons fresh lemon juice**

1 **teaspoon salt**

¼ **teaspoon freshly ground white pepper**

1½ **cups water**

Parsley sprigs to garnish

1 **pimiento-stuffed green olive**

Lemon-Parsley Sauce

½ cup butter, melted

1 garlic clove, crushed

⅓ cup minced fresh parsley

3 egg yolks

⅓ cup fresh lemon juice

½ teaspoon salt

⅛ teaspoon freshly ground white pepper

½ cup chopped, pitted olives

Rinse fish. Combine lemon juice, salt, and pepper in a small bowl. Brush surface and cavity of fish with mixture. Measure thickness of fish.

Place fish, cavity side down, in steam basket, curving fish along side of basket or placing across basket. Pour water into pressure cooker and insert steam basket. Secure lid. Over high heat, bring pressure up to medium-high. Reduce heat to maintain pressure and cook 2½ minutes per inch of fish. If you have a fish 3 inches thick, it will take about 7½ minutes (multiplying the thickest part by 2½ minutes).

Release pressure according to manufacturer's directions. Remove lid. Remove steam basket. Carefully transfer fish to a serving platter. Fish will remain curved. Peel skin from fish. Garnish gills with parsley. Cut a pimiento-stuffed olive in half and insert each half into eye cavities. Garnish platter with parsley sprigs. Keep fish warm.

Prepare sauce: Melt butter in a saucepan. Add garlic and parsley and sauté until softened. Gradually whisk in egg yolks, lemon juice, salt, and pepper. Cook, stirring, over low heat until thickened. Stir in olives.

Serve fish with sauce.

RICH FISH STOCK

This mild fish stock is quick and easy to prepare and is filled with flavor.

MAKES 1½ QUARTS

⅓ cup olive oil

2 medium leeks, thickly sliced

2 garlic cloves, unpeeled and quartered

1 large carrot, cut into 2-inch pieces

2 celery stalks, cut into 2-inch pieces

6 sprigs parsley

1½ pounds fish heads, tails, and bones (available from fish monger)

1 (8-ounce) bottle clam juice

2 cups white wine

4 cups water

1 tablespoon fresh lemon juice

1 teaspoon salt

¼ teaspoon white pepper

2 tablespoons bouquet garni in cheesecloth bag (page 205)

Heat oil in a pressure cooker over medium-high heat. Add leeks, garlic, carrot, celery, and parsley and sauté 3 minutes, stirring occasionally. Stir in fish pieces, clam juice, wine, water, lemon juice, salt, pepper, and bouquet garni. Secure lid. Over high heat, bring pressure up to medium-high. Reduce heat to maintain pressure and cook 10 minutes.

Release pressure according to manufacturer's directions. Remove lid. Strain stock through a cheesecloth-lined colander into large bowl. Using back of a large spoon, press vegetables and fish pieces to extract juices.

Use stock immediately in your favorite soup recipe, store in refrigerator up to 3 days, or freeze in airtight containers up to 3 months. Thaw in refrigerator.

COOK'S NOTE: Fish stock becomes bitter if overcooked.

SIDE DISHES AND MORE

Vegetables cooked in a pressure cooker are absolutely wonderful. The color remains vibrant, the nutrients are retained, and best of all, the flavors are more pronounced than in conventional cooking. Vegetables cook quickly and it is important to follow the timing chart precisely.

For successful pressure-cooked vegetables: Keep the vegetables uniform in size and use accurate minimum water amounts as recommended by the manufacturer. Timing begins after the pressure is reached. Reduce the steam quickly at the end of the cooking cycle, usually by releasing the pressure under cold running water.

SELECTING FINE VEGETABLES

When shopping, look for firm stems and leaves. If the vegetables appear wilted, do not buy them, as they have already lost nutrients. Refrain from purchasing vegetables with blemishes or large, dark holes or spots.

Layers of vegetables may be steamed or pressure-cooked together with very little mingling of flavors. Add the minimum amount of water required, according to the manufacturer's directions for your cooker. Insert the steam basket. Layer

VEGETABLE	CUT	MINUTES	WHOLE (MIN)	FROZEN (MIN)	PRESSURE
Acorn squash	halves	12			high
Artichoke	quartered	3	10	3	med-high
Asparagus			2	3	med-low
Beans, green		3			medium
Beets	½-inch slices	3	14	5	high
Broccoli	florets	3		3	med-high
Broccoli	spears	2			med-high
Brussels sprouts			4	5	med-high
Cabbage	quartered	6			med-high
Cabbage	shredded	2			med-high
Carrots	½-inch slices	3		4	high
Cauliflower	florets	2		3	med-high
Cauliflower	quartered	4			med-high
Celery	1-inch slices	2			med-high
Corn	ears	2		5	high
Eggplant	1-inch slices	2			medium
Endive			8		high
Escarole			8		high
Fennel root	½-inch slices	2	5		med-high
Okra	pods	3		4	med-high
Onion	1-inch slices	2			med-high
Parsnips	quartered	4	10		high
Peas	pods	2		4	med-low
Potatoes	2-inch cuts	7	10		high
Potatoes (new)	1½-inch–2-inch		8		high
Rutabagas	2-inch cuts	7		8	high
Spinach			3	4	med-high
Sweet potatoes	2-inch cuts	6	12		high
Tomatoes	quartered	2	5		med-high
Turnips	½-inch slices	2	10		high
Zucchini	1-inch slices	2			med-high

vegetables, separating with parchment paper or stacking in ovenproof containers.

Remember to release the steam quickly after timing is reached. Run cold running water over lid to quickly reduce the pressure or release according to manufacturer's directions.

BROCCOLI WITH GARLICKY CAESAR DRESSING

The dressing is pungent and delicious. It stores well in the refrigerator for up to four days.

MAKES 6 SERVINGS

4 cups broccoli florets

½ teaspoon salt

1 cup water

2 garlic cloves, crushed

2 canned anchovies, drained

1 tablespoon fresh lemon juice

1 large egg, boiled 3 minutes (see Egg Safety, page 16)

2 tablespoons mayonnaise

2 tablespoons freshly grated Parmesan cheese

¼ cup olive oil

Salt and freshly ground black pepper to taste

Place broccoli in a pressure cooker. Sprinkle with salt and pour water over top. Secure lid. Over high heat, bring pressure up to low. Reduce heat to medium to maintain pressure and cook 2 minutes.

Release pressure under cold running water. Remove lid. Drain broccoli and place in a serving bowl.

In a blender or food processor, process garlic,

anchovies, lemon juice, egg yolk, mayonnaise, and cheese until smooth. Drizzle olive oil into the mixture a little at a time. Season with salt and pepper. Drizzle dressing over broccoli and serve.

❑ ❑ ❑

BROCCOLI, BELL PEPPER, AND TOMATOES IN LEMON DRESSING

Broccoli is available in produce sections all year round. Select unblemished, firm stalks with perky florets. The color should be a deep green, without any yellow tinge. Broccoli can be stored in an airtight bag in the refrigerator for up to five days.
MAKES 6 SERVINGS

1 large head broccoli
1 yellow bell pepper, thinly sliced
1 cup water
2 medium tomatoes, coarsely diced
2 tablespoons fresh lemon juice
3 tablespoons olive oil
⅛ teaspoon salt
Dash freshly ground white pepper

Trim away tough outer layer from broccoli. Cut broccoli stalks in half. Place steam rack into the pressure cooker and layer broccoli and bell pepper in the rack. Pour water over top. Secure lid. Over high heat, bring pressure up to low.

Reduce heat to medium to maintain pressure and cook 2 minutes.

Release pressure under cold running water. Remove lid. Place broccoli, bell pepper, and tomatoes on a serving dish. Blend lemon juice, olive oil, salt, and pepper together. Drizzle dressing over top of vegetables and serve.

❑ ❑ ❑

CREAMY PEARL ONIONS

It's old-fashioned and delicious comfort food. Serve it as a side dish with ham, chicken, or fish.
MAKES 6 SERVINGS

3 cups pearl onions, peeled and bottoms scored
1 cup chicken broth
½ teaspoon salt
¼ cup half-and-half
¼ cup all-purpose flour or potato starch
Dash freshly ground white pepper
1 teaspoon sugar
2 tablespoons butter, melted

Combine onions, chicken broth, and salt in a pressure cooker. Secure lid. Over high heat, bring pressure up to low. Reduce heat to medium to maintain pressure and cook 3 minutes.

Release pressure under cold running water. Remove lid. Using a slotted spoon, remove onions from stock and set aside in a bowl. Whisk together half-and-half, flour, pepper, sugar, and butter until smooth. Pour into the onion juices and cook over high heat, stirring, until juices thicken. Pour over onions and serve hot.

□ □ □

GREEK-STYLE GREEN BEANS IN TOMATO SAUCE

This is a great side dish for lamb or chicken. Select long, firm, and slender beans, dark green in color. Fresh green beans store well in an airtight bag in the refrigerator for up to five days.

MAKES 6 SERVINGS

3 tablespoons olive oil

1 medium onion, coarsely diced

2 garlic cloves, crushed

4 cups fresh green beans, ends removed and
   cut in half

¼ cup chopped fresh parsley

1 stalk celery, coarsely chopped

1 cup canned diced tomatoes in sauce

1 teaspoon salt

Dash crushed red pepper flakes

2 teaspoons dill weed

¼ teaspoon dried oregano

1 teaspoon fresh lemon juice

Crusty Greek bread and feta cheese to serve

Heat oil in a pressure cooker over medium heat. Add onion and garlic and sauté 3 min-utes. Add remaining ingredients, except bread and cheese. Stir well. Secure lid. Over high heat, bring pressure up to medium. Decrease heat to medium to maintain pressure and cook 3 minutes.

Release pressure under cold running water. Remove lid. Transfer to a serving platter. Serve with bread and cheese.

□ □ □

ITALIAN BROCCOLI-CAULIFLOWER

Florets are the bud clusters of the vegetable. Trim away from tough stalk and gently shave off tough outer layer from the small stems. The stalk part is nutritious and wonderful chopped in a salad.

MAKES 6 SERVINGS

2 cups broccoli florets

2 cups cauliflower florets

1¼ teaspoons salt

2 cups water

3 tablespoons olive oil

3 tablespoons pine nuts

1 leek (white part only), rinsed and thinly sliced

2 garlic cloves, crushed

½ small red bell pepper, thinly sliced

½ small green bell pepper, thinly sliced

½ teaspoon ground fennel

½ teaspoon dried basil

Dash crushed red pepper flakes

2 tablespoons grated fontinella cheese

ombine broccoli, cauliflower, 1 teaspoon of the salt, and water in a pressure cooker. Secure lid. Over high heat, bring pressure up to medium. Reduce heat to medium to maintain pressure and cook 2 minutes.

Release pressure under cold running water. Remove lid. Drain vegetables and place on a serving platter.

Heat oil in a large skillet over medium heat. Add pine nuts and stir until golden in color. Remove with a slotted spoon and set aside. Add leek, garlic, bell peppers, fennel, basil, ¼ teaspoon salt, and pepper flakes. Stir well and cook over medium heat 4 minutes, or until veggies are wilted. Add pine nuts and stir well. Spoon mixture over broccoli and cauliflower. Toss gently to combine. Sprinkle cheese over top.

MARINARA SAUCE

Bell peppers are also known as sweet peppers and are available in all produce areas. This recipe calls for the red bell pepper because of its extra sweetness, and it also lends extra-rich color to the sauce.

MAKES 6 SERVINGS

2 tablespoons olive oil or canola oil

1 large onion, diced

4 garlic cloves, crushed

1 small red bell pepper, coarsely diced

⅓ cup minced fresh parsley

2 carrots, coarsely diced

½ teaspoon ground fennel

½ teaspoon dried oregano

1 teaspoon dried basil

1 bay leaf

1 teaspoon salt

Pinch crushed red pepper flakes

1 (15-ounce) can diced tomatoes in sauce

½ cup chicken broth

eat oil in a pressure cooker. Add onion, garlic, bell pepper, and parsley and sauté 2 minutes. Add remaining ingredients and stir well. Secure lid. Over high heat, bring pressure up to high. Reduce heat to medium to maintain pressure and cook 6 minutes.

Release pressure according to manufacturer's directions. Remove lid. Stir well. Process sauce in a blender or food processor until almost smooth, leaving a little texture. A hand blender also works very well. Serve over pasta, rice, or vegetables. Sauce freezes very well in a freezer container for up to 3 months.

VARIATION Eggplant with Marinara Sauce: Peel an eggplant. Cut into ¼-inch-thick slices and brush with olive oil and season with salt and freshly ground black pepper. Broil for several minutes on both sides, or until tender. Transfer to a serving dish. Spoon marinara sauce over eggplant and sprinkle with grated mozzarella cheese.

MUSTARD GREENS WITH BACON AND ONION DRESSING

Mustard greens have a peppery leaf. They are a member of the same family as broccoli, kale, and collard greens. The leaves are a rich dark green and should be crisp, not flabby. Store wrapped in a damp cloth in the refrigerator.

MAKES 6 SERVINGS

2 slices Canadian bacon or turkey bacon, coarsely diced

2 tablespoons olive or canola oil

1 small onion, thinly sliced

¼ teaspoon dried rosemary

½ teaspoon salt

⅛ teaspoon freshly ground white pepper

2 bunches mustard greens, rinsed well

2 cups water

1 tablespoon fresh lemon juice

Sauté bacon with oil in a pressure cooker over medium heat until crisp. Add onion and sauté 3 minutes. Add rosemary, salt, and pepper and stir well. Pour bacon mixture into a small bowl, including all oil and drippings, and set aside.

Add greens to the pressure cooker along with the water. Secure lid. Over high heat, bring pressure up to medium. Reduce heat to medium to maintain pressure and cook 5 minutes.

Release pressure under cold running water. Remove lid. Drain and press all excess water from greens. Transfer to a bowl and add bacon mixture.

Drizzle lemon juice over top and toss until greens are coated and bacon mixture is evenly distributed.

□ □ □

PUREED TURNIPS AND CARROTS

Buy firm, not spongy, turnips. Make sure they are free of blemishes. They keep well in a cool dry place for up to a week.

MAKES 6 SERVINGS

3 large turnips, peeled and quartered

4 large carrots, cut into 2-inch pieces

2 cups water

1 teaspoon salt

2 tablespoons olive oil

½ teaspoon freshly grated nutmeg

2 tablespoons sour cream

Place vegetables in the pressure cooker and cover with water. Sprinkle salt over top. Secure lid. Over high heat, bring pressure up to high. Reduce heat to medium to maintain pressure and cook 8 minutes.

Release pressure under cold running water. Remove lid. Drain vegetables. Using a potato masher or potato ricer, process vegetables until smooth. Stir together olive oil, nutmeg, and sour cream. Thoroughly blend into the vegetable mixture.

SPINACH WITH ONIONS AND FETA CHEESE

Spinach is found both fresh and in the frozen food area. Fresh spinach is available year-round and is a great source for iron. Look for firm dark green leaves. Avoid limp or wilted leaves. Because spinach is grown in a sandy soil, it is very gritty and should be rinsed at least two times in lukewarm water. The warm water will soften the leaves, releasing all grit that is lodged within the vegetable.

MAKES 6 SERVINGS

2 (10-ounce) packages fresh spinach, rinsed

2 cups water

1 teaspoon salt

2 tablespoons olive oil

1 medium onion, peeled and sliced fine

1 garlic clove, crushed

½ teaspoon dried dill weed

1 tablespoon fresh lemon juice

⅓ cup crumbled feta cheese

Trim away tough stems from spinach. Combine spinach, water, and salt in a pressure cooker. Secure lid. Over high heat, bring pressure up to medium. Reduce heat to medium to maintain pressure and cook 3 minutes.

Release pressure under cold running water. Remove lid. Drain. Press all excess water from spinach. Place in a serving bowl. Heat olive oil in pressure cooker over medium heat. Add onion and garlic and sauté 3 minutes. Add dill and

lemon juice. Stir well and add to spinach and toss to combine. Sprinkle feta cheese over top.

▢ ▢ ▢

AUTUMN RATATOUILLE

About ¼ cup Ratatouille folded into an omelet makes an out-of-this-world dish.

MAKES 6 TO 8 SERVINGS

¼ cup olive oil

2 large onions, sliced

3 garlic cloves, crushed

⅓ cup chopped fresh parsley

2 carrots, cut into ¾-inch slices

1 large eggplant, peeled and cut into 2-inch cubes

1½ pounds zucchini, cut into 2-inch pieces

1 (15-ounce) can whole peeled tomatoes, crushed

1 green bell pepper, sliced lengthwise

2 large potatoes, peeled and cut into ¼-inch slices

½ cup beef, chicken, or vegetable stock

1 tablespoon light brown sugar

1 teaspoon salt

¾ teaspoon crushed red pepper flakes

1 teaspoon dried leaf oregano

¼ teaspoon ground fennel

2 tablespoons bouquet garni (page 205) in cheesecloth bag

2 bay leaves

3 tablespoons butter, at room temperature

3 tablespoons all-purpose flour

Heat oil in a pressure cooker over medium heat. Add onions, garlic, parsley, and carrots and sauté 2 minutes. Add eggplant, zucchini, tomatoes, bell pepper, potatoes, stock, brown sugar, salt, pepper flakes, oregano, fennel, bouquet garni, and bay leaves. Stir well. Secure lid. Over high heat, bring pressure up to high. Reduce heat to maintain pressure and cook 6 minutes.

Release pressure quickly according to manufacturer's directions. Remove lid. Gently stir vegetables. Discard bay leaves. Combine butter and flour in a small bowl, making a paste; gradually add to vegetables, and cook, stirring, until slightly thickened.

VARIATION If you want to eliminate the butter in the flour paste, add ⅓ cup seasoned bread crumbs and stir a few seconds. This will thicken the ratatouille's extra juices.

▣ ▣ ▣

BEETS

Ruby-red fresh beets are available year-round in vegetable markets and produce departments. However, their flavor is best from May to November. Select beets with greens attached. Look for firm bulbs without blemishes.
MAKES 6 SERVINGS

2 cups water

6 (3-inch) whole beets, unpeeled, whole or quartered, greens removed

½ teaspoon salt

Pour water into a pressure cooker. Add beets and salt. Secure lid. Over high heat, bring

pressure up to high. Reduce heat to maintain pressure and cook whole beets 14 minutes or quartered beets 8 minutes.

Release pressure according to manufacturer's directions. Remove lid. Drain beets in a colander, then rinse under cold running water, rubbing to remove skins. The skins should release easily.

▣ ▣ ▣

BROCCOLI WITH LEMON BUTTER

Broccoli is available year-round in the United States, but the price may vary depending on the season. Look for a deep green color. Stalks should not be dry.
MAKES 6 SERVINGS

½ cup water

1 bunch broccoli, stems peeled and trimmed, split into serving pieces

3 tablespoons butter, melted

1 tablespoon fresh lemon juice

¼ teaspoon salt

¼ cup grated Asiago cheese (optional)

Pour water into a pressure cooker. Layer broccoli in steam basket and place in cooker. Secure lid. Over high heat, bring pressure up to high. Reduce heat to maintain pressure and cook 3 minutes.

While broccoli cooks, whisk butter, lemon juice, and salt together in a small bowl. Set aside.

Quickly release steam according to manufacturer's directions. Remove lid. Remove steam basket and carefully transfer broccoli to a serving dish. Spoon lemon sauce over broccoli and sprinkle with cheese (if using).

⊡ ⊡ ⊡

CAULIFLOWER AND BROCCOLI PARMESAN

What could be easier and more appetizing than this healthy side dish of deep green and contrasting white florets?

MAKES 6 SERVINGS

2 tablespoons olive oil

1 cup water or chicken broth or stock

2 tablespoons fresh lemon juice

2 tablespoons chopped fresh parsley

½ teaspoon salt

⅛ teaspoon freshly ground black pepper

½ teaspoon dried oregano

½ head cauliflower, cut into florets

½ bunch broccoli, stems peeled and trimmed, cut into florets

¼ cup freshly grated Parmesan cheese

Combine oil, broth, lemon juice, parsley, salt, pepper, and oregano in a pressure cooker. Stir well. Layer cauliflower and broccoli in steam basket and place in cooker. Secure lid. Over high heat, bring pressure up to high. Reduce heat to maintain pressure and cook 3 minutes.

Quickly release steam according to manufacturer's directions. Remove lid. Remove steam basket and place vegetables on a platter. Spoon ¼ of cooking liquid over vegetables and sprinkle with cheese.

COOK'S NOTE: Uncooked cauliflower and broccoli will hold five days in the refrigerator, unwashed. The vegetables should be stored in a plastic bag with a few sprinkles of water.

⊡ ⊡ ⊡

CAULIFLOWER WITH HERBED PEA SAUCE

This dish makes a lovely and colorful addition to any meal. The green pea puree is vibrant against the cauliflower.

MAKES 6 SERVINGS

¼ cup olive oil

3 green onions, minced

1 slice bacon, cut into ½-inch pieces

1 cup chicken broth or stock

2 cups frozen green peas

2 tablespoons fresh lemon juice

1 teaspoon salt

⅛ teaspoon freshly ground white pepper

½ teaspoon dried basil

1 large head cauliflower, stems trimmed and cut into florets

¼ cup sour cream

½ cup (2 ounces) shredded Cheddar cheese

Heat oil in a pressure cooker. Add green onions and bacon and sauté 2 minutes. Stir in broth, peas, lemon juice, salt, pepper, and basil. Layer cauliflower in steam basket. Place basket over pea mixture in cooker. Secure lid. Over high heat, bring pressure up to medium. Reduce heat to maintain pressure and cook 4 minutes.

Quickly release pressure according to manufacturer's directions. Remove lid. Remove steam basket and place cauliflower on a serving platter. Cover to retain heat.

Pour peas and cooking liquid into a food processor or blender. Add sour cream and ¼ cup of the cheese. Process until smooth. Spoon sauce over cauliflower and sprinkle with remaining cheese.

▫ ▫ ▫

GLAZED CARROTS WITH PECAN, APRICOT, AND RAISIN SAUCE

Carrots may be used in many vegetable medleys and seasoned with herbs and spices from every cuisine in the world. Serve this dish with roasted turkey, chicken, or pork.

MAKES 6 TO 8 SERVINGS

1 cup orange juice

1 pound carrots, cut julienne into 3-inch strips

¼ cup apricot preserves

½ cup golden raisins

1 teaspoon light brown sugar

⅛ teaspoon freshly grated nutmeg

1 tablespoon cornstarch mixed with 2 tablespoons cold water

⅓ cup toasted pecans, chopped (see Cook's Note, page 185)

Pour orange juice into a pressure cooker. Stir in carrots, preserves, raisins, brown sugar, and nutmeg. Secure lid. Over medium-high heat, bring pressure up to medium. Reduce heat to maintain low pressure and cook 3 minutes.

Quickly release pressure according to manufacturer's directions. Remove lid. Gently stir carrots. Stir ½ cup of cooking liquid into cornstarch mixture and stir to mix thoroughly. Stir into carrot mixture and cook over medium heat 1 minute. Stir in pecans.

GREEN BEANS WITH BASIL

Sometimes the simplest recipes are the tastiest, and this dish is a great accompaniment for any main dish.

MAKES 6 TO 8 SERVINGS

¼ cup olive oil

2 garlic cloves, crushed

1 pound green beans, ends removed

1 cup water or chicken broth

¾ teaspoon salt

⅛ teaspoon freshly ground black pepper

1 teaspoon dried basil

2 tablespoons butter (optional)

Heat oil in a pressure cooker over medium heat. Add garlic and sauté 1 minute. Stir in beans. Add water, salt, pepper, and basil. Stir well. Secure lid. Over high heat, bring pressure up to medium-high. Reduce heat to maintain pressure and cook 3 minutes.

Quickly release pressure according to manufacturer's directions. Remove lid. Stir beans, then drain in a colander. Place beans in a serving dish and dot with butter (if using).

COOK'S NOTE: Available all year round, green beans should be crisp, green, and free of dark spots.

POTATOES (AND SWEET) POTATOES

POTATOES

Russet potatoes, also called Idaho or Russet Burbank potatoes, are the number-one selling potato in the market and can be used successfully in most potato dishes. In addition to Idaho, potatoes also come from California, Washington, Michigan, Oregon, and Maine. Try the new Yukon gold potato. It has a lovely texture and a hint of butter flavor in its taste.

My preference is the White Rose potato, also called the Cal White or Long White. It has just a little more moisture than the russet and the texture is smoother and excellent for mashing. Use a russet or White Rose for baked potatoes. For stews and soups, the other varieties work fine. Try a variety of potatoes and form your own preferences. Potatoes are available in mesh bags or you may select your own. I prefer selecting my own. Look for firm potatoes with smooth skins without bruises or dark spots. Avoid green potatoes. Potatoes are very nutritious, high in vitamin C, and rich in minerals. Although many believe potatoes are high in calories, potatoes have only about 25 calories per ounce. So enjoy!

GARLIC-HORSERADISH MASHED POTATOES

There are a variety of potatoes in the marketplace, including the russet, a low-moisture and mealy potato, perfect for baking, but which can be used for other dishes. The White Rose potato is excellent for mashed potatoes. Mashed potatoes are a great side with roast beef or any meat, poultry, or fish dish.

MAKES 6 SERVINGS

5 medium white potatoes, peeled and cut into quarters

2 cups water

1⅛ teaspoons salt

1 tablespoon butter

3 garlic cloves, minced

Dash freshly ground white pepper

1 tablespoon horseradish

3 tablespoons sour cream

Combine potatoes, water, and 1 teaspoon of the salt in a pressure cooker. Secure lid. Over high heat, bring pressure up to high. Reduce heat to medium to maintain pressure and cook 7 minutes.

In the meantime, heat butter in a small skillet over medium-low heat. Add garlic and sauté 2 minutes. Remove from heat and add remaining ⅛ teaspoon salt, pepper, horseradish, and sour cream. Set aside.

Release pressure under cold running water. Remove lid. Drain potatoes. Put potatoes through a potato ricer, or mash with a masher. Stir in garlic mixture and blend with a fork until well incorporated and smooth in texture.

SKORDALIA

This authentic garlic and potato sauce is regularly found in Greek kitchens. It is delicious, and offers the magnificent flavor and essence of raw garlic. It is said the poor use all bread instead of potatoes, the rich use walnuts. This is the favored version. Serve with steamed vegetables or as a side dish.

MAKES 6 SERVINGS

3 medium potatoes, peeled and cut into quarters

1 cup water

3 slices rich bread, dried and crumbled

4 garlic cloves, crushed

¼ cup olive oil

2 tablespoons white wine vinegar

½ teaspoon salt

⅛ teaspoon freshly ground white pepper

Place potatoes and water in a pressure cooker. Secure lid. Over high heat, bring pressure up to high. Reduce heat to medium to maintain pressure and cook 5 minutes.

Release pressure according to manufacturer's directions. Remove lid. Drain potatoes. Place potatoes in a bowl and mash. Add bread crumbs, garlic, olive oil, vinegar, salt, and pepper. Blend well. Taste and correct seasoning. Store in airtight container in the refrigerator.

HUMMUS MASHED POTATOES

The garlicky and creamy hummus offers a new twist of flavors to mashed potatoes.

MAKES 6 SERVINGS

4 medium potatoes, peeled and quartered

1 cup water

1/2 teaspoon salt

1/2 cup Hummus (page 19)

2 tablespoons finely chopped fresh parsley

Place potatoes, water, and salt in a pressure cooker. Secure lid. Over high heat, bring pressure up to high. Reduce heat to medium to maintain pressure and cook 8 minutes.

Release pressure under cold running water. Remove lid. Drain. Put potatoes through a potato ricer, or mash with a masher. Stir in hummus until thoroughly incorporated. Sprinkle with parsley.

❑ ❑ ❑

POTATO AND GARBANZO BEAN RAGOUT

Ragout is a French word describing a stew with a combination of well-seasoned vegetables, meat, poultry, or fish. This is a healthy vegetable ragout to be enjoyed as a main dish or side dish.

MAKES 6 SERVINGS

1 cup dried garbanzo beans, soaked

2 tablespoons olive oil

2 medium onions, coarsely diced

2 garlic cloves, crushed

1 medium red bell pepper, coarsely chopped

1 pinch saffron

1/2 teaspoon sweet paprika

Pinch crushed red pepper flakes

1 teaspoon salt

2 cups chicken broth

1 cup canned diced tomato

3 medium potatoes, peeled and cut into 1-inch pieces

3 tablespoons seasoned bread crumbs

Drain garbanzo beans and set aside. Heat oil in a pressure cooker over medium heat. Add onions, garlic, and bell peppers and sauté 3 minutes. Stir well. Add garbanzo beans and remaining ingredients, except potatoes and bread crumbs. Secure lid. Over high heat, bring pressure up to high. Reduce heat to medium to maintain pressure and cook 10 minutes.

Release pressure under cold running water. Remove lid. Add potatoes and stir well. Secure lid. Over high heat, bring pressure up to high. Reduce heat to medium to maintain pressure and cook 5 minutes. Release pressure and remove lid. Stir in bread crumbs. Let stand 5 minutes, stir, and serve.

PARMESAN POTATOES WITH PESTO

Pesto is traditionally a mixture of fresh basil, freshly grated Parmesan cheese, lemon juice, oil, and garlic. It's a very aromatic mixture and is wonderful tossed into pasta or rice. It also gives meat, fish, or poultry an interesting flavor.

MAKES 6 SERVINGS

¼ cup plus 2 tablespoons olive oil

3 leeks (white parts only), rinsed and sliced

3 garlic cloves, crushed

⅓ cup chopped parsley

4 medium potatoes, peeled and cut into ½-inch
    slices

½ cup chicken broth or stock

1 teaspoon salt

¼ teaspoon freshly ground white pepper

¼ cup freshly grated Parmesan cheese

¼ cup minced fresh basil or 1 tablespoon dried
    sweet basil

1 tablespoon fresh lemon juice

Heat ¼ cup oil in a pressure cooker over medium heat. Add leeks, 2 of the garlic cloves, and parsley and sauté 3 minutes. Add potatoes and stir well. Add broth, salt, and pepper. Secure lid. Over high heat, bring pressure up to high. Reduce heat to maintain pressure and cook 5 minutes.

Release pressure according to manufacturer's directions. Remove lid. Drain potatoes in a colander and transfer to a flameproof platter. Preheat broiler. Combine cheese, basil, remaining 1 garlic clove, lemon juice, and 2 tablespoons oil in a small bowl. Add mixture to potatoes, tossing gently until potatoes are evenly coated. Broil until browned, 2 minutes.

SCALLOPED POTATOES

This popular dish can be made up to a couple of days ahead of time and refrigerated.

MAKES 6 TO 8 SERVINGS

1 cup chicken broth or stock

6 medium potatoes, peeled and cut into ¼-inch
    slices

½ teaspoon salt

⅛ teaspoon freshly ground white pepper

1 tablespoon chopped fresh chives

⅓ cup sour cream

⅓ cup milk

2 tablespoons potato starch or all-purpose flour

Dash of paprika

Pour broth into a pressure cooker. Add potatoes, salt, pepper, and chives. Secure lid. Over high heat, bring pressure up to high. Reduce heat to maintain pressure and cook 5 minutes.

Release pressure according to manufacturer's directions. Remove lid. Using a slotted spoon, transfer potatoes to a flameproof platter. Preheat broiler. Pour sour cream, milk, and potato starch into cooking liquid in cooker. Cook, whisking to blend, over high heat 1 minute. Pour over potatoes and use 2 forks to gently mix. Sprinkle with paprika and brown under broiler.

VARIATION By adding ½ cup shredded Cheddar cheese, the dish is transformed into easy au gratin potatoes. Either way, it's a favorite.

◻◻◻

MASHED SWEET POTATOES WITH BANANAS

A new twist for a wonderful sweet potato dish, the banana adds a lovely dimension. It's great with pork, chicken, or turkey.

MAKES 6 SERVINGS

2 large sweet potatoes, quartered

2 cups water

1 teaspoon salt

2 large ripe bananas, mashed

⅓ cup packed light brown sugar

4 tablespoons butter

2 tablespoons half-and-half

⅛ teaspoon ground cinnamon

1 cup toasted pecans, coarsely chopped

Place sweet potatoes, water, and salt in a pressure cooker. Secure lid. Over high heat, bring pressure up to high. Reduce heat to medium to maintain pressure and cook 12 minutes.

Release pressure according to manufacturer's

directions. Remove lid. Drain potatoes. Under cold running water, slide skins off the potatoes. Place in a heatproof bowl. Add bananas, brown sugar, butter, half-and-half, and cinnamon. Mash and mix until combined. Transfer mixture to a serving dish and sprinkle pecans over top.

◻◻◻

SWEET POTATO AND SAUSAGE WITH POACHED EGGS

This is a delicious alternative to traditional hash. It is full of fall flavors and ingredients.

MAKES 6 SERVINGS

1 large sweet potato

3 cups water

1 small onion, finely diced

2 small garlic cloves, crushed

½ red bell pepper, seeded and finely diced

¼ cup minced fresh parsley

1 teaspoon salt

⅛ teaspoon freshly ground white pepper

1 pound prepared breakfast sausage

2 tablespoons maple syrup

2 tablespoons butter

6 extra-large eggs

Cut sweet potato into quarters. Add water and sweet potato to the pressure cooker. Secure lid. Over high heat, bring pressure up to high.

Reduce heat to medium to maintain pressure and cook 8 minutes.

Release pressure according to manufacturer's directions. Remove lid. Drain sweet potato. Under cold running water, slide skin off. Set aside.

Heat pressure cooker and add onion, garlic, bell pepper, parsley, salt, white pepper, and sausage. Stir until well incorporated. Cook for 1 minute. Secure lid. Over high heat, bring pressure up to medium. Reduce heat to medium to maintain pressure and cook 3 minutes.

Release pressure according to manufacturer's directions. Remove lid. Stir well. Chop cooked sweet potatoes into small cubes. Add to the sausage mixture. Blend in syrup and butter. Cover and set aside.

Poach the eggs: Using an egg poacher put 2 inches water in bottom. Break eggs into each cup. Cover and bring water to a boil. Reduce heat to medium and cook until whites are set and yolks are of desired doneness. Divide potato-sausage mixture among 6 plates. Top each serving with a poached egg.

MANDARIN ORANGES AND SWEET POTATOES

The refreshing orange flavor of the sweet juice complements the delicate sweet potatoes.

MAKES 6 SERVINGS

¾ cup plus 2 tablespoons orange juice

4 medium sweet potatoes, peeled and cut into ½-inch slices

¾ cup firmly packed brown sugar

¼ cup butter

1 tablespoon cornstarch

1 (11-ounce) can mandarin oranges, drained

Pour ¾ cup of the orange juice into a pressure cooker. Place sweet potatoes in juice and sprinkle with brown sugar. Stir well. Secure lid. Over high heat, bring pressure up to high. Reduce heat to maintain pressure and cook 4 minutes.

Quickly release pressure according to manufacturer's directions. Remove lid. Using a slotted spoon, remove sweet potatoes and arrange on a platter. Dot sweet potatoes with butter.

Combine cornstarch and remaining 2 tablespoons orange juice in a small bowl. Stir into cooking liquid. Cook, stirring, until thickened. Fold in half of oranges. Ladle sauce over sweet potatoes and garnish with remaining oranges.

COOK'S NOTE: Most sweet potato recipes are sweet; however, this vegetable is delightful when mashed with just a dash of nutmeg and a little butter.

MAPLE PECAN SWEET POTATOES

Use pure maple syrup for the best flavor.

MAKES 6 SERVINGS

1 cup water

1 (1-inch) piece lemon peel

½ cup packed brown sugar

¼ teaspoon salt

3 medium sweet potatoes, peeled and cut into
   ½-inch slices

¼ cup butter

1 cup coarsely chopped pecans

¼ cup maple syrup

1 tablespoon cornstarch

Whole pecans to garnish

Pour water into a pressure cooker and add lemon peel, brown sugar, and salt. Stir in sweet potatoes. Secure lid. Over high heat, bring pressure up to high. Reduce heat to maintain pressure and cook 4 minutes.

Release pressure according to manufacturer's directions. Remove lid. Using a slotted spoon, transfer sweet potatoes to a serving dish.

In a skillet, melt butter, heating until bubbly. Stir in chopped pecans. Add syrup and corn-starch, stirring to blend. Add to liquid in cooker and cook over medium heat until thickened. Ladle over sweet potatoes. Garnish with whole pecans.

COOK'S NOTE: Select firm potatoes with smooth surfaces that are unblemished. It is best to look for evenly shaped potatoes for uniform cooking.

(BEANS)

BEAN AND LENTIL COOKING TIMES

Type of Beans	Minutes	Pressure
Black-eyed peas	10	high
Garbanzo beans	20	high
Kidney beans	12	high
Lentils	10	high
Lima beans	10	high
Michigan beans	12	high
Navy beans	15	high
Peas	10	high
Pinto beans	12	high
Turtle beans (black beans)	15	high

Conventional Soaking

Soak dried peas or beans overnight. Measure beans, place in a bowl, add water in twice the amount of the measured beans and 1 teaspoon salt. Let stand overnight or at least 6 hours. Drain, then cook as directed.

Pressure-Cooker Soaking (Quick Soaking)

Pour 4 cups water, 1 teaspoon salt, and 1 cup dried peas or beans into pressure cooker. Secure lid. Over high heat, bring pressure up to high. Reduce heat to maintain pressure and cook 2 minutes. Quickly reduce pressure by running cold running water over cooker. Remove lid. Drain peas or beans, then cook as directed.

Because beans are starchy and the starches can scorch, always use a heat diffuser between the pressure cooker and heat source after pressure is reached.

Allow 3 cups liquid for each 1 cup of soaked beans (see opposite). Add 1 tablespoon oil to the cooking water. This prevents excessive starchy foam. Allow steam to slowly reduce at the end of the cooking cycle; beans need the extra steam time and will improve in texture.

BOSTON BAKED BEANS

Great for barbecues and picnics, this dish will soon become a family favorite.

MAKES 6 SERVINGS

1 cup white beans, soaked
6 slices bacon, finely diced
1 large onion, finely diced
2 large garlic cloves, crushed
1½ cups tomato sauce
1 cup chicken broth
2 tablespoons dark molasses
1 teaspoon Dijon mustard
1 large bay leaf
1 tablespoon light brown sugar
½ teaspoon ground ginger
1 teaspoon dried thyme
1½ teaspoons salt
Dash crushed red pepper flakes

Drain beans and set aside. Cook bacon in a pressure cooker over medium heat until crisp. Add onion and garlic and sauté 2 minutes, scraping bottom of cooker with a wooden spoon to loosen any browned bits. Stir in remaining ingredients, including beans. Secure lid. Over high heat, bring pressure up to high. Reduce heat to medium to maintain pressure and insert a heat diffuser between pressure cooker and heat. Cook 12 minutes.

Release pressure according to manufacturer's directions. Remove lid. Discard bay leaf. Stir well.

▢▢▢

CUBAN BEANS

This Cuban bean dish is great as a side with chicken or pork dishes.

MAKES 6 SERVINGS

1 cup black beans, soaked

2 slices bacon, finely diced

3 tablespoons olive oil

1 large onion, finely diced

4 garlic cloves, crushed

1 small red bell pepper, finely diced

2 tablespoons apple cider vinegar

2 cups chicken broth

½ cup tomato sauce

Dash Tabasco sauce

1 tablespoon light brown sugar

¼ cup finely chopped fresh cilantro

Drain beans and set aside. Cook bacon with oil in a pressure cooker over medium heat until crisp. Add onion, garlic, and bell pepper and sauté 3 minutes, scraping bottom of cooker with a

wooden spoon to loosen any browned bits. Stir in beans and remaining ingredients, except cilantro. Secure lid. Over high heat, bring pressure up to high. Reduce heat to medium to maintain pressure and insert a heat diffuser between pressure cooker and heat. Cook 12 minutes.

Release pressure according to manufacturer's directions. Remove lid. Stir in cilantro.

▢▢▢

FAVA BEANS WITH VEGETABLES

Fava beans are a spring vegetable and are worth waiting for. The bean has a rich delicate flavor. They can be purchased in large quantities, blanched, and frozen for use during the year.

MAKES 6 SERVINGS

3 pounds fresh fava beans in the pods

3 tablespoons olive oil

1 small onion, finely diced

2 garlic cloves, crushed

2 large carrots, coarsely diced

1 large fennel bulb, trimmed and finely diced

1 cup chicken broth

1 tablespoon fresh lemon juice

1 teaspoon salt

½ cup minced fresh parsley

3 tablespoons butter

Slit side of each fava bean pod and remove the beans. Set beans aside.

Heat oil in a pressure cooker over medium heat. Add onion and sauté 2 minutes. Add garlic and carrots and sauté 2 minutes. Stir in fava beans. Add remaining ingredients, except parsley and butter. Secure lid. Over high heat, bring pressure up to medium. Reduce heat to medium to maintain pressure and cook 3 minutes.

Release pressure according to manufacturer's directions. Remove lid. Drain beans and transfer to a serving bowl. Stir in parsley and butter. Serve as a side dish.

MIDDLE EASTERN LENTILS WITH CARAMELIZED ONION

The lentil is part of the legume family and frequently found in recipes of Middle Eastern and Indian origin. Lentils are available dried in supermarkets and readily available in brown or yellow colors.

MAKES 6 SERVINGS

2 cups lentils, soaked

2 tablespoons olive oil

1 small onion, finely diced

4 garlic cloves, crushed

¾ cup long-grain white rice

½ teaspoon dried ground allspice

1½ teaspoons salt

⅛ teaspoon freshly ground black pepper

4 cups chicken broth

Caramelized Onion

1 tablespoon olive oil

1 small onion, sliced fine

½ teaspoon sugar

⅛ teaspoon salt

Dash freshly ground black pepper

Drain lentils and set aside. Heat oil in a pressure cooker over medium heat. Add onion and garlic and sauté 3 minutes. Add lentils, rice, allspice, salt, pepper, and chicken broth. Stir well. Secure lid. Over high heat, bring pressure up to high. Reduce heat to medium to maintain pressure and cook 8 minutes.

Release pressure according to manufacturer's directions. Remove lid.

To make Caramelized Onion: Heat oil in a skillet over medium heat. Add onion and sugar and sauté over medium heat 5 minutes, stirring frequently. Season with salt and pepper.

Transfer lentils to a serving bowl and gently toss in onion mixture. Serve as a side dish.

GARBANZO BEANS

Dried garbanzo beans, also known as chickpeas, are firmer, nuttier in flavor, and sweeter than the canned ones. They can be added to soups, stews, or salads, or used to make a delicious Hummus (page 19).

MAKES 4 CUPS

1 pound (2 cups) garbanzo beans (chickpeas)
4 cups water or chicken broth
1 teaspoon salt
⅛ teaspoon freshly ground white pepper

Place beans in a bowl with 6 cups water. Let stand 4 hours. Drain.

In a pressure cooker, combine beans, 4 cups water, salt, and pepper. Stir well. Secure lid. Over high heat, bring pressure up to high. Reduce heat to medium to maintain pressure and insert a heat diffuser between pressure cooker and heat. Cook 20 minutes.

Release pressure according to manufacturer's directions. Remove lid. Stir beans and let stand 2 minutes. Drain through a colander.

COOK'S NOTE: Garbanzo beans may be frozen up to 3 months. Thaw in refrigerator.

(PASTA)

PASTA COOKING TIMES

Type of Pasta	Minutes	Pressure
Cavatelli	18	high
Egg noodles	7	med-high
Elbow macaroni	7	med-high
Fresh noodles	5	med-high
Macaroni	8	high
Ravioli	4	med-high
Spaghetti	8	high
Spaghetti (thin)	7	high
Spinach noodles	6	med-high
Tortellini	5	med-high

Pasta is wonderful when prepared in a pressure cooker.

Be sure ingredients do not exceed half the capacity of the cooker. Always add 2 tablespoons oil to the cooking liquid to minimize the starchy foam that develops during cooking. Allow steam to reduce slowly at the end of the cooking cycle. Use a heat diffuser on the burner after pressure is reached.

COUSCOUS WITH HERBS

Couscous is a tiny pasta used frequently in North Africa. Available in whole wheat or regular, it is great with saucy stews.

MAKES 6 SERVINGS

4 tablespoons olive oil

1 small onion, finely diced

1 garlic clove, crushed

1 teaspoon dried mint flakes

1 teaspoon salt

1/8 teaspoon freshly ground white pepper

1 (12-ounce) box couscous

3 1/2 cups chicken broth or water

2 teaspoons fresh lemon juice

Heat 2 tablespoons of the oil in a pressure cooker over medium heat. Add onion and garlic and sauté 2 minutes. Add remaining ingredients, except lemon juice and the remaining 2 tablespoons olive oil. Secure lid. Over high heat, bring pressure up to high. Reduce heat to medium to maintain pressure and insert a heat diffuser between pressure cooker and heat. Cook 2 minutes.

Release pressure under cold running water. Remove lid. Stir in lemon juice and remaining olive oil.

FETTUCCINE WITH FENNEL AND SPINACH

Fennel is a vegetable with a celerylike stalk and an anise flavor. It is bright green in color and has feathery foliage on the ends of the stalks and large bulbs. It is frequently used in Italian dishes.

MAKES 6 SERVINGS

3 tablespoons olive oil

1 large onion, coarsely diced

3 garlic cloves, crushed

1/4 large red bell pepper, seeded and coarsely diced

4 cups chicken broth

1 large fresh fennel bulb, trimmed and thinly sliced

1 pound fettuccine

1 teaspoon salt

1/8 teaspoon freshly ground black pepper

1/4 cup finely chopped fresh parsley

1/2 cup pitted medium black olives

3 tablespoons grated fontinella cheese

Heat oil in a pressure cooker over medium heat. Add onion and sauté 2 minutes. Stir in garlic and bell pepper. Add broth, fennel, fettuccine, salt, and black pepper. Secure lid. Over high heat, bring pressure up to high. Reduce heat to medium to maintain pressure and insert a heat diffuser between pressure cooker and heat. Cook 6 minutes.

Release pressure according to manufacturer's directions. Remove lid. Stir in parsley and olives. Transfer to a serving platter and top with cheese.

PASTA FAGIOLI WITH SAUSAGE

Italian sausage is readily available at most deli and meat counters. It comes in two varieties. The sweet Italian sausage is seasoned with peppers, fennel, and garlic. The hot Italian sausage is flavored with hot red peppers.

MAKES 6 SERVINGS

1 cup white beans, soaked

4 tablespoons olive oil

2 medium onions, coarsely diced

4 garlic cloves, crushed

½ cup finely chopped fresh parsley

2 large carrots, cut into 1-inch-thick slices

1 medium red bell pepper, sliced

⅛ teaspoon freshly ground black pepper

Pinch crushed red pepper flakes

½ teaspoon salt

1 teaspoon ground fennel

2 cups penne or ziti

1½ pounds sweet Italian sausage, cut into 2-inch pieces

1 (15-ounce) can diced tomatoes with sauce

2 cups chicken broth

⅓ cup half-and-half

¼ cup seasoned bread crumbs

¼ cup freshly grated Parmesan cheese

Drain beans and set aside. Heat oil in a pressure cooker over medium heat. Add onions and sauté until limp. Stir in garlic, parsley, carrots, and bell pepper. Add beans and remaining ingredients, except half-and-half, bread crumbs, and cheese. Secure lid. Over high heat, bring pressure up to high. Reduce heat to medium to maintain pressure and insert a heat diffuser between pressure cooker and heat. Cook 10 minutes.

Release pressure according to manufacturer's directions. Remove lid. Stir well. Stir in half-and-half and bread crumbs. Cover and let stand 3 minutes. Stir once again. Transfer to a large pasta bowl and sprinkle cheese over top.

❑ ❑ ❑

PASTA WITH FRESH VEGETABLES

The process of interrupting the cooking process is used in this recipe. Many recipes call for this process to ensure that vegetables are cooked to perfection.

MAKES 6 SERVINGS

3 tablespoons olive oil

2 tablespoons pine nuts

1 large leek (white part only), rinsed and sliced

3 garlic cloves, thinly sliced

3 cups ziti pasta

2 cups chicken broth

2 large potatoes, peeled and cut into 1-inch cubes

2 large carrots, cut into 2-inch pieces

1 medium red bell pepper, thickly sliced into strips

1 (15-ounce) can chopped tomatoes in sauce

1 teaspoon dried basil

1½ teaspoons salt

⅛ teaspoon freshly ground black pepper

1 (10-ounce) bag fresh spinach, chopped

2 cups fresh green beans, ends removed

1 cup shaved Parmesan cheese

Heat oil in a pressure cooker over medium heat. Add pine nuts and sauté until golden. Remove with a slotted spoon and set aside. Add leek and garlic and sauté 3 minutes. Add ziti, chicken broth, potatoes, carrots, bell pepper, tomatoes, basil, salt, and black pepper and stir well. Secure lid. Over high heat, bring pressure up to high. Reduce heat to medium to maintain pressure and insert a heat diffuser between pressure cooker and heat. Cook 6 minutes.

Release pressure according to manufacturer's directions. Remove lid. Stir in spinach and green beans. Secure lid. Over high heat, bring pressure up to high. Reduce heat to medium to maintain pressure and insert a heat diffuser between pressure cooker and heat. Cook 2 minutes.

Release pressure under cold running water. Remove lid. Stir in pine nuts. Transfer to a large pasta bowl. Sprinkle half of the cheese over top and serve the rest of the cheese at the table.

PENNE WITH GORGONZOLA

Gorgonzola cheese is also known as Dolcelatte. It is soft with blue veins running throughout the cheese. The imported Gorgonzola is smoother and milder in flavor, and preferred to domestic Gorgonzola.

4 slices bacon, finely diced

1 medium onion, coarsely diced

4 garlic cloves, crushed

1 pound penne pasta

4 cups chicken broth

1 teaspoon salt

Dash crushed red pepper flakes

1 teaspoon dried sage

3 cups broccoli florets

¼ cup minced fresh parsley

¼ pound crumbled Gorgonzola

¼ cup half-and-half

Cook bacon in a pressure cooker over medium heat until crisp. Stir in onion and garlic and sauté 2 minutes. Add pasta, chicken broth, salt, pepper flakes, and sage. Stir well. Secure lid. Over high heat, bring pressure up to high. Reduce heat to medium to maintain pressure and insert a heat diffuser between pressure cooker and heat. Cook 7 minutes.

Release pressure according to manufacturer's directions. Remove lid. Stir broccoli into the pasta. Secure lid. Over high heat, bring pressure up to high. Reduce heat to medium to maintain pressure and insert a heat diffuser between pressure cooker and heat. Cook 2 minutes.

Release pressure under cold running water. Remove lid. Stir in parsley, cheese, and half-and-half. Transfer to a large pasta bowl and serve hot.

⬚ ⬚ ⬚

SPAGHETTI WITH PESTO AND RED PEPPERS

Pesto is a sauce made with fresh basil, garlic, pine nuts, and Parmesan cheese. Consider using it as a sandwich spread with chicken.

MAKES 6 SERVINGS

Sauce

3 tablespoons olive oil

¼ cup pine nuts

2 garlic cloves, crushed

½ large red bell pepper, sliced into medium strips

½ cup finely chopped fresh basil

2 teaspoons freshly grated Parmesan cheese

8 ounces thin spaghetti

6 cups water

1½ teaspoons salt

Dash crushed red pepper flakes

¼ cup freshly grated Parmesan cheese

Heat oil in a pressure cooker over medium heat. Add pine nuts and sauté until golden. Remove with a slotted spoon and set aside. Add garlic, bell pepper, and basil to the oil. Cook, stir-

ring, 1 minute. Transfer to a food processor or blender. Add pine nuts and Parmesan cheese. Process until blended but some texture remains. Set aside.

Combine spaghetti, water, and salt in a pressure cooker. Secure lid. Over high heat, bring pressure up to high. Reduce heat to medium to maintain pressure and insert a heat diffuser between pressure cooker and heat. Cook 6 minutes.

Release pressure according to manufacturer's directions. Remove lid. Drain well. Transfer spaghetti to a large pasta bowl and toss in the basil mixture. Sprinkle pepper flakes and Parmesan cheese over top.

⬚ ⬚ ⬚

THREE-CHEESE MACARONI CASSEROLE

There are many types, designs, and lengths of tube pastas in the marketplace. It is always fun to vary the pasta shape for this dish.

MAKES 6 SERVINGS

1 tablespoon olive oil

1 medium onion, finely diced

2 garlic cloves, crushed

2 cups elbow macaroni

3 cups chicken broth

1 teaspoon salt

⅛ teaspoon freshly ground white pepper

½ teaspoon dried basil

1 cup half-and-half

1 cup (4 ounces) grated Cheddar cheese

1 cup (4 ounces) shredded mozzarella cheese

½ cup (2 ounces) grated fontinella cheese

½ cup seasoned bread crumbs

2 tablespoons butter, melted

Dash paprika

Heat oil in a pressure cooker over medium heat. Add onion and garlic and sauté 2 minutes. Add macaroni, chicken broth, salt, pepper, and basil. Secure lid. Over high heat, bring pressure up to high. Slide a heat diffuser between pressure cooker and heat. Reduce heat to medium to maintain pressure and cook 6 minutes.

Release pressure according to manufacturer's directions. Remove lid. Drain and place in an ovenproof baking dish. Preheat broiler. Stir half-and-half into macaroni. Stir well. Mix together cheeses, reserving 2 tablespoons for topping, and mix cheese mixture into macaroni.

Toss bread crumbs with butter. Sprinkle over top of casserole. Sprinkle reserved cheese and paprika over top of bread crumbs. Broil until top is golden brown.

ORZO GRATIN

Orzo is a tiny, rice-shaped pasta. It may be substituted in most dishes for rice.

MAKES 6 SERVINGS

2 tablespoons olive oil

1 small onion, finely chopped

1 garlic clove, crushed

½ medium red bell pepper, coarsely chopped

½ medium green bell pepper, coarsely chopped

1 teaspoon salt

⅛ teaspoon freshly ground white pepper

1 teaspoon dried basil

¼ teaspoon dried oregano

3½ cups chicken broth

1½ cups orzo

2 tablespoons grated fontinella cheese

½ cup (2 ounces) grated Muenster cheese

Heat oil in a pressure cooker over medium heat. Add onion and sauté 1 minute. Add garlic, bell peppers, and seasonings. Stir well. Add chicken broth and orzo. Secure lid. Over high heat, bring pressure up to high. Reduce heat to medium to maintain pressure and insert a heat diffuser between pressure cooker and heat. Cook 8 minutes.

Release pressure according to manufacturer's directions. Remove lid. Preheat broiler. Combine cheeses and reserve ¼ cup for topping. Blend in remaining cheeses and transfer orzo mixture to a heatproof serving dish. Sprinkle reserved cheese over top and brown under broiler until golden.

ORZO WITH VEGETABLES AND SAUSAGE

This one-dish meal is full of well-balanced Mediterranean flavors.

MAKES 6 SERVINGS

2 tablespoons olive oil

1 large onion, coarsely diced

2 garlic cloves, crushed

2 pounds sweet Italian sausage, cut into 1-inch pieces

4 cups chicken broth

2 carrots, coarsely diced

¼ cup finely chopped fresh parsley

½ medium red bell pepper, coarsely diced

1 teaspoon dried basil

1½ cups orzo

1½ teaspoons salt

Dash crushed red pepper flakes

2 cups broccoli florets

2 tablespoons grated fontinella cheese

Heat oil in a pressure cooker over medium heat. Add onion and sauté 2 minutes. Stir in garlic and sausage and cook 1 minute. Combine remaining ingredients, except broccoli and cheese. Secure lid. Over high heat, bring pressure up to high. Insert a heat diffuser between pressure cooker and heat. Reduce pressure to medium to maintain pressure and cook 6 minutes.

Release pressure under cold running water. Remove lid. Stir in broccoli. Secure lid. Over high heat, bring pressure up to medium. Reduce heat to medium to maintain pressure and insert a heat diffuser between pressure cooker and heat. Cook 2 minutes.

Release pressure under cold running water and remove lid. Stir well. Transfer to a serving bowl and gently toss in the cheese.

□ □ □

FETTUCCINE WITH PARSLEY BUTTER

Pasta can be cooked in a pressure cooker just until tender to the bite if cooking times are followed correctly.

MAKES 6 SERVINGS

2 tablespoons olive oil

½ pound fettuccine

3 cups chicken broth or water

1 teaspoon salt

¼ teaspoon freshly ground white pepper

½ teaspoon dried summer savory, crushed

¼ cup butter, at room temperature

¼ cup chopped fresh parsley

¼ cup grated fontinella or Parmesan cheese

Heat oil in a pressure cooker over high heat. Stir fettuccine into oil. Add broth, salt, pepper, and savory. Secure lid. Over high heat, bring pressure up to high. Reduce heat to medium to maintain pressure and insert a heat diffuser between pressure cooker and heat. Cook 8 minutes.

Release pressure according to manufacturer's directions. Remove lid. Drain fettuccine through a colander and return to cooker. Add butter and parsley, mixing gently until fettuccine is well coated. Pour into a serving bowl. Sprinkle with cheese.

VARIATION Short egg noodles may be substituted in this delicate creamy dish.

NOODLES ALFREDO

Serve this marvelous creamy noodle dish as a main dish or side dish.

MAKES 6 SERVINGS

2 slices bacon, cut into 1-inch pieces

2 tablespoons olive oil

1 leek (white part only), rinsed and minced

1 garlic clove, crushed

1 carrot, coarsely diced

2 cups egg noodles

1½ cups chicken broth

1½ cups water

8 cherry tomatoes, cut into halves and seeds removed

1 teaspoon salt

⅛ teaspoon freshly ground white pepper

½ teaspoon dried leaf tarragon

1 cup frozen green peas

⅓ cup whipping cream or yogurt

⅓ cup freshly grated Parmesan cheese

3 tablespoons butter

2 tablespoons chopped fresh parsley to garnish

Sauté bacon with oil in a pressure cooker over medium heat until crisp. Add leek, garlic, and carrot and sauté 1 minute. Stir in noodles, broth, water, tomatoes, salt, pepper, and tarragon. Mix thoroughly. Secure lid. Over high heat, bring pressure up to high. Reduce heat to medium to maintain pressure and insert a heat diffuser between pressure cooker and heat. Cook 8 minutes.

Release pressure according to manufacturer's directions. Remove lid. Stir noodle mixture. Drain in a colander and return noodles to cooker. Stir in peas, cream, cheese, and butter. Cook over medium heat 1 minute, stirring. Transfer to a serving platter and garnish with parsley.

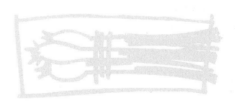

GRITS WITH BACON

Grits could be ground corn, oats, or rice, but here grits from dried hominy, or hominy grits, is used.

MAKES 6 SERVINGS

2 slices bacon, finely diced

2 tablespoons canola oil

1 small onion, finely diced

1 cup hominy grits

3 cups chicken broth or water

1 teaspoon sugar

1 teaspoon salt

⅛ teaspoon freshly ground white pepper

2 tablespoons butter

Sauté bacon with oil in a pressure cooker over medium heat until almost crisp. Add onion and sauté, scraping bottom of pan to loosen any brown bits, 1 minute. Stir in remaining ingredients, except butter. Secure lid. Over high heat, bring pressure up to high. Reduce heat to medium to maintain pressure and insert a heat diffuser between pressure cooker and heat. Cook 15 minutes.

Release pressure according to manufacturer's directions. Remove lid. Stir butter into grits. Serve hot in a heatproof bowl.

POLENTA

Polenta is from the northern part of Italy. Traditionally it is eaten hot; however, it may be cooled, cut into squares, and fried. Serve with meat, poultry, vegetables, or a sauce.

MAKES 6 SERVINGS

3 ounces prosciutto or bacon, finely chopped

1 small onion, finely diced

2 cups cornmeal

6 cups chicken broth

1½ teaspoons salt

⅛ teaspoon freshly ground white pepper

2 tablespoons butter

¼ cup freshly grated Parmesan cheese

2 tablespoons grated fontinella Cheese

Cook prosciutto in a pressure cooker over medium heat 2 minutes. Stir in onion and cook 1 minute, scrapping bottom of cooker with a wooden spoon to loosen any browned bits. Add remaining ingredients, except cheeses. Secure lid. Over high heat, bring pressure up to high. Reduce heat to medium to maintain pressure and insert a heat diffuser between pressure cooker and heat. Cook 15 minutes.

Release pressure according to manufacturer's directions. Remove lid. Stir in cheese. Cover and let stand 5 minutes.

(RICE)

RICE COOKING TIMES

Type of Rice	Minutes	Pressure
Arborio rice	15	high
Basmati rice	7	medium-high
Converted rice	7	medium-high
Long-grain brown rice	15	high
Long-grain white rice	7	medium-high
Wild rice	25	high

Rice is fluffy and perfect when prepared in a pressure cooker. Always use the heat diffuser on the burner after pressure is reached, or starches from the rice will settle on the bottom and scorch. Allow 2¼ cups water or broth for each 1 cup of rice, along with 1 teaspoon salt and 1 tablespoon oil. Allow steam to reduce slowly at the end of the cooking cycle. Grains like the extra moisture, and improve in texture.

CONFETTI BASMATI RICE

Basmati, a rice from the Himalayas, is an aged, long-grain rice, which decreases the moisture content. It has a nutty flavor and is oh so delicious.
MAKES 6 SERVINGS

2 tablespoons olive oil

1 medium onion, finely diced

1 garlic clove, crushed

2 medium carrots, coarsely diced

¼ cup coarsely chopped fresh parsley

½ medium red bell pepper, coarsely diced

1½ cups basmati rice

½ teaspoon dried basil

1 bay leaf

4½ cups chicken broth

1 teaspoon fresh lemon juice

1 teaspoon salt

⅛ teaspoon freshly ground white pepper

2 tablespoons grated fontinella cheese

Heat olive oil in a pressure cooker over medium heat. Add onion and sauté 1 minute. Stir in garlic, carrots, parsley, bell pepper, and rice. Cook for 1 minute. Stir in remaining ingredients, except the cheese. Secure lid. Over high heat, bring pressure up to high. Reduce heat to medium to maintain pressure and insert a heat diffuser between cooker and heat. Cook 8 minutes.

Release pressure according to manufacturer's directions. Remove lid. Stir with a fork. Transfer to a serving bowl and sprinkle with cheese.

CREOLE-STYLE RICE WITH RED BEANS

Creole cooking is a combination of Spanish, French, and African cuisines. It is generally rich and creamy, and less spiced than the Cajun flavors of the region.

MAKES 6 SERVINGS

1 cup red beans, soaked
2 slices bacon, finely diced
1 large onion, coarsely diced
3 garlic cloves, crushed
1 large celery stalk, coarsely chopped
1 cup long-grain rice
4 cups chicken broth
¼ cup half-and-half
1 teaspoon dried Creole seasoning
1½ teaspoons salt
⅛ teaspoon freshly ground white pepper
2 tablespoons butter
Crusty bread to serve

Drain beans and set aside. Sauté bacon in a pressure cooker over medium heat until crisp. Add onion, garlic, and celery. Cook 3 minutes. Stir in beans and remaining ingredients, except butter and bread. Secure lid. Over high heat, bring pressure up to high. Reduce heat to medium to maintain pressure and insert a heat diffuser between cooker and heat. Cook 9 minutes.

Release pressure according to manufacturer's directions. Remove lid. Stir in butter until blended. Serve with bread.

INDIAN RICE WITH PEAS

Basmati rice is easily found in grocery stores and in Middle Eastern markets.

MAKES 6 SERVINGS

3 tablespoons corn oil
1 medium onion, finely diced
2 cups basmati rice
5 cups chicken broth
1½ teaspoons salt
½ teaspoon ground cardamom
1 small cinnamon stick
½ teaspoon ground cumin
¼ cup golden raisins
2 cups frozen green peas

Heat oil in a pressure cooker over medium heat. Add onion and sauté 3 minutes. Add rice, chicken broth, salt, cardamom, cinnamon, and cumin. Stir well. Secure lid. Over high heat, bring pressure up to high. Reduce heat to medium to maintain pressure and insert a heat diffuser between cooker and heat. Cook 8 minutes.

Release pressure according to manufacturer's directions. Remove lid. Stir in raisins and peas. Cover and let stand 2 minutes. Transfer to a serving bowl.

RISOTTO WITH FRESH TOMATOES AND CHEESE

Risotto cooks exceptionally well in a pressure cooker, eliminating the labor-intensive stirring of the conventional method. The results are deliciously tender.

MAKES 6 SERVINGS

3 tablespoons olive oil

1 large onion, finely diced

3 garlic cloves, crushed

2 carrots, coarsely diced

1½ cups arborio rice

5 cups chicken broth

1 teaspoon salt

⅛ teaspoon freshly ground white pepper

2 large tomatoes, seeded and cut into eighths

1 cup (4 ounces) grated part-skim milk mozzarella cheese

⅓ cup freshly grated Parmesan cheese

Heat oil in a pressure cooker over medium heat. Add onion, garlic, and carrots and sauté 2 minutes. Stir in rice. Add broth, salt, and pepper. Secure lid. Over high heat, bring pressure up to high. Reduce heat to medium to maintain pressure and insert a heat diffuser between cooker and heat. Cook 12 minutes.

Release pressure according to the manufacturer's directions. Remove lid. Stir in tomatoes and mozzarella cheese. Cover and let stand 5 minutes. Sprinkle with Parmesan cheese.

RISOTTO WITH MOREL MUSHROOMS AND ASPARAGUS

Morel mushrooms, nature's gift of late spring, are considered by many as one of the most savored mushrooms due to the smoky, earthy flavor. They are found fresh in the marketplace during early May. They are also available canned or dried and packaged.

MAKES 6 SERVINGS

1 (1-ounce) package dried morel mushrooms

1 cup warm water

2 tablespoons olive oil

4 green onions, coarsely diced

2 medium carrots, coarsely diced

1 garlic clove, crushed

1½ cups arborio rice

4 cups chicken broth

1½ teaspoons salt

⅛ teaspoon freshly ground white pepper

1 bay leaf

½ teaspoon dried tarragon

12 spears fresh asparagus, trimmed and cut into 2-inch pieces

1 teaspoon fresh lemon juice

2 tablespoons freshly grated Parmesan cheese

Soak mushrooms in warm water 30 minutes. Drain and rinse well. Water will be very sandy. Slice mushrooms into thirds and set aside.

Heat oil in a pressure cooker over medium heat. Add green onions, carrots, garlic, and morels and sauté 2 minutes. Add rice and stir well. Stir in broth, salt, pepper, bay leaf, and tarragon. Secure lid. Over high heat, bring pressure up to high. Reduce heat to medium to maintain pressure and insert a heat diffuser between cooker and heat. Cook 10 minutes.

Release pressure according to manufacturer's directions. Remove lid. Discard bay leaf. Stir in asparagus and lemon juice. Cover and cook over medium heat 2 minutes. Sprinkle with Parmesan cheese.

RISOTTO WITH TURKEY SAUSAGE AND RED PEPPERS

Arborio or risotto rice is a firm rice that becomes creamy during cooking. The Italian arborio rice is the favored rice for most risotto dishes.

MAKES 6 SERVINGS

3 tablespoons olive oil

1 medium onion, finely diced

2 garlic cloves, crushed

½ pound Italian turkey sausage

1½ cups arborio rice

5 cups chicken broth

1½ teaspoons salt

⅛ teaspoon freshly ground white pepper

1 teaspoon dried basil

1 large red bell pepper, thinly sliced

⅓ cup finely chopped fresh parsley

¼ cup freshly grated Parmesan cheese

Heat oil in a pressure cooker over medium heat. Add onion and garlic and sauté 2 minutes. Add sausage, stirring to break up meat, and cook until beginning to brown. Stir in rice, broth, salt, white pepper, basil, and bell pepper. Secure lid. Over high heat, bring pressure up to high. Insert a heat diffuser between cooker and heat. Reduce heat to medium to maintain pressure and insert a heat diffuser between cooker and heat. Cook 8 minutes.

Release pressure according to manufacturer's directions. Remove lid. Stir in parsley. Sprinkle with Parmesan cheese.

VARIATION Milanese Risotto: Add a pinch of saffron.

ITALIAN RISOTTO WITH VEGETABLES

The texture of this dish is creamy and deliciously satisfying.

MAKES 6 TO 8 SERVINGS

2 tablespoons olive oil

¼ pound pancetta or bacon, cut into 1-inch pieces

6 green onions, coarsely chopped

3 garlic cloves, crushed

1 small carrot, thinly sliced

¼ cup chopped fresh parsley

1 cup arborio rice

2¾ cups chicken broth or stock

½ cup tomato sauce

1 tablespoon fresh lemon juice

1 tablespoon light brown sugar

1 teaspoon salt

¼ teaspoon freshly ground white pepper

1 teaspoon dried rosemary

1 bay leaf

1 cup frozen green peas

½ cup grated fontinella or Parmesan cheese

Heat oil in a pressure cooker over medium heat. Add pancetta, green onions, garlic, carrot, and parsley and sauté 3 minutes. Stir in rice and cook 1 minute, stirring. Add broth, tomato sauce, lemon juice, brown sugar, salt, pepper, rosemary, and bay leaf. Stir well. Secure lid. Over high heat, bring pressure up to high. Reduce heat to medium to maintain pressure and insert a heat diffuser between cooker and heat. Cook 13 minutes.

Release pressure according to manufacturer's directions. Remove lid. Discard bay leaf. Using a wooden spoon, stir rice mixture well. Stir in peas. Cook, uncovered, over medium-high heat 1 minute. Ladle rice into a serving bowl and sprinkle with cheese.

WILD RICE WITH PINE NUTS AND RAISINS

Allspice gives the rice dish a fragrant complex flavor of cinnamon, nutmeg, and cloves.

MAKES 6 SERVINGS

2 tablespoons olive oil

¼ cup pine nuts

1 small onion, coarsely diced

¼ teaspoon dried allspice

1½ cups wild rice

1 teaspoon salt

⅛ teaspoon freshly ground white pepper

4 cups chicken broth

½ cup raisins

Heat oil in a pressure cooker over medium heat. Add pine nuts and cook until golden. Remove with a slotted spoon to a dish and set aside. Add onion and sauté 2 minutes. Add remaining ingredients, except pine nuts and raisins. Secure lid. Over high heat, bring pressure up to high. Reduce heat to medium to maintain pressure, and insert a heat diffuser between cooker and heat. Cook 11 minutes.

Release pressure according to manufacturer's directions. Remove lid. Stir in raisins and pine nuts. Cover and let stand 2 minutes, allowing the steam to plump the raisins.

BROWN RICE WITH FRESH VEGETABLES

This easy dish using both rice and vegetables is prepared in half the time that brown rice usually takes.

MAKES 6 TO 8 SERVINGS

¼ cup olive oil

½ medium onion, diced

2 large garlic cloves, crushed

¼ cup minced fresh parsley

1 large carrot, cut into bite-size pieces

1½ cups long-grain brown rice

1 teaspoon salt

¼ teaspoon freshly ground white pepper

1 teaspoon dried leaf thyme

1 bay leaf

3½ cups chicken broth or stock

2 tablespoons fresh lemon juice

½ pound broccoli, stems peeled and trimmed,
   cut into bite-size pieces

Heat oil in a pressure cooker over medium heat. Add onion, garlic, parsley, and carrot and sauté 3 minutes. Add rice, salt, pepper, thyme, and bay leaf. Stir and cook 1 minute. Add broth and lemon juice. Secure lid. Over high heat, bring pressure up to high. Reduce heat to medium to maintain pressure and insert a heat diffuser between cooker and heat. Cook 15 minutes.

Release pressure according to manufacturer's directions. Remove lid. Add broccoli to rice mixture. Secure lid. Over high heat, bring pressure up to high. Reduce heat to maintain pressure, and insert a heat diffuser between cooker and heat. Cook 1 minute.

Quickly release steam according to manufacturer's directions. Remove lid. Discard bay leaf. Using 2 large forks, toss broccoli and rice mixture and spoon into a serving dish.

COOK'S NOTE: Stirring rice into oil will retard the foaming of the starch in the cooker during cooking.

▨ ▨ ▨

PRESSURE-STEAMED RICE

A basic recipe, it can be used as a foil to spicy dishes, or seasoned as described in the variation if serving with grilled meats, fish, or chicken.

MAKES 6 SERVINGS

2 tablespoons olive oil

1 cup long-grain white rice

2 cups beef or chicken broth or water

¾ teaspoon salt

2 tablespoons butter or olive oil

Dash freshly ground black pepper

Heat oil in a pressure cooker over medium heat. Stir rice into hot oil. Add broth and salt. Secure lid. Over high heat, bring pressure up to high. Reduce heat to medium to maintain pressure, and insert a heat diffuser between cooker and heat. Cook 8 minutes.

Release pressure according to manufacturer's directions. Remove lid. Add butter and pepper to rice. Toss to mix thoroughly. Serve hot.

VARIATION For a seasoned rice with international flair, select one of the following: 1 teaspoon dried dill weed, ½ teaspoon dried oregano, 1 teaspoon dried basil, or 1 teaspoon curry powder.

SAVORY RICE WITH BUTTERED PEAS

This colorful dish is good with almost any grilled meat or fish. It's a fool proof way to perfect rice.
MAKES 6 SERVINGS

3 tablespoons olive oil

2 green onions, minced

1 garlic clove, crushed

1 cup long-grain white rice

2 cups chicken broth or water

1 teaspoon salt

¼ teaspoon freshly ground white pepper

¼ teaspoon dried tarragon

3 tablespoons butter

1 cup frozen green peas, thawed

Heat oil in a pressure cooker over medium heat. Add green onions and garlic and sauté 1 minute. Stir in rice and cook 1 minute. Add chicken broth, salt, pepper, and tarragon. Secure lid. Over high heat, bring pressure up to high. Reduce heat to medium to maintain pressure, and insert a heat diffuser between cooker and heat. Cook 7 minutes.

Release pressure according to manufacturer's directions. Remove lid. Using a fork, add butter a little at a time and toss to blend with rice. Gently toss in peas.

VARIATION Experiment by using basmati rice or brown rice in this recipe. Refer to the rice chart for timing (page 175).

DESSERTS

Pressure cooking becomes sweet in this chapter filled with a mouthwatering array of lovely, traditional desserts.

Following these tested recipes, you will realize the heights pressure cooking can reach. Who would imagine creamy cheesecakes, lovely moist bread pudding with a velvety sauce, and lemon curd all cooked to perfection under pressure?

There are several cheesecake recipes that are rich, creamy, and delicious in flavor. The pan size required must fit inside your pressure cooker. Consider using the steamer basket insert that may have come with your unit. Simply line the basket with microwave-safe plastic wrap or foil, then proceed with the recipe.

PEAR BREAD PUDDING WITH VANILLA YOGURT SAUCE

There are a variety of pears in the produce department. Select one that has a smooth skin, no blemishes, and has a slight give. If the pears seem too firm, place them in a paper bag for 36 hours to ripen. Pears, unlike other fruit, improve in flavor over time.

MAKES 6 SERVINGS

2 cups half-and-half or evaporated milk

2 large eggs

¼ cup packed light brown sugar

¾ cup granulated sugar

2 large ripe pears, peeled, cored, and cut into
    1-inch cubes

1 teaspoon grated orange zest

1 teaspoon vanilla extract

4 cups 2-inch pieces rich cinnamon bread

1 cup almonds, toasted and coarsely chopped

1 (8-ounce) container vanilla-flavored yogurt mixed
    with 1 teaspoon granulated sugar

Prepare the harness illustrated on page 197. In a large bowl, combine half-and-half, eggs, brown sugar, granulated sugar, pears, orange zest, and vanilla. Mix well. Add bread and almonds and mix well. Let soak 5 minutes. Spoon mixture into a 7- or 8-inch ovenproof pan and cover with foil.

Pour 1 cup water into the pressure cooker and insert steam rack. Lift baking pan, using the harness, into the pressure cooker. Secure lid. Over high heat, bring pressure up to high. Reduce heat to medium to maintain pressure. Cook 18 minutes.

Release pressure according to manufacturer's directions. Remove lid. Allow steam to dissipate. Grasp the harness, and lift pudding out of the pressure cooker. Place onto a cooling rack. Cool 15 minutes. Spoon yogurt mixture into a serving bowl. Spoon bread pudding into serving dishes and place a dollop of yogurt on top.

❑ ❑ ❑

APPLE RUM CINNAMON BREAD PUDDING

Moist with apples and scented with spices, this pudding topped with a dollop of Chantilly Cream is heavenly. The recipe will quickly become a family favorite.

MAKES 6 TO 8 SERVINGS

½ cup butter, melted

1 cup half-and-half or milk

1 teaspoon rum flavoring

2 large eggs, lightly beaten

1 cup granulated sugar

½ cup packed light brown sugar

1½ teaspoons ground cinnamon

¼ teaspoon grated nutmeg

1 large Granny Smith or McIntosh apple, peeled
    and cut into 1-inch cubes

½ cup raisins

¾ cup chopped toasted walnuts (see Cook's Note,
    page 185)

8 cups (2-inch cubes) Italian or French bread

1½ cups water

Chantilly Cream (optional) to serve

2 cups whipping cream

⅓ cup powdered sugar, sifted

¼ teaspoon vanilla extract

Dash ground cinnamon

Butter an 8-inch round baking pan or steam basket from pressure cooker (page 6) with some of melted butter. If using steam basket, cover outside of basket with foil. Combine remaining butter, half-and-half, rum flavoring, eggs, sugars, cinnamon, and nutmeg in a bowl. Beat until thoroughly blended.

Combine apple, raisins, walnuts, and bread in a large bowl. Pour egg mixture over bread mixture. Toss until bread is well moistened and fruit is thoroughly mixed. Spoon mixture into prepared pan. Pour 1½ cups water into pressure cooker. Insert steam rack. Prepare foil harness (page 197). Place pan in center of harness and lower into pressure cooker. Fold harness to make a handle over bread pudding. Secure lid. Over high heat, bring pressure up to high. Reduce heat to maintain pressure and cook 12 minutes.

Release pressure according to manufacturer's directions. Remove lid. Lift pan from pressure cooker and place on a wire rack to cool.

Prepare Chantilly Cream (if using): Whip cream until it begins to thicken. Add powdered sugar, vanilla, and cinnamon. Whip 1 minute, or until soft peaks form. Spoon into a serving bowl and refrigerate until ready to serve.

Serve pudding hot or cold with Chantilly Cream (if using).

COOK'S NOTE: To toast nuts, preheat oven to 350 degrees F. Place nuts in a shallow baking pan and bake 7 to 8 minutes, or until golden and fragrant.

BLUEBERRY BREAD PUDDING

Serve pudding hot or cold with a dollop of Chantilly Cream (page 185), ice cream, or warm milk poured over the top.

MAKES 6 TO 8 SERVINGS

½ cup butter, melted

1 cup half-and-half or milk

1½ cups sugar

2 large eggs, lightly beaten

1 teaspoon vanilla extract

½ teaspoon ground nutmeg

2 cups blueberries

8 cups (2-inch cubes) Italian or French bread

Butter an 8-inch round baking pan or steam basket from pressure cooker (page 6). If using steam basket, line basket, cover outside of basket with foil.

Combine butter, half-and-half, sugar, eggs, vanilla, and nutmeg in a bowl. Beat until smooth. Stir in blueberries. Place bread cubes into a large bowl. Pour fruit mixture over bread cubes. Toss until bread is well moistened. Spoon mixture into prepared pan.

Pour 1½ cups water into pressure cooker. Insert steam rack. Prepare foil harness (page 197). Place pan in center of harness, lower into cooker, and loop top of harness into a handle. Secure lid. Over high heat, bring pressure up to high.

Reduce heat to maintain pressure and cook 15 minutes. Release pressure according to manufacturer's directions. Remove lid. Lift pan from cooker and place on wire rack to cool.

VARIATION The pudding may be prepared with fresh or frozen blueberries. If frozen blueberries are used, drain excess liquid after thawing.

□ □ □

SOUTH PACIFIC BREAD PUDDING WITH PINEAPPLE SAUCE

The tropical flavors of coconut and pineapple are refreshing and delicious. The Pineapple Sauce is great as an ice-cream topping, too!

MAKES 6 TO 8 SERVINGS

1 (16-ounce) can cream of coconut

1 cup half-and-half

3 large eggs, beaten

½ cup butter, melted

¾ cup sugar

1½ teaspoons rum flavoring

¼ teaspoon grated nutmeg

1 (20-ounce) can pineapple chunks, drained and juice reserved

1¼ cups toasted coconut (see Cook's Note, page 187)

8 cups (2-inch cubes) Italian or French bread

Pineapple Sauce

¼ cup butter

¾ cup sugar

1 (20-ounce) can crushed pineapple, undrained, plus reserved pineapple juice from pudding recipe, to measure 3 cups

½ teaspoon grated orange zest

1 tablespoon plus 2 teaspoons cornstarch mixed with ¼ cup pineapple juice

Butter an 8-inch round baking pan or steam basket from pressure cooker (page 6). If using steam basket, cover outside of basket with foil.

Combine cream of coconut, half-and-half, eggs, butter, sugar, rum flavoring, and nutmeg in a bowl. Beat thoroughly. Mix in pineapple and 1 cup of the coconut. Place bread in a large bowl. Pour creamed mixture over bread. Toss until bread is well moistened and mixed. Spoon mixture into prepared pan or basket.

Pour 1½ cups water into pressure cooker. Prepare foil harness (page 197). Place pan in harness and lower into cooker. If using basket, place a metal measuring cup in bottom of cooker and set steam basket, filled with bread pudding, on measuring cup. Secure lid. Over high heat, bring pressure up to high. Reduce heat to maintain pressure and cook 12 minutes.

Release pressure according to manufacturer's directions. Remove lid. Remove pan from pressure cooker and place on wire rack to cool. Sprinkle with remaining coconut.

Prepare Pineapple Sauce: In a saucepan, combine butter, sugar, pineapple, 3 cups pineapple juice, and orange zest. Mix well and bring to a boil. Stir cornstarch mixture and add to pineapple mixture. Cook, stirring, until thickened. Serve pudding warm, or chilled with sauce.

COOK'S NOTES: To toast coconut, scatter evenly on a baking sheet. Preheat oven to 375 degrees F. Bake 4 minutes or until golden brown.

The quality of the bread is extremely important in all bread pudding recipes and should not be overlooked.

▢ ▢ ▢

CHOCOLATE BREAD PUDDING WITH CHOPPED PECANS

If a richer, more pronounced chocolate is preferred, substitute the milk chocolate chips with dark sweet chocolate chips. Any toasted nut, such as almonds or walnuts, may also be substituted.

MAKES 8 SERVINGS

4 cups rich white bread, torn into pieces
1 cup half-and-half

¼ cup light brown sugar
½ cup granulated sugar
2 tablespoons unsweetened cocoa powder
1 teaspoon rum flavoring or vanilla extract
2 large eggs, beaten
¼ teaspoon ground cinnamon
½ cup pecans, toasted
½ cup milk chocolate chips
Chocolate Sauce (page 188) to serve

Place bread pieces into a large bowl. Beat half-and-half, sugars, cocoa powder, flavoring, eggs, and cinnamon in a medium bowl until blended. Pour over bread and toss until bread is coated. Let stand 4 minutes. Mix one more time.

In the meantime, toast pecans in a preheated 375 degree F oven 5 minutes. Cool and coarsely chop. Toss into the bread mixture along with the chocolate chips. Spoon bread mixture into a 7- or 8-inch ovenproof pan. Cover securely with foil.

Pour 1 cup water into the pressure cooker and insert steam rack. Prepare harness on page 197 and place it around the pan. Lift into the pressure cooker and secure lid. Over high heat, bring pressure up to high. Reduce heat to medium to maintain pressure. Cook for 15 minutes.

Release pressure according to manufacturer's directions. Remove lid. Lift pudding out of pan and place on cooling rack 10 minutes. Serve cool or warm with a little Chocolate Sauce.

CHOCOLATE SAUCE

Delicious rich-flavored sauce is perfect for ice-cream desserts, bread-pudding toppings, cake, or any dessert. It makes a great hostess gift.

MAKES 10 SERVINGS

1 cup half-and-half

⅛ teaspoon ground cinnamon

Dash nutmeg

½ cup sugar

½ cup dark corn syrup

10 ounces dark sweet chocolate, coarsely grated

1 teaspoon vanilla extract

In a 1-quart saucepan, combine half-and-half, cinnamon, nutmeg, sugar, and corn syrup. Bring to a gentle boil and cook over medium heat 2 minutes. Stir well and remove from heat. Add chocolate and stir until chocolate melts and syrup is formed. Stir in vanilla. Sauce may be bottled and stored for up to a month in the refrigerator.

VARIATION Dark sweet chocolate may be substituted with milk chocolate for a more delicate-flavored sauce.

COCONUT RICE PUDDING

There are many rice variations in the marketplace. A favorite among cooks is the medium-grain rice from Louisiana. The rice is not as starchy, is moister, and is fairly fluffy.

MAKES 8 SERVINGS

½ teaspoon salt

1 cup medium-grain white rice

1 cup sweetened shredded coconut

½ cup coconut milk

¾ cup sugar

2 large egg yolks

1 large egg

1 teaspoon coconut flavoring

1 tablespoon butter

1 (8-ounce) can pineapple chunks

In a pressure cooker combine 4 cups water, salt, and rice. Secure lid. Over high heat, bring pressure up to high. Reduce heat to medium to maintain pressure and insert a heat diffuser between cooker and heat. Cook 16 minutes.

Release pressure according to manufacturer's directions. Remove lid. Set aside, loosely covered.

Preheat oven to 350 degrees F. Place coconut on a baking sheet and toast 2 to 3 minutes, or until golden. In a bowl, combine coconut milk, sugar, egg yolks, egg, coconut flavoring, and butter. Whisk until blended. Stir in 1 cup hot rice and pour mixture into the pressure cooker and stir well, until blended. Place over medium heat and cook, stirring, 3 minutes. Pour into small ramekins or serving bowls. Top with toasted coconut. Drain pineapple and place one piece in center of each pudding. Cover each serving with plastic wrap and refrigerate until chilled.

VARIATION Vanilla Rice Pudding: Substitute vanilla extract for coconut flavoring and milk for coconut milk. Omit shredded coconut. Sprinkle with a mixture of 1 tablespoon sugar and 1/8 teaspoon ground cinnamon.

GREEK RICE PUDDING WITH CINNAMON SUGAR TOPPING

Greek rice pudding is everyone's favorite. The spices are representative of Greece. The flavors of cinnamon, nutmeg, and orange are found in most desserts.

MAKES 6 SERVINGS

1 teaspoon salt

1 cup long-grain white rice

Peel of 1 orange (orange part only), cut into strips

1/2 cup half-and-half

3 large egg yolks

1 cup granulated sugar

Dash freshly grated nutmeg

2 tablespoons light brown sugar

1/2 teaspoon ground cinnamon or to taste

Heat 4 cups water and salt in a pressure cooker. Stir in rice and orange peel. Secure lid. Over high heat, bring pressure up to high. Reduce heat to medium to maintain pressure and insert a heat diffuser between cooker and heat. Cook 18 minutes.

Release pressure according to manufacturer's directions. Remove lid. Discard orange peel. Stir well.

Whisk together half-and-half, egg yolks, 3/4 cup of the granulated sugar, and nutmeg. Ladle 1 cup of hot rice into the egg mixture. Stir well and transfer mixture into the pressure cooker. Over medium heat, cook 2 minutes, stirring. Transfer rice pudding into 6 (6-ounce) ramekins. Cover. Cool to room temperature. Mix together brown sugar, remaining 1/4 cup granulated sugar, and cinnamon. Sprinkle over top of each rice pudding. Refrigerate until chilled. (Additional cinnamon sugar may be added when serving.)

PUMPKIN CRÈME BRÛLÉE WITH TOASTED PECANS

There is a great difference in flavor between purchased grated nutmeg and freshly grated nutmeg. The flavor of freshly grated is more delicate and fragrant. There are a variety of graters and planes available in cook's departments, and they are relatively inexpensive. A nutmeg grater is a must for all cooks.

MAKES 6 SERVINGS

1½ **cups half-and-half**

½ **cup canned pumpkin**

2 **large eggs**

½ **cup plus** 1 **tablespoon granulated sugar**

⅛ **teaspoon ground cinnamon**

⅛ **teaspoon ground ginger**

Pinch freshly grated nutmeg

1 **cup pecans, toasted**

¼ **cup light brown sugar**

Place steam rack into pressure cooker along with 1 cup water. Have 6 ramekins ready.

In a bowl, mix together half-and-half, pumpkin, eggs, ½ cup granulated sugar, cinnamon, ginger, and nutmeg.

Preheat over to 350 degrees F. Place pecans on a baking sheet and toast 5 minutes, or until fragrant. Coarsely chop and mix with brown sugar and 1 tablespoon granulated sugar. Place 1 tablespoon of the nut mixture in the bottom of each ramekin. Ladle the pumpkin mixture over the top of the nuts, filling ramekins three-fourths full. Tightly cover top of each ramekin with a square of foil.

Place the ramekins on the steam rack, forming a pyramid. Secure lid. Over high heat, bring pressure up to high. Reduce heat to medium to maintain pressure and cook 8 minutes.

Release pressure according to manufacturer's directions. Remove lid. Allow steam to dissipate. Carefully remove ramekins onto a cooling rack. Cool and refrigerate, covered, up to 3 days.

◻ ◻ ◻

APPLESAUCE

You'll never buy applesauce again once you've tried this recipe. The cinnamon hearts add a lovely blush and a spicy flavor.

MAKES 6 SERVINGS

2 **pounds McIntosh or Granny Smith apples, peeled, cored, and cut into** ½-**inch slices**

1 **cup canned apple juice**

2 **tablespoons fresh lemon juice**

¼ **cup granulated sugar**

⅓ **cup packed brown sugar**

½ **teaspoon grated nutmeg**

¼ **teaspoon ground cinnamon**

⅓ **cup red cinnamon candy (optional)**

In a pressure cooker, combine apples, apple juice, lemon juice, sugars, nutmeg, cinnamon, and candy (if using). Secure lid. Over high heat, bring pressure up to medium-high. Reduce heat to maintain pressure and cook 4 minutes.

Release pressure according to manufacturer's directions. Remove lid. Drain apples through a colander. Place apples in a food processor, blender, or food mill and process until smooth. Serve warm or cold. Store in airtight container in refrigerator up to 3 days.

LEMON CURD

This tangy English lemon curd is refreshing and delicious after a meal. Served with blueberries or strawberries, it is pretty as well.

MAKES 6 SERVINGS

3 large eggs

1 egg yolk

¼ cup butter, at room temperature

¾ cup fresh lemon juice

1 teaspoon grated lemon zest

1⅓ cups superfine sugar

Butter 6 custard cups or ramekins. Combine eggs, egg yolk, butter, lemon juice, lemon zest, and sugar in a bowl. Mix gently but thoroughly. Pour ½ cup of mixture into each cup. Cover with microwave-proof plastic wrap or foil.

Pour 2 cups water into pressure cooker. Insert steam basket. Place cups in basket, pyramid style, beginning with three cups at bottom. Secure lid.

Over high heat, bring pressure up to medium-high. Reduce heat to maintain pressure and cook 9 minutes.

Release pressure according to manufacturer's directions. Remove lid. Carefully remove cups to a wire rack. Remove plastic wrap. Using a tiny whisk or small fork, gently whisk filling. Refrigerate at least 4 hours. Serve chilled.

COOK'S NOTE: Superfine sugar can be easily made in the blender or food processor from regular granulated sugar.

FUDGY PEANUT BUTTER CHEESECAKE

What could be better than peanut butter and chocolate? This creamy peanutty cheesecake will be favored by all!
MAKES 6 TO 8 SERVINGS

Peanut Crust
1 cup ground toasted unsalted peanuts (see Cook's Note, page 185)
¼ cup packed light brown sugar
1 tablespoon unsweetened cocoa powder
3 tablespoons butter, melted

1 cup peanut butter
2 (8-ounce) packages cream cheese, softened
½ cup packed light brown sugar
½ cup powdered sugar, sifted
2 tablespoons cornstarch
2 large eggs
¼ cup sour cream
1 (12-ounce) package semisweet chocolate chips, melted
Whipped cream to decorate
Chocolate curls to decorate

Prepare crust: Combine peanuts, brown sugar, cocoa, and butter in a small bowl. Press into a 7-inch springform pan, covering bottom and 1 inch of sides. Set aside.

Using an electric mixer, blend peanut butter, cream cheese, sugars, and cornstarch together in a bowl until smooth. Beat in eggs, 1 at a time, and blend in sour cream. Pour in chocolate and blend on low speed until thoroughly mixed. Pour batter into crust. Cover with 2 layers of paper towels, top with foil, and crimp along edge to seal.

Pour 2 cups water into pressure cooker. Insert steam basket. Prepare foil harness (page 197). Place pan in harness and lower into cooker. Loop top of harness into a handle. Secure lid. Over high heat, bring pressure up to high. Reduce heat to maintain pressure and cook 22 minutes.

Release pressure according to manufacturer's directions. Remove lid. Lift pan from cooker and place on wire rack. Refrigerate at least 4 hours. Remove cover.

Decorate with whipped cream and chocolate curls.

COOK'S NOTE: Unsalted peanuts are available at supermarkets.

LEMON CHEESECAKE

Almonds and lemon are a delight together, as in this lemon-flavored cheesecake with an almond crust. Blueberries are great with this cheesecake.

MAKES 6 TO 8 SERVINGS

Almond Crust

1 cup toasted blanched almonds, ground

3 tablespoons granulated sugar

3 tablespoons butter, melted

Dash nutmeg

2 (8-ounce) packages cream cheese, softened

1⅓ cups powdered sugar, sifted

1 teaspoon grated lemon zest

2 tablespoons cornstarch

2 large eggs, at room temperature

⅓ cup fresh lemon juice

Prepare crust: Combine almonds, sugar, butter, and nutmeg in a mixing bowl. Blend thoroughly. Press into a 7-inch springform pan, covering bottom and 1 inch of sides. Set aside.

Using an electric mixer, blend cream cheese, powdered sugar, lemon zest, and cornstarch together in a bowl 1 minute. Beat in eggs, 1 at a time, beating thoroughly after each addition. Drizzle lemon juice into creamed mixture and beat at low speed until blended.

Pour batter into crust. Cover with 2 layers of paper towels, top with foil, and crimp along edge to seal. Pour 1 cup water into pressure cooker. In-sert steam rack. Prepare foil harness (page 197). Place pan in harness, folding top of harness into a handle, and lower into cooker. Secure lid. Over high heat, bring pressure up to high. Reduce heat to maintain pressure and cook 22 minutes.

Release pressure according to manufacturer's directions. Remove lid. Remove cheesecake and place on wire rack. Refrigerate at least 4 hours. Remove cover. Serve chilled.

COOK'S NOTE: Lemon zest is the yellow outer skin of the lemon, grated off with a traditional grater or with a gadget called a lemon zester. Be careful, however, not to dig into the white layer under the yellow skin. It will give a bitter flavor.

PUMPKIN CHEESECAKE

This autumn dessert is a favorite, filled with all the lovely spicy flavors of the season.

MAKES 6 SERVINGS

Pecan Crust

½ cup graham cracker crumbs

⅓ cup granulated sugar

½ cup toasted pecans, finely chopped
   (see Cook's Note, page 185)

½ teaspoon ground cinnamon

¼ cup butter, melted

2 (8-ounce) packages cream cheese, softened

1¼ cups powdered sugar

1 teaspoon grated orange zest

2 large eggs, at room temperature

1 cup canned pumpkin

2 tablespoons butter, at room temperature

3 tablespoons cornstarch

1 teaspoon ground cinnamon

½ teaspoon ground nutmeg

⅛ teaspoon ground ginger

Spiced Whipped Cream

1 cup whipping cream

3 tablespoons powdered sugar

⅛ teaspoon ground cinnamon

Prepare crust: Combine crumbs, sugar, pecans, cinnamon, and butter in a small bowl. Press crumbs into bottom of 7-inch springform pan. Set aside.

Using an electric mixer, beat cream cheese, sugar, and orange zest together 1 minute. Beat in eggs, 1 at a time, beating thoroughly after each addition. Beat in pumpkin, butter, cornstarch, cinnamon, nutmeg, and ginger, beating just until smooth.

Pour batter over crust. Cover with 2 layers of paper towels, top with foil, and crimp along edge of pan to seal.

Pour 1 cup water into pressure cooker. Insert steam basket. Prepare foil harness (page 197). Place pan in harness, lower into cooker, and loop top of harness into a handle. Secure lid. Over high heat, bring pressure up to high. Reduce heat to maintain pressure and cook 25 minutes.

Release pressure according to manufacturer's directions. Remove lid. Lift cheesecake from cooker and place on wire rack. Refrigerate at least 3 hours. Remove cover.

Prepare Spiced Whipped Cream: Using an electric mixer, beat cream in a medium bowl until it begins to thicken. Add powdered sugar and cinnamon and whip until thickened.

Serve whipped cream with cheesecake.

▫ ▫ ▫

DRIED FRUIT COMPOTE

Serve this wonderfully delicious compote in winter when good fresh fruit is unavailable. It makes a wonderful breakfast dish or light dessert.

MAKES 6 SERVINGS

1 cup golden raisins

1 (8-ounce) package dried apricots

1 (8-ounce) package dried peaches

1½ cups orange juice

⅔ cup sugar

1 cinnamon stick

4 whole cloves

In a pressure cooker, combine fruit, orange juice, sugar, and spices. Secure lid. Over high heat, bring pressure up to high. Reduce heat to maintain pressure and cook 3 minutes.

Release pressure according to manufacturer's directions. Remove lid. Continue cooking over medium heat 2 more minutes, stirring occasionally.

Store in a covered bowl in the refrigerator up to 1 week.

▫ ▫ ▫

FRESH PEAR CUPS WITH ZABAGLIONE CREAM AND RASPBERRIES

This delicate dessert is Italian in origin and deliciously beautiful to serve. Select firm pears, free of blemishes and soft spots. The Bosc pear works very well in this recipe; it has a sweet-tart flavor and holds its shape while cooking.
MAKES 6 SERVINGS

6 ripe pears, peeled

½ cup pear liqueur or Grand Marnier

1 cup sugar

4 large egg yolks

⅓ cup half-and-half or milk, mixed with 2 teaspoons cornstarch

2 cups fresh raspberries or blueberries

2 tablespoons raspberry liqueur

Cut pears in half horizontally (crosswise). Remove core and some pulp from bottom halves, leaving bottoms intact and sides ½ inch thick. Pear bottoms should resemble small cups. Eat pear tops or discard.

In a pressure cooker, combine pear liqueur, ¼ cup water, sugar, and pear bottoms. Secure lid. Over high heat, bring pressure up to high. Reduce heat to maintain pressure and cook 4 minutes.

Release pressure according to manufacturer's directions. Remove lid. Using a slotted spoon, transfer pears to a serving dish.

Whisk egg yolks in a small bowl. Whisk ¼ cup hot pear liquid into egg yolks, then pour egg mixture into liquid in cooker. Cook over medium heat, stirring frequently, until thickened and bubbles disappear. Add half-and-half mixture. Cook, stirring, 2 minutes, or until thickened. Spoon sauce into pear cups. Cover with plastic wrap and refrigerate. Combine raspberries and raspberry liqueur. Serve with raspberries sprinkled over filled pears.

STEAMED CHRISTMAS PUDDING

Forget about hours and hours of steaming Christmas pudding. This family favorite is completed in less than half the time, and the result is a pudding with a delicate, delicious texture and flavor that will delight everyone.

MAKES 8 TO 12 SERVINGS

1 cup toasted pecans, coarsely chopped (see Cook's Note, page 185)

1 cup candied red or green cherries

½ cup currants

½ cup mixed candied fruit

1½ cups all-purpose flour

½ cup corn oil

1½ cups powdered sugar, sifted

2 teaspoons grated orange zest

2 eggs

2 teaspoons baking powder

1 teaspoon ground cinnamon

½ teaspoon ground allspice

½ teaspoon grated nutmeg

3 tablespoons orange liqueur

¼ cup molasses

Orange Vanilla Sauce (optional)
1½ cups milk

1 cup sugar

2 tablespoons cornstarch

3 tablespoons butter

2 tablespoons orange liqueur

1 teaspoon vanilla extract

1 egg yolk

Combine pecans and fruit in a large bowl. Sprinkle with ½ cup of the flour, tossing until fruit is thoroughly coated. Set aside.

Using an electric mixer, beat oil, powdered sugar, and orange zest together 1 minute. Beat in eggs, 1 at a time, beating well after each addition. Combine remaining 1 cup flour, baking powder, and spices in a small bowl. Alternately add liqueur and dry ingredients to egg mixture, beating well. Beat in molasses. Fold batter into fruit.

Spray a 6-cup tubular steamed pudding mold with nonstick cooking spray. Pour batter into mold. Tap mold several times on work surface and seal with lid of the mold or cover with foil.

Pour 3 cups water into pressure cooker. Insert steam basket. Lower pudding mold into basket. Secure lid. Over high heat, bring pressure up to high. Reduce heat to maintain pressure and cook 50 minutes. Decrease pressure to medium according to manufacturer's directions and cook 20 minutes.

Release pressure according to manufacturer's directions. Remove lid. Remove pudding mold and place on a wire rack to cool. Let stand 15 minutes. Wrap in cheesecloth soaked in bourbon. Seal in foil. Store in a cool, dry place up to 2 months, or at least 24 hours. Invert on a round serving platter.

Prepare Orange Vanilla Sauce (if using): In a saucepan, combine milk, sugar, cornstarch, and butter. Cook over medium-high heat, stirring often, until mixture begins to thicken. Whisk liqueur, vanilla, and egg yolk together in a bowl. Pour ¼ cup hot milk mixture into yolk mixture and blend together. Whisk yolk mixture into milk mixture and cook over medium heat, stirring, until it begins to bubble.

Serve pudding with sauce (if using).

COOK'S NOTES: The fruit is coated with flour at the beginning so when added to the rest of the ingredients, the flour enables the fruit to attach to the batter and not sink to the bottom of the pan. To flame the pudding tableside, heat 2 tablespoons 80-proof bourbon. Place 2 sugar cubes in center of pudding in a tiny flameproof container. Pour heated bourbon over sugar cubes and ignite.

HARNESS FOR REMOVING PANS FROM PRESSURE COOKER

A harness made of foil strips is extremely useful in transferring pans or other dessert containers into and out of the pressure cooker.

Tear a 30-inch length of foil. Cut in half lengthwise. Fold each strip into thirds lengthwise.

Crisscross the two folded strips and tape at the center to secure.

Set pan or container in center of crossed strips, bring ends together over top of pan or containers and fold to secure.

CHUTNEYS AND JAMS

Chutneys are composed of a variety of fruits and vegetables. Explore chutney flavors by taking the combinations beyond conventional components: try plums, squash, tomatoes, and berries, adding zest with garlic, chives, peppercorns, and mustard.

Select unblemished fresh fruit and vegetables. When using dried fruit in a recipe calling for fresh fruit, increase the liquid by 1 cup for each pound of dried fruit.

Always use cooking utensils of nonreactive materials such as ceramic, stainless steel, or enamel for cooking mixtures containing vinegar.

Serve chutneys hot or cold with meat, poultry, rice, or casseroles. Chutneys also add flavor to stuffings.

The jams can be frozen or processed for longer storage. To can the jams, fill sterilized jars to within ¾ inch of the rims. Clean rims and seal. Place a steam basket in a pressure cooker with 1 inch water. Pyramid filled jars in pressure cooker. Secure lid and bring pressure up to high. Reduce heat and cook 2 minutes. Release pressure naturally and use tongs to transfer jars to a towel-covered countertop. Allow to cool.

CHERRY-RHUBARB CHUTNEY

This lovely chutney will keep well in an airtight container for up to four weeks. As a side dish or garnish, the delightful combinations will complement pork, ham, chicken, turkey, or may be used as a barbecue sauce.

MAKES 6 SERVINGS

1 cup dried tart cherries

2 cups fresh or frozen chopped rhubarb

1 small onion, finely diced

1 large apple, peeled, cored, and cubed

½ teaspoon ground ginger

1 cup packed light brown sugar

½ cup granulated sugar

½ teaspoon ground cinnamon

2 tablespoons apple cider vinegar

½ cup apple juice

2 whole cloves tied in cheesecloth

Combine cherries, rhubarb, and remaining ingredients in a pressure cooker. Stir well. Secure lid. Over high heat, bring pressure up to medium. Reduce heat to medium to maintain pressure and cook 5 minutes.

Release pressure according to manufacturer's directions. Remove lid. The sugar syrup in the chutney will be dangerously hot. Stir carefully. Discard whole cloves. Ladle into sterilized canning jars or into a heatproof bowl. Cover and refrigerate up to 4 weeks.

CORN AND BEAN RELISH

Any variation of bean may be substituted in this recipe. The combination is colorful and the tangy sauce makes it most appetizing.

MAKES 12 SERVINGS

Dressing

¼ cup olive or canola oil

2 teaspoons apple cider vinegar

1 teaspoon sugar

⅛ teaspoon salt

⅛ teaspoon freshly ground black pepper

½ teaspoon dried tarragon

½ teaspoon prepared mustard

½ teaspoon prepared creamy horseradish

1 red bell pepper, diced medium

1 small onion, finely diced

1 cup navy beans, soaked

4 cups water

1 teaspoon salt

3 cups frozen whole-kernel corn

¼ cup minced fresh parsley

Make the dressing: In a small bowl, combine oil, vinegar, sugar, salt, pepper, tarragon, mustard, and horseradish. Whisk until well blended.

Add bell pepper and onion to a medium bowl. Add dressing and toss to combine.

Drain beans. Transfer beans into a pressure cooker along with water and salt. Secure lid. Over high heat, bring pressure up to high. Reduce heat to medium to maintain pressure and insert a heat diffuser between cooker and heat. Cook 10 minutes.

Release pressure according to manufacturer's directions. Remove lid. Drain beans. Add beans and corn to bell pepper and onion. Toss gently. Sprinkle parsley over top.

▫ ▫ ▫

CRANBERRY-PINEAPPLE RELISH

The high temperatures while under pressure will develop the sugar and juices into a syrup resembling a sauce. This relish is a grand side dish for holiday poultry dishes, and also makes a lovely hostess gift presented in an old-fashioned canning jar.

MAKES 6 SERVINGS

1 (10-ounce) package fresh cranberries

1 teaspoon grated lemon zest

1 cup orange juice

1 cup granulated sugar

½ cup packed light brown sugar

½ teaspoon ground ginger

1 small cinnamon stick

1 cup walnuts, toasted (see Cook's Note, page 185) and chopped very coarse

1 (20-ounce) can crushed pineapple with juice

Combine all ingredients into the pressure cooker, except walnuts and pineapple. Stir well. Secure lid. Over high heat, bring pressure up

to high. Reduce heat to medium to maintain pressure and cook 5 minutes.

Release pressure according to manufacturer's directions. Remove lid. The mixture can be dangerously hot. Carefully stir in walnuts and crushed pineapple. Let stand 5 minutes. Stir once again. Ladle into sterilized airtight jars. Store in the refrigerator up to 1 month.

▫ ▫ ▫

PEACH-PINEAPPLE CHUTNEY

A great barbecue side dish, the fresh flavors are perfect with spareribs, chicken, or sausage. It stores well in an airtight container in the refrigerator for up to a month.

MAKES 6 SERVINGS

1 pound freestone peaches, peeled

1 small onion, diced

¼ cup chopped red bell pepper

¼ teaspoon ground ginger

Dash crushed red pepper flakes

½ cup packed light brown sugar

½ cup granulated sugar

¼ teaspoon ground cinnamon

1 teaspoon grated lemon zest

½ cup citrus marmalade

1 cup crushed pineapple, with juice

2 tablespoons apple cider vinegar

Place whole peaches in a pressure cooker and pour enough hot water into the pot to cover. Secure lid. Over high heat, bring pressure up to medium. Reduce pressure to medium to maintain pressure and cook 1 minute.

Release pressure according to manufacturer's directions. Remove lid. Drain into colander and run cold running water over peaches. Skins should slide off very easily. Cut peaches into large wedges. Combine all ingredients, except pineapple and vinegar, in the pressure cooker and secure lid. Over high heat, bring pressure up to medium-high. Reduce heat to medium and cook 4 minutes.

Release pressure according to manufacturer's directions and stir in pineapple and vinegar. Stir well. Transfer chutney to a heatproof bowl or sterilized canning jar. Cover and refrigerate.

CRANBERRY CHUTNEY

A family favorite, I share this with everyone, especially at holiday time when cranberries are available. Bottled with a colorful bow around the top the chutney makes a welcome hostess gift that everyone raves about.

MAKES 8 CUPS

1½ cups walnut pieces, toasted (see Cook's Note, page 185)

1 pound cranberries

1 cup golden raisins

1 small red onion, sliced

½ cup orange marmalade

½ cup orange juice

2 tablespoons grated orange zest

⅓ cup white wine vinegar

1 cup granulated sugar

½ cup packed light brown sugar

½ teaspoon salt

¼ teaspoon red (cayenne) pepper

½ teaspoon ground ginger

1 cinnamon stick

1 bay leaf

In a pressure cooker, combine walnuts, cranberries, raisins, onion, marmalade, orange juice, zest, vinegar, sugars, salt, spices, and bay leaf. Stir well. Secure lid. Over high heat, bring pressure up to medium. Reduce heat to maintain pressure and cook 5 minutes.

Release pressure according to manufacturer's directions. Remove lid. Remove cinnamon stick and bay leaf from chutney. Stir well. Pour hot chutney into sterilized jars with lids. Store in refrigerator up to 3 to 4 weeks.

BLUEBERRY JAM

Make this delicious jam when blueberries are at their peak.

MAKES 8 (½-PINT) JARS

4 cups blueberries

4 cups sugar

1 cup orange juice

1 teaspoon grated orange zest

½ teaspoon grated nutmeg

1 (6-ounce) bottle pectin or 1 (1¾-ounce) package dry pectin

In a pressure cooker, combine blueberries, sugar, orange juice, orange zest, and nutmeg. Stir well. Secure lid. Over high heat, bring pressure up to medium. Reduce heat to maintain pressure and cook 2 minutes.

Release pressure according to manufacturer's directions. Remove lid. Stir blueberry mixture well. Process in a food mill, over a bowl, separating seeds from pulp. Return pulp to pressure cooker. Over high heat, stir pectin into pulp and bring to a rolling boil. Cook, stirring with a long-handled wooden spoon, 1 minute.

Ladle jam into 8 sterilized ½-pint jars, filling to 1 inch below rim and being careful not to splash on rim or upper inch of jar. Use damp cloth to wipe rim and inside of jar before sealing.

Store in refrigerator up to 3 to 4 weeks. Blueberry jam may also be frozen in freezer containers for 6 to 8 months. Or process according to directions on page 199.

☒ ☒ ☒

GINGER PEAR JAM

Use your favorite pears, selecting ripe pears that are free of blemishes or dark spots.
MAKES 8 (½-PINT) JARS

2½ pounds pears, peeled, cored, and thinly sliced
4 cups sugar
½ cup orange juice
1 teaspoon grated fresh ginger
1 (6-ounce) bottle pectin

In a pressure cooker, combine pears, sugar, orange juice, and ginger. Stir well. Secure lid. Over high heat, bring pressure up to high. Reduce heat to maintain pressure and cook 6 minutes.

Release pressure according to manufacturer's directions. Remove lid. Using a slotted spoon, transfer pears to a food processor, blender, or food mill. Process until coarsely pureed. Return to pressure cooker. Cook pear mixture over medium heat 1 minute. Stir in pectin and bring to a full boil. Cook 1 minute, stirring with a long-handled wooden spoon to avoid being splattered by bubbling mixture.

Remove from heat. Ladle into 8 sterilized ½-pint jars, filling to 1 inch below top. Avoid dripping pear mixture on rim or upper inch of jar. Use a damp cloth to wipe away any pear mixture or juice on rim or inside of jar before sealing.

Store in refrigerator up to 3 to 4 weeks. Pear jam may be frozen in freezer containers 6 to 8 months. Or process according to directions on page 199.

PEACH-APRICOT PRESERVES WITH ALMONDS

The toasted almonds add a nutty flavor that comes from the oils during the toasting process. When combined with the flavor of the apricots and peaches, it makes a delightfully flavored topping for toast.

MAKES 8 (½-PINT) JARS

6 whole fresh peaches

1 cup water

1 (8-ounce) package dried apricots, chopped

½ cup almonds, toasted (see Cook's Note, page 185), coarsely chopped

1½ cups orange juice

4½ cups sugar

2 whole cloves

1 cinnamon stick

1 (1¾-ounce) package pectin powder

Pierce peaches with cake tester or skewer. Pour water into a pressure cooker. Place peaches in water. Secure lid. Over high heat, bring pressure up to high. Reduce heat to maintain pressure and cook 3 minutes.

Release pressure according to manufacturer's directions. Remove lid. Place peaches into a bowl filled with cold running water. Peel peaches. Slice peaches into wedges.

In a pressure cooker, combine peaches, water, apricots, almonds, orange juice, sugar, cloves, and cinnamon. Stir well. Secure lid. Over high heat, bring pressure up to medium. Reduce heat to maintain pressure and cook 2 minutes.

Release pressure according to manufacturer's directions. Remove lid. Stir fruit mixture thoroughly. Remove cloves and cinnamon stick. Sprinkle pectin over fruit and stir well. Cook over medium-high heat 2 minutes.

Ladle preserves into 8 sterilized ½-pint jars, filling to 1 inch below rim. Use a damp cloth to wipe away any peach mixture or juice on rim or inside of jar before sealing. Store in refrigerator up to 3 to 4 weeks. Preserves may be covered and frozen, or process according to directions on page 199.

(HERBS)

FRESH HERBS

If there is a choice, select fresh herbs over dried. The flavor is pure, fresh, and more pronounced. Store the fresh herbs by rinsing in cool water. Wrap stems in a damp paper towel and place them in a plastic bag or wrap loosely in plastic wrap.

SUBSTITUTING FRESH FOR DRIED HERBS

The rule for substituting fresh herbs in a recipe is to triple the amount specified. Example: 1 teaspoon dried dill or 3 teaspoons (1 tablespoon) fresh dill.

Bouquet garni: a delightful combination of herbs used to enhance the flavors of soups, stews, and sauces. In the summer, when fresh herbs are available, tie together, with cotton twine, 2 sprigs parsley, 1 sprig thyme, 1 sprig marjoram, and 1 bay leaf. Add to the ingredients while cooking your favorite dish.

It's easy to keep dried bouquet garni on hand during the winter months. Simply mix together in a jar 3 crumbled bay leaves, ¼ cup dried parsley, 2 tablespoons dried thyme, and 2 tablespoons marjoram. Keep it stored in a pantry for future use. Make sure there is a tight lid on the jar.

HERBS: A LOVELY TOUCH TO A SIMPLE RECIPE

BEEF

Bay leaf

Black peppercorns

Cayenne

Cumin

Garlic

Marjoram

Oregano

Paprika

Rosemary

Red pepper flakes

Sage

Tarragon

PORK

Allspice

Bay leaf

Cayenne

Celery seed

Cloves

Curry powder

Ginger

Oregano

Parsley

Paprika

Mustard (dired)

Rosemary

Sage

LAMB

Basil

Bay leaf

Black pepper

Curry

Dill

Fennel

Ginger

Marjoram

Parsley

Oregano

Red pepper flakes

Rosemary

Spearmint

Thyme

VEAL/POULTRY

Basil

Bay leaf

Cayenne

Chervil

Fennel

Marjoram

Oregano

Paprika

Rosemary

Sage

Tarragon

Thyme

White pepper

FISH

Basil

Bay leaf

Cayenne

Celery seed

Chervil

Cilantro

Dill

Fennel

Peppercorns

Oregano

Paprika

Savory

Thyme

White peppercorns

VEGETABLES

Basil

Bay leaf

Chervil

Dill

Fennel

Garlic

Marjoram

Oregano

Parsley

Red pepper flakes

Rosemary

Tarragon

White peppercorns

PASTA/RICE

Basil

Dill

Fennel

Marjoram

Oregano

Saffron

Savory

White

METRIC CONVERSION CHARTS

COMPARISON TO METRIC MEASURE

When you know	Symbol	Multiply By	To Find	Symbol
Teaspoons	tsp.	5.0	milliliters	ml
Tablespoons	tbsp	15.0	milliliters	ml
Fluid ounces	fl. oz.	30.0	milliliters	ml
Cups	c.	0.24	liters	l
Pints	pt.	0.47	liters	l
Quarts	qt.	0.95	liters	l
Ounces	oz.	28.0	grams	g
Pounds	lb.	0.45	kilograms	kg
Fahrenheit	F	5/9 (after subtracting 32)	Celsius	C

FAHRENHEIT TO CELSIUS

F	C
200–205	95
220–225	105
245–250	120
275	135
300–305	150
325–330	165
345–350	175
370–375	190
400–405	205
425–430	220
445–450	230
470–475	245
500	260

LIQUID MEASURE TO MILLILITERS

¼ teaspoon	=	1.25	milliliters
½ teaspoon	=	2.50	milliliters
¾ teaspoon	=	3.75	milliliters
1 teaspoon	=	5.00	milliliters
1¼ teaspoons	=	6.25	milliliters
1½ teaspoons	=	7.50	milliliters
1¾ teaspoons	=	8.75	milliliters
2 teaspoons	=	10.0	milliliters
1 tablespoon	=	15.0	milliliters
2 tablespoons	=	30.0	milliliters

LIQUID MEASURE TO LITERS

¼ cup	=	0.06	liters
½ cup	=	0.12	liters
¾ cup	=	0.18	liters
1 cup	=	0.24	liters
1¼ cups	=	.30	liters
1½ cups	=	.36	liters
2 cups	=	.48	liters
2½ cups	=	.60	liters
3 cups	=	.72	liters
3½ cups	=	.84	liters
4 cups	=	.96	liters
4½ cups	=	1.08	liters
5 cups	=	1.20	liters
5½ cups	=	1.32	liters

INDEX

Michael Reynold

Toula Patsalis is instructor of cooking and former program director of four successful cooking schools affiliated with quality cookshops in the state of Michigan. She has studied cooking both in the United States and abroad. Toula is considered a culinary authority and has appeared regularly on television and various media talk shows. Besides being a chairperson for cookbook projects to benefit the American Cancer Society and a local Greek Orthodox cathedral, Toula Patsalis is a member of the International Association of Culinary Professionals.